StuG III Brigade 191, 1940–1945

StuG III Brigade 191, 1940–1945

The Buffalo Brigade in Action in the Balkans, Greece and from Moscow to Kursk and Sevastopol

Bruno Bork

Foreword by Anthony Tucker-Jones

Greenhill Books

StuG III Brigade 191, 1940–1945: The Buffalo Brigade in Action in the Balkans, Greece and from Moscow to Kursk and Sevastopol

Greenhill Books

First published by Greenhill Books, 2021
Greenhill Books, c/o Pen & Sword Books Ltd,
47 Church Street, Barnsley, S. Yorkshire, S70 2AS
For more information on our books, please visit
www.greenhillbooks.com, email contact@greenhillbooks.com
or write to us at the above address.

Copyright © Verlagshaus Würzburg GmbH & Co. KG
Flechsig Verlag, Beethovenstraße 5B, D-97080 Würzburg, Germany
www.verlagshaus.com

This edition © Greenhill Books, 2021
Anthony Tucker-Jones foreword © Greenhill Books, 2021

PUBLISHING HISTORY
StuG III Brigade 191, 1940–1945 was originally published in 1977 by Verlagshaus
Würzburg GmbH & Co. KG with the title *Die Sturmgeschützbrigade 191:
Die 'Büffelbrigade' im Einsatz auf dem Balkan und in den Weiten Russlands 1940–1945*,
with a revised edition in 2009. This edition has a new foreword by Anthony Tucker-Jones.

CIP data records for this title are available from the British Library
ISBN 978-1-78438-695-5

Typeset by JCS Publishing Services Ltd
Typeset in 11/15pt Adobe Caslon Pro
Printed and bound in Great Britain by TJ Books Ltd

Contents

Preface

It has been the wish of many surviving members of StuG Brigade 191 to have a cohesive documentary record of their experiences in the war years 1941 to 1945. This publication completes the work begun by the first commanding officer of our Abteilung, the late Generalmajor Günter Hoffmann-Schoenborn.

The aim of this book is to present in a simple format the development of the self-propelled assault gun described herein, to make its tactical significance clearly recognizable and to honour the achievements of the members of our Abteilung.

The background is set down factually with the reports and personal experiences of our men being built into the text. Unfortunately, many documents, particularly action reports, were not available and I was obliged to put together the brigade history from anecdotes, war communiqués, the published literature and personal accounts. It has also proved difficult to obtain photographs suitable for use.

If this record can be a memorial to the men of our brigade who fell, then I believe that this brigade history will have fulfilled its purpose.

Bruno Bork,
December 1977

Note to the 2009 Edition

After the death of the author of the original chronicle several years ago, two former brigade members supplied photographs which provided the incentive for this expanded new edition. Frau Bork delivered some previously unpublished photographs from her husband's literary estate so that the volume is now richly illustrated. Our very grateful thanks go to Hermann Röhm and Pacco Hofmann for making the photographs available.

The Publishers,
August 2009

Foreword

A Breed Apart

Bruno Bork was a veteran of the Buffalo Brigade, so named after the charging buffalo emblem of the 191st Assault Gun Battalion. He completed the task, started by its commander Major Hoffmann-Schoenborn, of chronicling the unit's extensive combat experiences during the Second World War. Originally published in German in the late 1970s, following Bork's death in 1996 a new lavishly illustrated edition was produced in 2009. Now available in English for the very first time thanks to Greenhill, it is the sort of memoir that provides not only a tactical unit history but also a 'blood and guts' ground-level view of the war. *StuG III Brigade 191* offers a fascinating snapshot into the lives of those who fought with what eventually became the expanded 191st Assault Gun Brigade. This unit saw widespread action in both the Balkans and on the Eastern Front. It miraculously avoided becoming trapped in the Crimea in mid-1944, successfully escaping from Sevastopol thanks to the desperate Axis naval evacuation across the Black Sea.

One of the first things that strikes you about this book, apart from its scope, is the wealth of photos which show the brigade serving in all sorts of climatic conditions. These range from the positively tropical to the terrifyingly bitter winters endured by Mother Russia. Interestingly, judging by the early images the men of the 191st seem to have worn both the black panzer and grey assault gun crew uniforms, more of which later. The unit first came into being as the 191st Sturmgeschütz (StuG or assault gun) Battalion after the invasion of France. Then in April 1941 it took part in Hitler's Blitzkrieg against Greece, where its crews had to battle both the local terrain and the Greek Army. It suffered some of its first losses piercing the Greek Metaxas Line and forcing the Rupel Pass. This action doomed Greek resistance.

The Buffalos' role was to support various infantry divisions. Notably for the invasion of Russia in June 1941 they fought alongside the 298th Infantry Division. They then fought their way to the very gates of Moscow. This time the battalion found itself divided up supporting both the 3rd and 258th Infantry Divisions. Before the Russian capital the battalion encountered the Red Army's new T-34 medium tank for the very first time. This was superior to the early model StuGs, which were only armed with a short 75-mm support gun. However, they fought back as the 258th Infantry noted, 'A T-34 approaching the StuGs was so badly damaged by the first round fired by 3 Battery (Oberleutnant Göring) that the cover of the gun structure flew with the result that the tank turned away at once and fled.' The deepening snow of the oncoming winter and Russian partisans became their greatest enemy. The battalion's assault guns were deployed to protect local strongpoints behind their lines where German troops tried to ride out the cold weather. By this stage the battalion had suffered 221 killed and wounded plus 150 sick.

In the summer of the following year the Buffalos were sent south into the mountains of the Caucasus in an effort to capture the region's vital oilfields. At first the Red Army withdrew in the face of Hitler's renewed onslaught. However, Stalin gave orders that Grozny must be held at all costs to protect Baku and Tbilisi. As a result, German victory proved elusive in the face of stubborn Russian resistance. They stalled before Grozny at Mozdok and Nalchik and could get no further. Panzer divisions were in short supply in the Caucasus campaign, which meant the assault gun battalions supporting the infantry were always in great demand.

After the catastrophic German defeat at Stalingrad in early 1943 the battalion along with the other German forces in the Caucasus were forced to retreat into the fortified Kuban bridgehead opposite the Crimea. At which point the unit received the much-improved StuG III Ausf. G, which was armed with a dedicated long-barrelled 75-mm anti-tank gun. Bruno Bork was wounded during the fierce fighting in the Kuban. In the Crimea the brigade served with the remains of the 73rd Infantry Division. After escaping from Sevastopol in May 1944, the 191st withdrew steadily up through Yugoslavia and into Austria where it surrendered at the end of the war.

Initially the assault gun was intended as a close support weapon for the infantry, but it increasingly became an anti-tank platform. The assault gun differed from a tank in that it did not have a turret. Instead the main armament was installed within the fighting compartment of the hull and importantly had an armoured roof. Self-propelled guns by contrast had open fighting compartments and typically carried artillery pieces rather than anti-tank guns, though this was not always the case.

German StuG units were first organized into battalions and then from 1944 into brigades and were known as Sturmartillerie or assault artillery. StuG crews were considered gunners and not Panzertruppen. This was a crucial difference. The assault gun crews were a breed apart from Hitler's Panzerwaffe. They came under the control of the German Army's artillery. Many senior German generals were former career artillery officers so were happy to see assault guns remain under the artillery and not transferred to the control of the panzers. As the Second World War progressed the independent StuG brigades and assault gun detachments shouldered a greater and greater burden of the fighting, making them ever more important.

To emphasize that they were not Panzertruppen the assault gun crews were not allowed to wear the black panzer uniform. Instead they wore exactly the same style short double-breasted *Feldjacke*, loose trousers gathered at the ankle and *Feldmütze* sidecap or Einheitsfeldmütze cap – but in field grey. As the war went on there were inevitable shortages so Sturmartillerie crews in some instances resorted to panzer black or wore a combination of both styles depending on what was available. Likewise, they did not qualify for the Panzer Assault Badge, but instead were awarded the General Assault Badge, which was granted to anti-aircraft, anti-tank, artillery and engineer troops.

The backbone of the Sturmartillerie were the StuG III, StuH42 and StuG IV fully enclosed assault guns, which employed the Panzer III and Panzer IV chassis respectively. The Panzerjäger or tank hunter and the Jagdpanzer or 'hunting tank' armoured vehicles were dedicated tank killers and were mainly crewed by the Panzer Arm. The larger assault gun units were deployed as army- or corps-level assets, but as the war progressed they were increasingly deployed as battalion-strength units forming integral parts of the infantry, panzergrenadier and panzer divisions. Between 1942 and 1945 up to thirty independent assault gun units were deployed on the Eastern Front. In the summer of 1944 eight independent StuG brigades fought with Army Group Centre in Russia and three fought with Army Group B in Normandy.

Much to General Heinz Guderian's irritation, when he was appointed Inspector General of Armoured Troops in early 1943 the assault artillery was not included within his remit. One of the reasons for this, noted Guderian, was that 'the assault artillery was the only weapon which nowadays enabled gunners to win the Knight's Cross.' This situation was not remedied until the end of the year by which time it was way too late. Although he may have disliked the dissipating effect assault gun and self-propelled gun production had on Germany's tank force, the reality was that by the end of the war these weapons had surpassed the utility of the panzers. By 1944 Sturmartillerie crews claimed to have destroyed 20,000 enemy tanks. The men of the Buffalo Brigade helped to achieve that remarkable score as the following fascinating account explains.

Anthony Tucker-Jones

Introduction

The experience gained in the last years of the 1914–1918 war was the incentive for the creation of the Sturmgeschütz (StuG) assault gun just before the Second World War. It had been seen that there was a need to provide the frontline infantry not only with strong fire protection but also with the capability to overwhelm new targets of opportunity and heavy weapons. The improvement in machine guns and the beginning of the material battles in 1916 made a solution to the problem more urgent. Therefore horse-drawn light field guns, 'infantry escort batteries', were formed to advance at the gallop alongside the foremost infantry lines, swiftly take up position and open fire. This was an imperfect solution more akin to a suicide mission as heavy losses had to be expected in the approach and unlimbering, but the effect was impressive; the enemy did not like coming under direct high-explosive (HE) shellfire from 400 metres.

After the First World War, tacticians and technicians gave much thought to the question of supporting the frontline infantry with heavy weapons. The experience with tanks had shown that only motorized, easily manoeuvrable armoured vehicles were worth considering for the purpose. The tactical experiments were undertaken by the Reichswehr. Under the Treaty of Versailles the 100,000-man army was not allowed to have real panzers and so exercises and manoeuvres were carried out using motorized vehicles clad with pasteboard upper structures to resemble 'escort panzers'.

Once these limitations were removed in 1935, the idea of the assault gun was adopted. General von Manstein wrote a memorandum to the Chief of the General Staff and Commander-in-Chief of the Army, Generaloberst von Fritzsch, proposing that every active infantry division should have an Abteilung consisting of three batteries of six guns per battery by 1939. The suggestion was approved by the General Staff but the project met substantial delays following the resignation of von Fritzsch and the departure of von Manstein from Army High Command (OKH) at about the same time. This was both unnecessary and disadvantageous in that it led to the planning being heavily cut back by von Brauchitsch, the successor to von Fritzsch.

Brauchitsch wanted only a small number of StuG Abteilungen. The Panzer Arm under the leadership of General Guderian must have been seen as the hindrance, for Guderian was averse to the StuG, fearing the new weapon was a competitor that would interfere with the production of the standard panzer. Heated discussions ensued and even the Artillery Inspectorate was initially not keen on the idea of motorized assault guns. Accordingly by the summer of 1940 only a few batteries had come into existence despite the armament capacity being sufficient to fulfil the original programme.

In October 1937 the first experimental unit, 7 Battery under Hauptmann Steinkopf, was formed at the Artillerie-Lehrregiment, Jüterbog, where the first officers and gun crews were trained. Trials at Döberitz were very satisfactory. The new StuG was based on the proven chassis of the Mk III panzer. Without the revolving turret, the vehicle had a lower profile and better mobility across country. The reduction in weight permitted the inclusion of thicker frontal armour. The design was fitted with a 7.5-cm (3-inch) L/24 cannon with little elevation or traverse movement in a casemate. To engage a target the whole StuG had to be aimed at it. The development and testing of the new weapon concluded in 1938, and it would have been available in large numbers when war broke out if the cessation of all further testing had not been ordered in the autumn of 1938 when the existing StuGs disappeared.

The Polish campaign in the autumn of 1939 proved the need for armoured heavy weapons to protect the infantry, and OKH now ordered the formation of 'independent StuG batteries' and the resumption of training. At VI Artillerie-Lehrregiment, Hauptmann Steinkopf had charge of three batteries designated 'StuG-Lehr und Reserve Abteilung'. The depot with modern workshop was located in the new Adolf Hitler Lager situated on the Jüterbog firing range, in its grounds to the north. 16 Artillerie-Lehrregiment trained the commanders, platoon leaders and radio operators, 18 Artillerie-Lehrregiment the gun crews and drivers. Everybody set about the task with enthusiasm. StuG men were issued with the black panzer uniform initially, later the same style was retained but in field-grey cloth.

VI Artillerie-Lehrregiment had until the French campaign in 1940 to prepare. Five independent batteries had been formed by then and saw service as follows:

640: Commander, Oberleutnant Freiherr Eggloffstein: attached to Infanterieregiment (Inf.Regt) *Grossdeutschland*.

659: Oberleutnant Freiherr Frauenberg. The battery saw action in France where the commander fell. His successor was Oberleutnant Schaupensteiner.

660: Commander, Oberleutnant Tolkmitt. Battery served in France.

665: Commander, Oberleutnant Speyerer. Battery served with success in France.

666: Commander, Oberleutnant Alfred Müller, later Commander, StuG Brigade 191. After the French campaign the battery was transferred to Belgium as part of Operation *Sealion*, the invasion of England.

So outstandingly had they performed during the French campaign that a start was made at Jüterbog immediately, with the formation of more Abteilungen. The Sturmartillerie training continued at VI Artillerie-Lehrregiment. Only volunteers from artillery regiments who were qualified or assessed as suitable for the new weapon were accepted. The first StuG Abteilungen had three

A StuG hardly recognizable amidst a pine wood.

batteries, each of six vehicles and a Staff Battery with workshop platoon. These Abteilungen were numbered 184, 185, 190 and 191.

The time that had been lost could not be made up but at least Abteilungen 190 and 191 were able to take part in the Balkan campaign against Greece in the spring of 1941. At the beginning of the war against the Soviet Union a further six operational Abteilungen were ready, to be supplemented in quick succession for the Eastern Front.

The StuG of the Abteilungen formed between 1941 and 1943 were continually improved during the course of series production but essentially resembled the 1937 prototype. The main weapon remained the 7.5-cm L/24 cannon except for a few StuGs armed with the 10.5-cm L/25 howitzer. The years 1942/43 then saw significant changes, the vehicles deployed from now on being armed with the 7.5-cm Kampfwagenkanone (Kpw) L/48 cannon with a longer barrel.

Storing the ammunition in the vehicle was more problematic for the latter because, while 120 rounds of L/24 could be accommodated without holding supports, the number of L/48 shells which could be carried was 90, or at a stretch 100. In either case it was normal for the crew to sit on the ammunition.

The commander's hatch cover was replaced by a rotatable turret rim with angled mirrors so that even when the turret hatch was closed the area could be surveyed with scissor binoculars and around the vehicle using the mirrors.

The L/24 or L/48 cannon on the Mk III panzer chassis was outstanding and made for probably one of the most well-balanced armoured vehicles. The enemy was extremely respectful of the StuG; the men had a good *ésprit de corps*, made their presence felt and could be switched from one division to another 'like a fire brigade'.

Around 1943/44 the StuG Abteilungen were expanded into StuG brigades. A brigade had, in addition to the three fighting batteries and the Staff Battery, a 'grenadier escort battery' consisting of three platoons of grenadiers equipped with the Sturmgewehr 44, and a platoon of engineers. These three fighting batteries had ten StuGs each and one for the Brigade Staff so that the strength was thirty-one StuGs in all. This grouping proved itself but came too late.

The Army Sturmartillerie brigade even had an authorized strength of forty-five StuGs. From 1944 only a few StuG brigades were increased to Sturmartillerie brigades.

Photographer under scrutiny from the Kfz 15 Staff car. The radio equipment can be seen behind the driver.

The centre of the StuG Arm had begun with 7 Battery/Artillerie-Lehrregiment, progressed to VI Artillerie-Lehrregiment and later III Artillerie-Lehrregiment 2 (mot.) with the StuG instructor staff and remained at Jüterbog until 1943, when the first units occupied its own StuG School at Burg bei Magdeburg. The Burg school was enlarged very quickly under the later General Hoffmann-Schoenborn to accommodate the Command Staff with an experimental group, press office, one tactical and one Technical Training Staff – Commanding Officer Major Haarberg – an instruction Abteilung and an installation staff. Its area of responsibility included the entire Sturmartillerie of the Feldersatzheer – field reserve army – the training and education of recruits of the branch of service and the instruction of delegations from the Axis states. Furthermore at Burg, as at all other weapons schools, experience reports were evaluated, technical innovations developed, traditions encouraged, publicity made to attract new recruits and a troop welfare office operated.

Immediately subordinate to the school were the reserve Abteilungen – 200 at Schweinfurt, later transferred to Schieratz in Warthegau – 300 at Neisse –

400 at Hadersleben in Denmark – 500 at Posen and 600 at Deutsch Eylau, the Training Staff West at Tours in France (personnel only) and the Training Staff Altengrabow – since 1943 responsible for all equipment at all new installations – at Lehrbrigaden.

The successor to Generalmajor Hoffmann-Schoenborn was Oberstleutnant Alfred Müller, Commanding Officer of 'Buffalo' Brigade 191. On 29 March 1945 he received the order to make all battleworthy parts of the school operational as 'Kampfgruppe Burg'. The remainder was transferred to Austria, where instruction continued. Through the merging of a whole series of Kampfgruppen, 'Division Schill' was formed under Major Müller. Within the framework of Armee Wenck, this division had the task of prising open the Soviet encirclement of Berlin at the south-west. The objective met with failure, and thereafter the division fought a rearguard battle to the Elbe north of Magdeburg, where on or about 7 May 1945 the greater part surrendered to American forces. Some of the prisoners were handed over to the Soviets by the Americans. Thus what remained battleworthy of the StuG School at Burg met its end near its place of origin.

Translator's Note

The Army gives orders and so does the Armee. To avoid confusion I have translated the word 'Heer' meaning Army in the sense of Army, Navy and Air Force as 'Army'. I have left untranslated the German word 'Armee', for example 6 Armee, 17 Armee, to distinguish the subsidiary Armee units which made up the whole.

The ranks of officer in the Abteilung and brigade ran Leutnant, Oberleutnant, Hauptmann, Major etc. as per the standard Army practice. The 'other ranks' started off as 'Kanonier' (gunner recruit), 'Funker' (wireless operator recruit) and so forth. 'Gefreiter' was a trained Private, usually with a few years' service. Obergefreiter, the next rank up, was a senior Private or 'Lance Corporal' with some powers of command but no status as an NCO.

The lowest rank of NCO was Unteroffizier (Corporal) but a man had to go through a training course as such before being appointed one.

Probably to reflect the cavalry role taken over by the StuG panzer in mutual support of infantry, the sergeants were given cavalry ranks: Wachtmeister (sergeant), Oberwachtmeister (senior sergeant) and Hauptwachtmeister (sergeant major), equivalent to a First Warrant Officer or Second Warrant Officer. An NCO had to be saluted but the extent to which this was necessary is not certain.

The 'Tross' supported the fighting staff with its immediate needs in ammunition, provisions and combat supplies. The author, Bruno Bork, was for some time the Hauptwachtmeister in charge of the Tross at Abteilung 191 but when the need arose he commanded an StuG and was eventually seriously wounded in battle.

The typical StuG of the early war years with the 7.5-cm L/24 'stump cannon'.

After the bitter experiences in the Russian campaign, the StuG of the later war years was equipped with the 7.5-cm L/48 long barrel.

Hermann Röhm was a member of 9 StuG Artillerie-Lehrregiment 2 (mot.) at Jüterbog.

Hermann Röhm in 'normal' Army uniform with puttees.

The military career of Hermann Röhm until 9 December 1941 as set out in a field postcard. He supplied this book with many interesting photographs from Jüterbog and StuG Abteilung 191 from 1942 to 1944. His text *My Time as a Recruit from 2 Oct 1941* reads: 'I had to report to Essling (Vienna) on 2 Oct. 1941. From 2 to 6 Oct. infantry training at Ludwigsburg (Baden-Württemberg) with the [illegible] artillery. 7 and 8 Oct. transferred to Epinal (Vosges, France) with heavy artillery Ersatz Abt. 61, mot. Training as a Wehrmacht driver from 9 Oct. until 1 Dec. 1941. From 2 to 6 Dec. by train to Jüterbog, Berlin. On 8 Dec drafted to Sturmartillerie. 15/12 took over vehicle and service with Sturmartillerie. Following pictures show my subsequent life as a soldier.'

Song of the Sturmartillerie.

Hermann Röhm in black StuG blouse. The uniform of the StuG Abteilungen resembled that of the Panzer Arm but the collar patches lacked the death's head symbol.

The barracks of 9/StuG Artillerie-Lehrregiment 2 (mot.), Adolf Hitler Lager, Jüterbog, south of Berlin.

Christmas festivities in December 1941 with a circle of comrades. At the same time on the Eastern Front, the German armies were suffering heavy losses as their advance faltered for the first time.

The richly spread table of presents, Christmas 1941. The tree is splendidly adorned with silver tinsel.

The Leutnant with his soldiers. He wears the ribbon of the Iron Cross II, and therefore has already had experience at the front.

A finely painted shield on the barracks wall. The StuG had long since matured into a branch of the artillery.

The soldiers' cinema in the Adolf Hitler Lager at Jüterbog.

In the harsh winter of 1941 everything at Jüterbog was heavily blanketed with snow, as the outdoor swimming pool is here.

Supply lorries neatly lined up before the halls.

To spare wear and tear on the StuG tracks during road travel, the special trailer (Sonderanhänger 116) of 22-tonne carrying capacity was used. The rear pair of wheels could be steered. The driver sat in the open air or within a removable cabin.

A Skoda Praga Type 6 towing machine snowed in at the barracks.

Hermann Röhm in battle dress by a training StuG.

A whole row of StuGs (C and D versions) alongside the halls.

The most frequently deployed StuG of the war years 1940 to 1942 was armed with the 7.5-cm short-barrel L/24 cannon.

Hermann Röhm (second from left) with colleagues in the squad room.

Spring 1942, leaving on manoeuvres, the motorcycle rider included.

A command/observation vehicle built especially for the StuG Arm was the Sd.Kfz 253, developed on the chassis of the light Sd.Kfz 250 (armoured infantry-carrier). In action the vehicle proved too lightly armoured.

In this photo is an StuG, a light ammunition transporter Sd.Kfz 252 and a Magirus lorry of the Lehrkompanie. On all vehicles, 'L' signified 'training' ('Lehrkompanie').

(above) A pause during training and (below) fooling around for the camera.

Hermann Röhm in the armoured ammunition vehicle Sd.Kfz 250/6. The motor is running and blows the exhaust out laterally.

February 1942: battle training in the extensive pine woods of Mark Brandenburg.

The plan included infantry training. Here, a light machine-gun team with the MG 34.

End of the exercise! The StuGs, ammunition vehicles and lorries arrive back at barracks.

Comrades of the motorcycle units and workshop platoon.

StuG version F with muzzle cap on the stump barrel.

The 7.5-cm short-barrel muzzle of a StuG.

Steel helmets loose on the gun. They had to be carried but were very cumbersome in action.

The despatch rider has on the sidecar of his BMW R12 the 'L' indicating 'Lehrkompanie'.

Hermann Röhm on sentry duty at one of the many outer gates of the Adolf Hitler Lager, Jüterbog.

The two-part barrel cleaner for the 7.5-cm barrel is located here above the track guard.

During the very harsh winter of 1941 snowdrifts cut off surrounding villages and StuGs were detailed to assist. Before departure the map is studied to pinpoint the precise locations.

The journey involves crossing country lying under deep snow in order to reach farmsteads cut off from the outside world.

Sentry duty during the bitterly cold winter of 1941 was not enjoyable.

A training StuG 'L' with identification letter 'B'.

Hermann Röhm on StuG 'B'. The chassis number is very difficult to make out.

March 1942: StuGs parked in the halls.

A robust 8-tonne towing machine Sd.Kfz 7 in the terrain. These tugs were widely used by the Wehrmacht and were often the last recourse in thick mud.

A group photo by the towing machine. Hermann Röhm is indicated by an 'X'.

During the long winter evenings of 1941/42 men of the StuG Lehrkompanie worked on an StuG model, made from metal parts, complete with 'garage'.

The garage with 'smoking forbidden' notice on the door.

The StuG model demonstrates its power 'in the terrain'.

The size of the model in comparison
with its builder.

Hermann Röhm in black field blouse, tie and
steel helmet.

The track members were made of wire. It was a fine piece of work, the fate of which is
unfortunately not known.

In the spring of 1942, damaged vehicles from StuG Abteilung 191 returned to Jüterbog from the Eastern Front. In the photo is a command/observation half-track Sd.Kfz 253.

Hermann Röhm with the unloading crew. In the photo is command vehicle No. 21. Because of bad experiences with these command vehicles in action, from 1942/43 the leaders of each StuG Abteilung were allocated their own StuG with expanded radio equipment.

A light armoured command vehicle Sd.Kfz 253, apparently with motor damage, being pulled by a truck. StuG Abteilung 191 was at Mogilev for a refresher course from April to May 1942. Still usable vehicles were no longer sent back to Germany.

The engine compartment of this vehicle was destroyed by fire. All reusable parts had already been removed by the Abteilung in Russia.

Hermann Röhm on the 18-tonne Famo towing machine (Sd.Kfz 9), the most powerful tug available to the Wehrmacht.

Even the frontal plating has been removed from this gutted observation vehicle.

The removal of a 'tin can' like this one was no problem for the Famo.

Heinz Bethge and Hans Büsing.

All wear the black panzer uniform but with field-grey field cap. The collar patches have (artillery) red edging (not pink as the Panzer Arm had).

A pose in the Jüterbog barracks.

Competitors in front of an inn, the 'Berliner Schlossbräu'.

A queue of vehicles on a cobbled street in the camp, June 1942. The Artillerie-Lehrabteilung carried out demonstrations for foreign visitors.

Group photo at the lorry park.

At the Artillerie-Lehrabteilung, Jüterbog, 'secret weapons' were tested, here one of two self-propelled gun carriages with the powerful 10.5-cm K 18 cannon.

A powerful leap in development from the 7.5-cm stump cannon to this giant gun.

The two cannons were mounted respectively on a converted Panzer Mark IV frame and box chassis. Both prototypes were tested in 1942 by 3 Panzer Division in the East, where they were found to be too heavy and lacking mobility in action.

Forty winks near a light ammunition panzerwagen Sd.Kfz 250/6. A steel helmet is hung up on the MG 34.

Hermann Röhm in regular field-grey StuG uniform which had the same style as the Panzertruppe issue.

Command personnel play a hand of skat near the barracks entrance, identities unfortunately no longer known.

An interesting view through the rear loading hatch into the interior of an armoured ammunition-carrier. The driver's seat is to the left, the radio operator's to the right. In the foreground are the closed flaps of the ammunition container. These vehicles could tow a trailer.

View into the engine compartment of an armoured ammunition-carrier. Two oil caps can be seen on the cylinder head cover.

Opened ammunition trailer (Sd.AnH 32A) with 7.5-cm HE shell 34. Sixty-four shells were carried in two chambers. A light armoured ammunition-carrier Sd. Kfz 252 could transport about 150 rounds.

The driver of a Kfz 15 Staff car. There is a good view of the instrument panel.

Hermann Röhm standing by an armoured ammunition-carrier (Sd.Kfz 252).

Wehrmacht Army registration plate and 'L' for Lehrabteilung clearly seen here.

Manoeuvres in the sand of Mark Brandenburg close to a ruined bunker, end of May 1942.

A comrade of the service team with screwdriver.

Apparently little
enthusiasm for
maintenance.

A view over the boiler
mounted on the field-
kitchen lorry.

The 3-tonne Magirus Klöckner Deutz lorry with which the Lehrabteilung was uniformly equipped.

These reliable lorries were produced between 1941 and 1943.

Time for a quick smoke by a lorry. On its roof is a triangular reflector.

View of the driving position of an StuG with open driver's shield. The driver is holding the left steering lever which works on the steering brake. To the right of the picture is the crank to elevate the cannon.

Close-up of an StuG's 7.5-cm L/24 stump cannon. From mid-1942 StuGs at the front were fitted with the long-barrel L/48 which increased firepower sufficiently to engage the Russian T-34 tank.

Hermann Röhm shortly before leaving Jüterbog.

The last evenings in a warm bed. From 21 December 1942 the company loaded up and moved out for Russia.

Chapter One

The Formation of StuG Abteilung 191 at Jüterbog, October–December 1940

StuG Abteilung 191 – known as the Sturmartillerie Abteilung until January 1941 – was one of the first four Abteilungen to be formed at the Artillerie-Lehrregiment at Jüterbog after the campaign in France in 1940.

The first course began in August 1940. Some of the radio operators were trained at the Army Signals School, Halle. The basic training at Jüterbog lasted about six weeks and from this course the core group was chosen for the four new Abteilungen.

On 1 October 1940 the formation of StuG Abteilung 191 at Jüterbog Old Camp was begun; the NCOs and men arrived and were assigned to their respective batteries. They were volunteers from artillery and motor vehicle units from all areas of Greater Germany. The knowledge that they belonged to a completely new, special Arm, initially secret, bonded the men together.

Our first Abteilung commanding officer was Hauptmann Hoffmann-Schoenborn, a career soldier from an old Posen military family who later settled in Lower Silesia. In 1924 he had joined Art.Regt 3 as an officer cadet; during the French campaign he was awarded the Iron Cross First Class and Second Class.

Once the authorized strength in personnel had been reached, the batteries were put together. Vehicles and equipment were fetched from the works and supply compounds, the StuGs from the Altmark track factory, Alkett in Berlin, and automobiles from Magdeburg. Each battery received six StuG assault guns armed with the 7.5-cm cannon, and the corresponding number of armoured half-track command and ammunition vehicles. A specially designed plan had as many men under training at a time as possible.

During this formation period we got to know our commanding officer. He visited every man at his position and discussed his opinion of the new weapon. He had a friendly word for everyone, praised achievements, rebuked shortcomings and errors. From these encounters the respect of the men for the commander grew.

The symbol for StuG Abteilung 191, a buffalo in attack mode, was approved and painted on all vehicles. To distinguish the individual batteries the emblem was coloured: Staff Battery bright blue, 1 Battery red, 2 Battery dark blue, 3 Battery yellow. It was a good choice of symbol, from which the honourable name 'Buffalo Brigade' was derived and which during the war – it is fair to say – became a byword. Once the formation of the Abteilung was completed, it transferred into the Adolf Hitler Lager where the batteries underwent battle training, the high point being the firing of live ammunition across the wide expanses of the training depot.

StuG Abteilung 191 – Occupation of Posts (as at October 1940)
Commanding Officer: Hauptmann Hoffmann-Schoenborn
Adjutant: Oberleutnant Anacker
1 Staff Officer: Leutnant Heise
2 Staff Officer: Leutnant Barths
Supplies Officer: Leutnant Pantel
Medical Officer: Stabsarzt Dr Gräve
Paymaster: Oberzahlmeister Feulner
Troop Engineer: Kriegsverwaltungsrat Mayr
Technical Inspector: Oberinspektor Heder
Foreman: Unteroffizier Knubben

Staff Battery
Battery Commander: Oberleutnant Möller
Reconnaissance Officer: Leutnant Hoppenstedt
Senior Radio Operator: Oberfunkmeister Gutowski
Artificer: Unteroffizier Kala
Armourer: Wachtmeister Weindl
Company Sergeant Major: Hauptwachtmeister Bork
Motor Pool Intendent: Oberschirrmeister Wohllaib
Vehicle Recovery Leader: Wachtmeister Immler

1 Battery

Battery Commander: Hauptmann von Schönau
Platoon Leaders:
Oberleutnant Vaerst,
Leutnatn Kollböck,
Leutnant Scheermann,
Leutnant Stoll,
Leutnant Berendes
Battery Sergeant Major: Hauptwachtmeister Genz
Motor Pool Intendent: Oberschirrmeister Spintig (now) Wohlt

2 Battery

Battery Commander: Oberleutnant Kapp
Platoon Leaders:
Oberleutnant von Bockum-Dolffs,
Leutnant Lützow,
Leutnant Vollrath,
Leutnant Nordhoff, plus one drafted
Battery Sergeant Major: Hauptwachtmeister Gotsch
Motor Pool Intendent: Schirrmeister Hammerstein

3 Battery

Battery Commander: Oberleutnant Haarberg
Platoon Leaders:
Leutnant Heinrich,
Leutnant Götz,
Leutnant Heinzle,
Leutnant Fuchs,
Leutnant Bingler
Battery Sergeant Major: Hauptwachtmeister Preine
Motor Pool Intendent: Oberschirrmeister Wieckmann

Meanwhile, on instructions from above, an advance party was assembled 'on the quiet'. A member of this special squad was our comrade Kingler (3 Battery). This is his account:

Kitchen NCO: 'Where the hell are the iron rations?'

It was in December when Hauptwachtmeister Preine told me that I was to be discharged from the Wehrmacht on the grounds of my age. I should go home to fetch civilian clothing for my demob. I did as he said and returned a few days later believing that I was to be discharged. However, it turned out differently. I was asked on the spot if I would volunteer to be the driver for an advance party led by Leutnant Berendes (1 Battery), I would find out who its other members were in due course. At first I felt disappointed but soon the business began to capture my interest. Leutnant Berendes let me in on the secret and introduced me to three uniformed officers, for whom I was to be the driver.

I took over a Horch (civilian car) and prepared. On 12 December we set off for Vienna. At the Command HQ there we received fresh orders and were issued passports and rations for several days. Our next stop was the town of Sinaia in Romania. We crossed the Hungarian and Romanian borders without incident. The tension grew. In Sinaia we had to report to 16 Panzer-Div. which was stationed here in Romania to train the local army. Apparently we were still not at our destination, however. After a few days' rest – I used the time to get to know the mountainous region with the king's residence – I was given the job of driving engineers to the Ploesti oilfields north of Bucharest. I had never seen anything like it before. Everywhere were great drilling derricks and conveyor systems to bring up the oil.

Our engineers were to take over from New Zealanders – enemy engineers – as a measure to protect the oilfields against seizure and sabotage. I knew now that this operation was of the highest political importance.

I spent Christmas and New Year as a guest in civilian clothing and at the beginning of January was relieved to be among people I knew when the real advance party of our Abteilung arrived. I was now under its orders, accommodations had to be found and after 3 Battery turned up I put on my uniform, reported back and resumed as a driver, and later became senior service driver.

Most members of the Abteilung would have known nothing of this operation, which is why our comrade Kingler's account is published here.

Chapter Two

Operations in the Balkans, Spring 1941

The Lehrtruppe in Romania, January and February 1941

Shortly before Christmas 1940 exercises at Jüterbog troop depot were followed by an inspection. We felt sure that this heralded the move out. Our Abteilung Commanding Officer Hoffmann-Schoenborn was promoted to Major. Some men were given Christmas leave, those who remained spent a noisy, restless time.

At New Year the Abteilung received orders. Preparations and loading up went ahead without incident. On New Year's Day 1941 the entire Abteilung rolled south-east aboard several railway transporters. Apart from sentries accompanying the vehicles, all members of the unit travelled in the trains' passenger carriages. Our destination was unknown and we were not allowed to send mail.

We rattled through Prague, Vienna, Pressburg, Budapest, Arad, Medias, Sibiu, through the Red Tower Pass in the Romanian Carpathian mountains, beyond Pitesti to Grivina, south of Ploesti, in the centre of Romania. Here a harsh midwinter was making itself felt with heavy snowfall. The transporter trains were unloaded in the worst conditions of snow and bitter cold: for us a foretaste of the far worse winter which awaited us later in the year in Russia.

The men were given emergency accommodation locally to be followed later by a difficult 50-kilometre trudge to quarters in the oilfield region at Ploesti. The Staff Battery, of which more shortly, was at Mislea. 1, 2 and 3 Batteries were at Scorteni, Tueni and Tintea respectively. Each battery had the task of making its allocated quarters inhabitable to some extent. Stoves, sacks of straw, firewood, petroleum lamps and much else had to be bought and soon our quarters were winterproof. Later large hangars with retractable roofs were erected for the vehicles.

The worst quarters were at Mislea in an evacuated women's prison. The building was antiquated and susceptible to minor earthquake activity. The community room and cells looked as though they dated from the Middle Ages. There was no alternative, though, and so I as the 'Spiess' – Company Sergeant Major (CSM) – had to get the men to make do as best they could. A thorough cleaning operation aimed at vermin control, particularly to stamp out the fleas and bugs, was not successful. Our hearts went out to all the women who had had to serve time in this place.

Only a third of our wage was paid in the local currency, 'lei'. We could buy anything but were not allowed to send home packets or parcels. For supplies and tactically the Abteilung was attached to Panzer Gruppe 1 at Bucharest. The roads to the capital were monitored by a motorcycle combination of the reconnaissance troop led by Wachtmeister Zinnecker. This troop also carried out courier duty.

Our relationship with the local population was good. We made excursions to Sinaia, Campina, Ploesti and Bucharest to get to know the land and people. We were shocked at the lack of cleanliness in houses and surroundings, both in town and in the villages. The great class difference between rich and poor, not only in civilian life but in the Romanian Army too, appalled us.

The inexhaustible oil reserves of Ploesti which we had come to protect convinced us of the economic potential of Romania. The oilfields were of outstanding strategic significance. For us 'young' StuG III gunners it was important to familiarize ourselves with the terrain at the foot of the Carpathian mountains. We exercised across a theatre of narrow, iced-over paths and snow-covered fields. Many of the tracked vehicles slid into wayside ditches.

From the *Bukarester Tageblatt*, a newspaper published in German, we learned of the political instability of Romania. The forced territorial concessions to the Soviet Union, Hungary and Bulgaria in 1940 had shattered the structure of this scarcely twenty-year-old Balkan state. Accordingly, on 6 September 1940 the government under General Ion Antonescu had joined the Axis, and German troops were being stationed in the country by invitation, including StuG Abteilung 191. With Hitler's support, Antonescu had been able to put down the rebellion of the Iron Guard which assisted him in the 1940 *coup d'état*. We sat out the crisis but in a state of immediate readiness to intervene. On 23 January, order was restored. Young King Michael remained king, but without power. The present leaders ruled Romania as dictators and later led it on Germany's side against the Soviet Union.

Danger threatened next in the Aegean, from where Great Britain was poised to move its forces against certain Balkan states. More German troops arrived in Romania, and as the winter slackened, great new preparations were put in hand for the year 1941.

The March through Bulgaria, March 1941

Bulgaria joined the Axis on 1 March 1941. As agreed with its government, German forces crossed the Danube the following day in order to protect Bulgarian interests and oppose the British Empire's intentions to extend the war into the Balkans. Britain immediately broke off diplomatic relations with Bulgaria. In an official note, the Soviet Union disapproved of the Bulgarian action but without mentioning Germany.

After receiving orders on 1 March to cross into Bulgaria, StuG Abteilung 191 reached the temporary bridge over the Danube at Giurgiu erected by German sappers on 2 March and crossed the 1-kilometre wide frontier river. The crossing went ahead without a hitch while the Bulgarians looked on smiling.

The icy cold of the previous night, which had been spent in our vehicles on the Rustchuck–Tarnavo road, turned into mild March sunshine. The population showered us with flowers, nuts and dried fruit. How different they were from the reserved Romanians. Through Tarnavo, the former Bulgarian capital, we continued into the Yantra Valley with its narrow, precipitous, jagged walls on one side and the torrential river on the other – which we had crossed by means of an ancient arched bridge at Gabrovo.

After some hold-ups in the column, finally on 5 March we reached the crest of the Shipka Pass at 1,338 metres, with its incredible panorama of the snow-covered peaks of the great Balkan mountains. A memorial stone there records the brave resistance of Russian troops against the invading Turks in 1877. Swathes of mist drifted over the snowy passes. Our StuGs had made the strenuous climb without incident and, despite the clouds of dust which reduced visibility, suffered no damage on the way down by keeping our distance.

At Rosental, Kasanlik, we emerged into the sunny climate of more southerly terrains, though the flowers of the valley were not yet in bloom. At Panicerevo and Zmeynovo the batteries made their first long stops and spent fourteen days there to rest while the vehicles were overhauled and repaired. The populace was well disposed towards us, inviting us into their clean and comfortable houses and showing us Bulgarian hospitality at its best. The people of these mountains and valleys were known then as the 'Prussians of the Balkans', a judgement we were happy to endorse. The meals of mutton and the high-percentage plum schnapps moved even the toughest panzer driver to tears of gratitude. There were thermal baths at Panicerevo and at Stara Zagora, a friendly township south of the mountain range and at lower altitude. Our men spent their leva, the national currency, on civilian enjoyments: apparently it did not buy much.

On 16 March 1941 the Otto motors of our panzers roared and we set off up the Maritza Valley via Plovdiv, the ancient city of Philippopolis dating from the fourth century BC, to Pazardshick and over the Trayans Pass into the basin of Sofia, the Bulgarian capital. We could not delay there long; our journey continued northwards through the Isker Valley to Kurilo, Ilyanzt and Kumariza, where we laid up. As we pulled out, 2 Battery suffered its first mortality when Obergefreiter Lüders was crushed to death by a StuG in a collision with his motorcycle. He was buried in the cemetery at Zmeynovo.

'A rolling stone gathers no moss.' Only fleeting images remain in our minds. This was the case in Sofia: we remembered little of this interesting city: the clean, modern streets, the castle of the tsars, the Alexander Nevsky Cathedral, the mosques … we forgot them all when we set off once more on 25 March southwards towards the Greek frontier. Our stops were at Pernik, Radomir, Dupnitza, Gorna Dyumaya. We followed the river Struma through the narrow Kresna Pass while the western foothills of the Rhodope mountains seemed to loom larger, in great massifs up to 3,000 metres high.

Two kilometres south of Livunovo we reached the readiness area of Inf.Regt 125. Our 1 Battery left us on 26 March for Nevrokop, a town amid the Rhodopes, and 72 Infanterie-Division (Inf.Div.). After a run of nearly 220 kilometres we made a peaceful bivouac stop near the Greek frontier. It lay a little to one side of our route of advance into Greece, at the foot of a mountain with a near-dry river, the Melnitza, which flowed into the Struma at Kula. We arranged the vehicles into a laager with tents at the centre. The men passed the time around the campfire. Here in the readiness area, in sight of the snow-covered mountain ranges surrounding us, the Abteilung passed relaxing sunny days. The high point was a merry evening spent in a gulch shaped like an amphitheatre. An infantry band provided the music. Sporting events, especially football matches, were held during the day. The light entertainment was accompanied by croaking frogs in the flickering firelight. W. Seibokat rounded off the event with his rendition of the Wehrmacht soldier's song, 'Es ist so schön Soldat zu sein, Rosemarie …'

The following morning brought the reality nearer. All the indications were that we would be involved in operations against the Metaxas Line, and against the most difficult part of it protecting the Bulgarian–Greek mountain range, the Rupel Pass position, the gateway created by the Struma.

12 Armee under Feldmarschall List had the task, supported by Luftflotte 4, of carrying out attacks against Skopye in southern Yugoslavia and Salonika on a broad front over the Greek frontier to the south. The objective was quickly to occupy the northern coast of the Aegean from Salonika to the Turkish border in order to secure the Romanian oilfields. 5 Gebirgs-Div. had the difficult task of forcing open the strongly fortified Rupel Pass.

The whole 155-kilometre long system was called the Metaxas Line after Minister President General Metaxas who, after employing Europe's most capable fortress builders for the job for six years, had announced to the king and cabinet that the wall was impregnable. Metaxas's confidence was based on his having led the scattered Greeks to victory against Mussolini who, in October 1940, had brought Greece into the war by attacking it from Albania. The ignominious defeat of the Italian invaders had forced Hitler to make war in the Balkans in support of his ally. The section of the Metaxas Line which interested us was a rectangular area 12 kilometres long and 5 kilometres wide at over 300 metres altitude, consisting of a string of forts and armoured cupolas equipped with the most modern armaments, arsenals with ammunition supplies and weapons in reserve, anti-tank obstacles and wire fencing. Each section was connected to the next by tunnels and had rooms which extended 80 metres into the mountains to provide accommodation for the crews, provisions stores and dressing stations. The defence force was sixty officers and 3,000 men, the elite of the Greek Army. 5 Gebirgs-Div. now had orders to prepare and carry out the attack on this section of the Metaxas Line.

The Greek Campaign, April 1941

The Attack on the Metaxas Line at the Rupel Pass, 6–10 April 1941

Combat Mission, Battle Organization and Deployment

Our Abteilung was attached to 12 Armee/XVIII Armeekorps for the impending attack. The Korps had placed two StuG batteries with Inf.Regt 125, and one battery with 72 Inf.Div., each with repairs detachments and recovery vehicles.

After reaching the readiness area south of Livunovo on 27 March, they were given their orders the same day at Inf.Regt 125. These orders specified that they were to:

(a) Provide support for the breakthrough to the Struma bridge by three attack groups (concentration of effort on left side), east of Neo Petritsi at the forefront of Inf.Regt 125.
(b) Eliminate enemy heavy weapons not destroyed by artillery and Stukas.
(c) Maintain closest cooperation with infantry which will have broken through.
(d) Secure the bridgehead with all available weapons.

The Abteilung Commanding Officer suggested the following organization (the direction of the attack was southwards):

1 Attack Group West: Along the road close to the west side of the Struma, 3 Battery (less one platoon) with four StuGs (Oberleutnant Haarberg).
2 Attack Group Centre: Along the Struma Valley road, one platoon of 3 Battery with two StuGs (Leutnant Heinrich).
3 Attack Group East: Support for the concentration of effort group via Height 350, Height 322 north-east of Klidi, Height 520 (north-east of Lutra) to the bridgehead to the east. Staff and 2 Battery with six StuGs (Oberleutnant Kapp).
4 Regimental Command Post: Report Centre (Oberleutnant Göring) in radio contact with Abteilung CO and all batteries involved. The CO in person to be with Attack Group East Battery.

This suggestion was adopted. The battery commanders and the 3 Battery platoon leader joined their attack groups and made their survey and reconnaissance reports. The Abteilung CO controlled the reconnaissance work and reported personally on the possibilities for the StuGs to cross the river Bistritza south-east of Kulata.

On 2 April, 3 Battery fighting unit/Attack Group West advanced to a readiness area west of the Struma so as not to endanger the operation by blocking the shaky bridge west of Marinopole on the eve of the attack.

Towards evening on 5 April 1941 the Abteilung received from Division the order to advance and that night the troops of the attack groups moved out and fighting vehicles rolled into the readiness areas. The night was bright with good visibility and headlights were not used. The Staff combat train of which I had charge went forward with provisions for the Battle Staff and motorcycle riders. So far no shot had been fired. Each man was given rations, cigarettes, chocolate and a quarter-litre of pear schnapps. Since nobody could sleep, the men passed the time playing cards. Meanwhile the CO attended the final operational conference at Inf.Regt 125 (Oberst Petersen).

The regiment had decided for the time being to send only one StuG battery towards the height over the Rupel Pass. It would be the job of the artillery to give this battery fire support. The Armee knew of the difficulties which the Abteilung had to face but insisted nevertheless that the StuGs would fight in the foremost line because only they would be in a position to destroy the strong bunker installations.

At about 0300 hrs the German side switched off all engines. Total silence returned to the valleys and mountaintops. No Very lights were fired, a hush descended over the whole front. Even the repairs detachments, the indefatigable servants of the StuGs, relaxed. They had done all they could to ensure that the vehicles were operational and battleworthy. Oberwachtmeister Immler's 18-tonne towing machine proceeded to the Bistritza to be on hand should any StuG require extraction from the river.

At 0515 hrs we greeted the dawn. Rifle fire came from Height 1224, then silence fell once more. The endless waiting got very much on one's nerves. I took my men of the combat train to the adjacent mountaintop to observe the attack.

At 0530 hrs the sun rose blood red in the east. The first of our anti-tank guns – Pak – fired. Precisely as the second hand reached the top of the dial, the silence of the morning was broken by the thunder of 250 artillery and flak barrels.

The attack began. Shellfire resounded, whizzed and whistled through the valley of the Struma. Within a few minutes Height 350 became enveloped in swathes of smoke, accompanied by explosive flashes. The barrage lasted thirty minutes. After this the Greek bunker positions were no longer recognizable. It seemed almost as if we had dealt the enemy a mortal blow, for they had not returned fire. They remained silent and we could not understand why. Through field glasses we saw how the area was pock-marked with countless shell craters, but not a single lump of concrete. Our offensive against the Metaxas Line had apparently failed.

Our Stukas came droning over. They climbed to altitude, the first tipped over the wing, then the second followed, their 'trumpets of Jericho' howling. Now we were entertained to a half-hour of bursting bombs, rising mushroom clouds of smoke, walls of fumes, and an inferno of crashing and smashing. Once the Stukas had dropped their payloads they retired and now finally the Greeks responded with artillery aimed at our height, and which began to fall ever closer as they got the range. In haste we sought shelter in the extensive mountain galleries.

Some of our vehicles received shrapnel damage from the shelling. The radiator of the field kitchen was hit and the water drained out. Our cook, Gefreiter Lempfuhl, lamented the loss of some of the coffee because of this. We could count ourselves lucky that the Greek surprise fire had not come down in the gully. Flak and Pak hammered out from our mountain heights: the Greeks responded with machine guns and mortars.

Far below, the first German assault troops crossed the frontier at the river Bistritza. The customs and guard houses were swiftly occupied but had already been abandoned. The assault companies prepared for their advance. Four flame-thrower squads made their way slowly uphill. Machine-gunners took up position and awaited the order to move. The spearhead of the company lay about 200 metres short of the bunkers.

Once the Stukas were out of sight, the infantry received the order to attack. Every man rose from cover and made a determined sprint to cover the dangerous open ground to the bunkers. After the first 50 metres they received heavy bursts of machine-gun fire from Greeks who were dug in above the slope: the zone could not be covered without heavy losses. The company commander fired up a double red Very light, the signal for the battalion which meant, 'We hold our ground, enemy fire too strong.'

At once Battalion radioed his request for the StuGs. From the alarm report, Major Hoffmann-Schoenborn saw that the company had moved back in order to avoid being wiped out. The Germans had fallen for the Greeks' bluff of lying low; the bombardments by Stukas and artillery had been without effect.

The Experience of Attack Group East

2 Battery formed part of Attack Group East alongside Inf.Regt 125. Its orders were:

(1) To support the attack up to Height 350 with three platoons, i.e. nine StuGs.
(2) After reaching Height 350, (1) two platoons were to support the advance to the bunker at Height 322 and (2) one platoon was to attend the breakthrough by II/Inf.Regt 125 at Klidi.
(3) All available StuGs including those of 3 Battery were to advance from Klidi on the Struma road to the bridge at the southern end of the Struma Valley.

Acting on the report from Battalion that the StuGs were required forward urgently, the Abteilung CO passed the order to 2 Battery (Oberleutnant Kapp) who placed himself and his Command Staff at the head of the three platoons of StuGs. Immediately the column stopped at the ford over the Bitritsa where the CO reminded all StuG commanders to 'keep precisely to the line of markers'. An 18-tonne recovery vehicle supervised by Oberwachtmeister Immler with the Abteilung CO and adjutant aboard then forded the river, which was 1.2 metres deep.

The first StuG followed, the driver set his course, the assault gun descended into the gurgling, foaming water and ploughed across the mountain river to reach the rocky bank on the far side without a problem. The major, his adjutant, Oberleutnant Anacker and the commanders had watched the manoeuvre intently. The other guns followed in line equally successfully until, just as the CO was about to board the command vehicle, a mishap occurred. StuG 567 had just entered the ford when its left-side track slid over the rocks into deep water. The vehicle listed severely and water entered the crew area. Immler and his driver Grosskopf now put their expertise to the test, got the StuG to a sandbank, and from there to the other side by hawser. The gun crew used their steel helmets to bail out the water and StuG 567 was under way again two hours later. The supply vehicles and motorcycle outriders crossed by the emergency bridge.

Meanwhile the three StuGs of 1 Platoon had made for Height 350 and reached the infantry readiness area by way of a narrow path. On the way they came under machine-gun fire from the Greeks but it failed to penetrate their armour. Under cover Oberleutnant Kapp conferred with the officer commanding the assault company and through their field glasses they studied the incessant spray of machine-gun fire from the enemy bunkers. Having assessed the situation, Kapp hurried to explain it to the platoon leaders and crews of his StuGs and issued his orders. The StuGs fanned out wide and proceeded to ascend the hill. At this the enemy machine-gun fire stopped for several minutes. Apparently this was the first time that the defenders had seen this kind of armoured vehicle. When the machine-gunners resumed they fired at the now stationary StuGs with all available barrels but again saw no effect on the armour.

For the first time, the enemy was experiencing the firepower of a StuG battery. After a few minutes of pounding by direct hits, several of the concrete bunkers were out of action, smoke billowing from their interiors accompanied by the sound of exploding ammunition. After ten minutes, Height 350 was shrouded in smoke and fumes. Now was the moment for the German infantry to become involved. The Very signal to attack having been given, the infantry stormed the height in a 400-metre-long broad front and took it with only token resistance. The Greeks had already vacated all the bunkers, taking their dead and wounded with them. The first objective of the attack had therefore been achieved with few German casualties.

The battalion infantry was allowed only a short breather before continuing, and then its troops came under heavy fire from the direction of the Rupel Pass and were forced to withdraw. Another scouting party sent out by Battalion to reconnoitre the bunkers and find routes of advance less exposed to the view of the enemy reported on its return that the strip to be attacked by the regiment lay in the field of fire of at least seventeen bunkers equipped with cannons or anti-tank guns. There was also a gully so precipitous as to be impossible for the StuGs to cross. Furthermore its far end was in range of heavy mortars which could be expected to cause heavy losses.

After Battalion CO Major Ens had related the situation by radio-telephone to Major Hoffmann-Schoenborn, the Abteilung CO gave Oberleutnant Kapp the task of finding a way around the gully to link up with the foremost infantry groups. Kapp described his next actions thus:

There was no possibility of getting StuGs across the gully. We continued over trackless rocky terrain, my thinking being that perhaps we might cross the gully somehow on the other side of the mountain. This idea was brought to a sudden end by a heavy, splintering explosion. My StuG had been penetrated by anti-tank fire and caught fire immediately. I managed to bring out my radio operator and the fatally wounded driver.

Meanwhile my StuGs were returning fire at a bunker on the far side of the gully from which anti-tank guns were continuing to shoot. Six or seven more bunkers were close by it. A few well-aimed rounds silenced them, but scarcely had one ceased fire than another took up the exchange. This high ground bristled with fighting posts. During reconnaissance of a track leading to Height 322, platoon leader Oberleutnant von Bockum-Dolffs, who had dismounted from his command vehicle, was struck and killed by shrapnel from a shell, in addition to which another StuG commander and gunlayer NCO were seriously wounded.

After a quarter of an hour more I broke off the engagement since there seemed little point in going on with it. Under the protective fire of two StuGs I sent the others back into the woods. The regiment called a halt to the advance for the time being until all StuGs were out of the field of fire. The new attack would commence at 1730 hrs with Stuka and artillery support promised.

I set out on foot to look for a place which the assault guns might be able to negotiate. Gasping for breath and dripping with sweat, I climbed a path to where our infantry battalion was grouped. New men were coming here from the gully to tuck themselves away right under the saddleback, the Rupel central defensive position. There was no possibility of moving up on the other side, anybody seen would have been shot down for sure. I had no alternative: if my StuGs were to assist our infantry, they had to climb this path. It was just wide enough but took hours to achieve. Our losses were one command vehicle overturned and one StuG stuck in the gully with track damage. By 1700 hrs the four surviving StuGs stood camouflaged and ready for action on the edge of the gully.

The Stukas appeared on time. Before the first wing plunged towards the bunkers and bombed, our artillery opened fire. Stuka bombs fell in the hail of shellfire, we saw lightning flashes through the wall of smoke, heard deafening explosions resound from the rocky walls. The shellbursts and general cacophony drowned out every word. From a distance we watched this theatre of destruction aghast, and felt a sense of relief once it was over. Several bunkers received direct hits.

By regimental orders the StuGs were to form the foremost line. I gave the signal and they rolled forwards slowly, the tracks grinding laboriously through the scree. The path was uphill, then came a 300-metre stretch, a kind of rocky ridge with a 70- to 80-metre drop either side. This was the critical spot. If the enemy anti-tank guns had the precise range we stood no chance. The StuGs advanced nose-to-tail and reached the narrow backslope of the rocky plateau from where we were to operate. Here I halted them and advised Battalion by radio, 'Have reached backslope before the pass Height 322. So far without receiving fire.'

The infantry came up behind us and assumed readiness behind the edge of the height. Space was too limited for StuGs and infantry together and so I ordered the four panzers forward. They rolled across the plateau and tipped cautiously forward at the edge. Below them lay the whole line of bunkers. The StuGs sheered apart, aimed at their respective targets and belched fire at the Greek bunkers. Now the German infantry advanced, followed by pioneers with their flame-throwers and explosive charges.

Suddenly the air was filled with such noise that I thought my eardrums would burst. The ground shook. The Greeks had brought to bear at the rounded mountaintop every gun they had available. Shells of all calibres exploded around us. The quantity of their armament surprised our infantry as much as it did us. The infantry sprinted to the backslope for shelter, but many failed to make it.

For several minutes all four StuGs were enveloped in dust and dirt. Deafening hits hammered our armour. In all honesty I thought my last hour had come. To turn about in this situation was impossible. The Abteilung CO ordered the StuGs to reverse behind the edge of the height and remain there for up to four days as moral support for the infantry on the downhill path. The gunloader of the first StuG was our only fatality. As for the four StuGs, all sheet metal, track covers and superstructure had been holed, ripped or torn away, but the armour plates had held.

Thus ends the report of Oberleutnant Kapp. To sum up, the first day in action had not left us with much to celebrate. The objective had not been achieved despite the massive support of our artillery and Stukas, and the involvement of our StuGs in which we had placed such hopes of great support for the foot soldiers. After sunset, provisions, fuel and ammunition were brought forward by the 18-tonne recovery vehicle, which then returned with the wounded. The repairs detachment worked through the night to get the StuGs repaired and battleworthy for the next day. At the regimental command post a situation-and-operations conference was held.

Division had ordered by radio that that night a volunteer assault troop should pass through the enemy lines in order to capture the southern end of the Struma Valley bridge by surprise. The officer in charge was Major Ens, commander of II/Inf.Regt 125, who volunteered to lead it himself. Twenty men stepped forward as volunteers for this risky attempt. Ens collated all reports and held his own conference at 1900 hrs. He had not been granted an StuG, and only one radio NCO with equipment from our Abteilung was made available. The raiding party set off at 2100 hrs. The weather was more favourable than expected. It began to rain and the sky was overcast with low cloud. [The author has omitted any further information regarding this operation. – *Trans.*]

III Battery assumed a defensive position at the edge of the gully. Our Abteilung CO defended towards Height 322 with 11 Company and one platoon of pioneers. The night of 7 April 1941 passed quietly except for a lot of Greek nuisance fire. Otherwise the enemy made no preparations for a counter-attack and remained passive. Major Hoffmann-Schoenborn had let the debacle of the opening day serve as a warning. The next day he was content to use only a couple of StuGs for a series of so-called outpost skirmishes. Individual Greek fighting bunkers had been discovered in a side valley: suddenly the StuGs appeared, fired salvoes at the enemy and then withdrew. Four bunkers were put out of action. The Greek response was nervous with heavy defensive shooting.

Originally Division had decided to assault the Rupel Pass positions again on the afternoon of 7 April. Not all of the damaged StuGs of Kapp's battery had been repaired successfully and so the attack was postponed. Therefore the second day concluded without success.

During the night the drizzle became gradually heavier. A situation-and-operations conference was held at the Abteilung command post in which it was decided to begin an assault troop operation on the morning of 8 April. It would consist of one StuG battery and one company of infantry, its purpose being to determine if the Greeks had sufficient firepower to endanger an operation of StuGs attacking en masse. That morning Hoffmann-Schoenborn decided to send one StuG forward as a decoy. If the enemy failed to respond, or replied only weakly, the whole force of assault guns would move up and attempt to overrun the bunkers at a stroke, supporting the advancing infantry with unbroken fire. That was the plan.

The decoy was the StuG commanded by Oberwachtmeister Bauer of 2 Battery. The preparations for the attack were completed and the infantry stood ready. Bauer's StuG rolled up to the saddleback and opened fire. The enemy ignored it for two or three minutes but then let loose at him with all heavy weapons in the bunkers. Oberleutnant Kapp, observing this dangerous operation, called Bauer back at once, which he managed unscathed. Kapp shook his hand and said, 'You and your crew have performed bravely, Bauer! In half an hour we shall try it again. Meanwhile our artillery will give them a hammering and try to silence the enemy batteries.'

Bauer merely looked at his battery commander and replied, '*Zum Befehl, Herr Oberleutnant!*' The second attack was a repeat of the first, Bauer was pulled back again unscathed and no impression was made on the Greek defensive front.

The Experience of Attack Group Centre

Attack Group Centre, made up of the reinforced I Battalion, Inf.Regt 125, carried out a push ordered along the Struma Valley road. Leutnant Heinrich, command of 3 Platoon (two StuGs), 3 Battery/StuG Abteilung 191, submitted the following report at 2230 hrs on 5 April 1941.

Situation Before the Beginning of the Advance

Towards 2230 hrs on 5 April 1941 the platoon, consisting of two StuGs, a command vehicle, an ammunition vehicle, a repairs truck and two motorcycle riders moved up from Kulata to the readiness position.

Group East, which had been put together from I/Inf.Regt 125 and strengthened by one company of pioneers, one platoon of 10-cm cannons and a flak company, had the task of:

(1) Destroying the defensive development on the Usita, which consisted of numerous bunkers and fighting positions.
(2) To advance via Klidi, wiping out the fighting positions there in cooperation with the advancing battle group on the west bank as far as the Struma bridge at Neo Petritsi, and establishing a bridgehead there.

Battle Objective of 3 Platoon

(1) To cover the advance by 1 and 2 Companies/Inf.Regt 125 to Promachon and eliminate the white bunker, the spotter post and the known field positions south-east of Promachon.

(2) After reaching the western slope of Usita with 3 Company, to form an assault spearhead and advance to the bridge.

All details of this attack, such as demolition of anti-panzer obstacles, and mine clearance, were carefully reviewed with the pioneers.

Enemy Strength

Based on data from Inf.Regt 125, the strength of the enemy in the eastern sector was estimated at one reinforced battalion. The other fortifications were staffed only by crews serving the position without assault reserves. These crews moreover were older Greek soldiers put in as replacements because of suspected unreliability. The fortifications themselves had been built very sparingly: the overall opinion was that they would not be able to withstand a powerful attack using modern weapons.

The Course of the Attack

The attack was timed to commence at 0530 hrs. At 0400 hrs elements of 2 Company set up outposts at the Bistritza bridge, cooperating with 3 Company advancing west if it. By 0520 hrs the pioneers (2/70) had erected a temporary bridge for the StuGs and a footbridge for the infantry.

At 0530 hrs, the two StuGs together with an 8.8-cm flak and a platoon of 2-cm flak overcame the frontier bunker and crossed the Kulata bridge to the road. The pioneers had already demolished the first anti-tank obstacles there; the infantry followed close behind in the shelter provided by the two StuGs.

Everything went to plan initially. Three to four kilometres south of Promachon, Leutnant Heinrich met up with the company led by Oberleutnant Schulz at which point the defensive fire, from all sides including the west bank, suddenly concentrated on the already weakened assault spearhead. The ammunition truck was blown up by a direct hit from an anti-tank gun. The driver was killed. German artillery fire, which according to the orders should have been on call was not effective because the positions of the enemy artillery spotters could not be identified. The commander and driver of one StuG were wounded. After consulting with Oberleutnant Schulz, Leutnant Heinrich set out to reconnoitre without infantry. Under heavy fire from east and west he had advanced 400 metres to the road before coming to an area damaged by explosives that led down to the river Struma and was impassable for StuGs.

Meanwhile, the second StuG had become involved with a number of bunkers. Though seriously damaged by shell hits, it managed to reach cover. Leutnant Heinrich returned safely from his scouting expedition but the attack spearhead had halted, the battalion's progress being prevented by three bunkers. Leutnant Heinrich removed the ammunition from the immobile StuG and then pulled back 200 metres with the still viable StuG in order to engage these three bunkers.

One of the three was eliminated but the StuG then received two hits from anti-tank rounds, one to the commander's hatch and the other in the chassis. Damage to the gun recoil could be repaired in cover: when the StuG moved forward again, however, it received further hits from anti-tank fire, this time to the control surfaces, and the damaged hatch was blown off completely. As the StuG pulled back again its commander was fatally wounded by shell shrapnel.

Leutnant Heinrich's command vehicle was a total write-off; while attempting to re-establish physical contact with Battalion, the officer received a shrapnel wound to his left arm.

Attempts to get the crippled StuG operational failed and under cover of darkness the platoon retired, leaving the foremost StuG where it stood. Leutnant Heinrich reported back to Regiment to prepare his initial report.

Experience of Attack Group West, Operation Involving 3 Battery (Oberleutnant Haarberg) at the Rupel Pass, 6 April

Battle Group West was composed of three companies of Inf.Regt 100, two companies of Pioneer Battalion 659, one and a half flak batteries and three light field-howitzer batteries, and two platoons of 3 Battery/StuG Abteilung 191 to start west of the river Struma.

Objective of this Battle Group

(1) To disable three steep heights with strong anti-tank defences and wire obstacles, field positions and about twenty-five bunkers.

(2) Break through to the west bank of the Struma after overcoming dragon-tooth obstacles, minefields and at least ten more bunkers.

(3) Sixteen assault boats on the Struma, manned by two platoons of pioneers and one infantry group, were to navigate to a place about 3 kilometres beyond the first dragon-tooth obstacle in order to support the assault group advancing along the riverbank road.

This battle group was led by Major Geiger, commander of the pioneer battalion and included the two platoons of 3 StuG Battery.

Objective of the Assault Artillery Platoons

(1) Provide protective fire for the pioneers during their demolition of the dragon-tooth anti-tank obstacles.

(2) Engage the enemy bunkers during the breakthrough to the west bank of the Struma.

(3) Running support of the two pioneer platoons proceeding down-valley until joining the group of assault boats.

The Course of the Attack

The two platoons of 3 Battery StuGs went forward at first light into the reconnoitred advanced battle positions using bush and tree cover ahead of the first dragon-tooth obstacles. 1 Platoon of the pioneers (Leutnant Hansberg) was already present.

At 0520 hrs the artillery and flak began range-finding and then went over directly to effective heavy fire against the heights, which were bristling with bunkers. The Greeks made no attempt to reply. The conference with the commander of the pioneer platoon about the terrain, the indication of the targets to the gun commanders, a last few calming words and the whole business went ahead untroubled 'as if it were a shooting exercise on the training grounds at Jüterbog'.

At 0615 hrs the StuGs and all other fighting units emerged from cover and opened fire at the nearest bunkers, the Greeks replying with machine guns, anti-tank and artillery, aiming at anything which moved. Like great rocks in the surf, the StuGs stood on the open plain in a hail of hits, and returned fire. Hit after hit on the Greek positions was observed, nevertheless the enemy maintained continuous fire with enormous expenditure of ammunition. Three StuGs received serious hits but were able to continue.

The pioneers had settled in holes and whatever cover was available and dared not stand up. The platoon commander came running and shouted to the Abteilung CO that there was no possibility of demolishing the dragon-tooth obstacles at this exposed site, he had to pull out his men and seek another position. The CO accepted and by radio ordered the StuGs to pull back to the nearest cover on the mountain slope. The CO and platoon commander had spotted a nearby projection higher up. Access was by a steep, narrow path, and blocked by dragon-tooth obstacles as aerial photos showed, though trees and bushes provided some cover. While the reconnaissance was carried out and the explosives prepared, two StuG crews worked to change damaged tracks and reload ammunition. When Leutnant Hansberg reported that a line of dragon-tooth obstacles had been cleared, Leutnant Fuchs measured the breach and reported that it was passable.

Towards 0800 hrs the second breakthrough was attempted. The CO placed 1 Platoon at the head, followed by StuGs 1 and 3 (commanded by Oberwachtmeister Düring and Oberwachtmeister Klose respectively), and two command vehicles (Leutnant Fuchs and the CO respectively). The vehicles had to be strung out so as to widen the enemy's field of fire, the pioneers keeping as close as possible to the vehicle on which they had stowed their heavy gear. Platoon leader Heinzle had the task of taking both StuGs up a slope in order to draw the fire from an identified enemy position on a mountain spur, thus protecting 1 Platoon and the pioneers, and following when they were clear.

Düring's StuG set off, negotiated the narrow gap created by the removal of the dragon-tooth obstacles and then followed the winding path to a very steep slope which he began to ascend towards the Fort 2 fortification. Here he came under furious machine-gun fire and then well-aimed anti-tank fire to his left flank from the bunkers along the path. A hit on the armour plating shot three bolts into the back of driver Unteroffizier Leidel and also damaged the brake lever and gearing and caused the brake fluid to drain out. The StuG could now only be steered dead ahead or to the right. As and when he could, Düring managed to fire off two rounds while his driver struggled to get the vehicle to the nearest blind spot and was then removed with difficulty from his seat.

Unteroffizier Schurig, the reserve driver for the towing vehicle, took over from Leidel and was immediately ordered by Düring to bring the 'ruin' of the StuG out on two further occasions 'in order to finish off the anti-tank guns' He succeeded in doing this at the second attempt and returned to make his report with some satisfaction that 'the way ahead was through the dragon-tooth obstacles and not in the direction ordered'. The CO then pulled back the platoons in order to blow the way clear at a more suitable place.

For the third breakthrough attempt, after discussions with Leutnant Hansberg, the CO decided that the blockade would be destroyed by having two StuGs bring the demolition squads to the dragon-tooth obstacles and then provide them with fire support. StuGs 1 and 3 led by Leutnant Fuchs as platoon leader went as close as he could to the obstructions and dropped off the pioneers in their shadow. The Greeks at once began to fire down from all bunkers. This did not frighten the StuG men but disconcerted the pioneers very much. Major Geiger, officer in charge of the whole operation, observing the situation alongside Oberleutnant Haarberg, recognized at once that it was impossible for Hansberg and his men to carry out the demolition work under fire so heavy, and ordered it broken off, stating that a breakthrough had to be tried from better cover closer to the foot of the mountain slope.

It was difficult to extract the StuGs and pioneers from the hail of fire. Radio communication had failed and a runner had to be used instead. Gefreiter Steinbeck carried out this duty with outstanding courage. The StuGs and all pioneers were then pulled out.

The fourth breakthrough attempt was a non-starter after Major Geiger rejected the reconnaissance report regarding the proposed site.

The fifth breakthrough attempt had looked suicidal at the outset but was achieved easily. When Leutnant Fuchs stated that he believed it still possible that the remaining intact StuGs, once through the first demolition gap, could descend the steep slope by way of trees and undergrowth, the CO gave his agreement at once while Major Geiger approved the decision and went off.

1 StuG (Leutnant Fuchs), 3 StuG (Oberwachtmeister Piotrowitz), the command vehicle (CO) and the recovery vehicle ascended the steep path. Scarcely had they passed through the breach than the Greeks opened fire with all barrels. The leading StuG slipped and slid down the steep slope and then got hopelessly stuck.

Piotrowitz's StuG held to the right and descended successfully; the command vehicle followed but halfway down ended up resting against a tree stump. With great presence of mind, Piotrowitz pulled back and used the steel hawser to haul free 1 StuG and the command vehicle, Gefreiter Sablatnik doing sterling work here. Thus all four vehicles arrived on the plain beyond the surviving dragon-tooth obstructions, headed straight for the bunkers and field fortifications on the riverside road, constantly shooting as they passed, intending to use the mountain to shelter from the enemy forts. After covering the first 400 metres, however, to his horror the CO observed that a pioneer sergeant was clinging to the rear of 3 StuG while hits rained against its armour and that of the command vehicle. The CO considered that since the group was also short of ammunition, it was best to call a halt to the progress and bring the two StuGs to safe cover. There was still no radio connection between the command vehicle and the StuGs and Gefreiter Sablatnik had to act as messenger. There was now a mildly disastrous situation.

The pioneer sergeant who had been clinging to StuG 3 lit a smoke candle to envelope the panzer against enemy fire. Unfortunately this obscured the vision of its driver and a collision occurred with the command vehicle. At the same time a shell hit the steering gear of the recovery vehicle, bringing it to a permanent stop. The StuGs disappeared into a copse but the recovery vehicle became a sitting duck for the Greek guns. 'Everybody out with your weapons!' the CO ordered. For once he had luck on his side and scarcely a minute later his two men joined him in cover between a tree trunk and stump of a tree. The CO, the two crew of the command vehicle and the pioneer sergeant dug in with the help of a pocket knife while under machine-gun and artillery fire. After a while they were overjoyed to hear the roar of StuG rounds fired at the enemy positions.

After two hours in their precarious position the CO began to experience some disquiet. Calling to the others to stay low, he ran a zig-zag course from bush to bush to escape the pursuing Greek fire, heading for the StuGs positioned behind a mountain projection. About 80 metres short of it he ran out of cover. Leutnant Fuchs saw him lying by the last bush, hand signals were exchanged and then 1 StuG roared over the open ground and turned about in such a way that the CO could shelter ahead of the StuG as he ran back. The Greeks maintained fire but to no effect.

After a brief update, the CO had the following scenario: both StuGs were in good cover about 100 metres on the enemy side of the obstacles.

They had sustained no casualties but received many hits. There were two pioneers nearby.

The CO now worked his way back in leaps and bounds under artillery fire up the slope, through the breach and down the path to the readiness position where the immobile 2 StuG stood. Scattered around were small groups of pioneers and mountain troops: Hauptmann Dietrich and Leutnant Hansberg both lay here wounded. The remainder of the two platoons of pioneers had dug in together with 2 Platoon about 400 metres back in the so-called 'green gully' having suffered heavy losses.

No more attacks were made on this day and I Battalion/Inf.Regt 100 ordered security positions to be set up for the night. The disabled StuG was isolated and could not be protected by infantry. A pioneer detachment and a group from Inf.Regt zbV 800 had finally blown the desired gap at the foot of the mountain and drew back on the night of 7 April into the Blütenmulde (gully of blossoms). A double sentry post was set up on the crest of the height about 100 metres ahead of the intact StuGs.

The Judgement of Battle: The Greek Northern Army Capitulates

On account of the extraordinary strength of the enemy's fortifications, the ineffectiveness of the Stukas and artillery, the lack of reserves with I/Inf.Regt 100, it was decided not to mount further attacks in this sector, and the battalion went on the defensive. After a situation conference at Division it had been decided to start a fresh attack on 9 April, but by then the Greek Army had capitulated. The apparently impossible had become reality. On the early morning of 9 April, elements of II Battalion/Inf.Regt 125 were behind the bunker complexes of the Metaxas Line and had pushed forward as far as the destroyed bridge. Elements of II Battalion/Inf.Regt 100 had also penetrated behind these bunkers. This fact and other circumstances of which we had little knowledge had motivated the Greek Northern Army to surrender, and the bunker crews along the Struma also gave in on 10 April. From the bunkers which had made our task so difficult we led away 600 Greeks. Major Ens, battalion commander of II/Inf.Regt 125, was awarded the Knight's Cross.

StuG Abteilung 191 had fifteen dead and thirty-seven wounded in the fighting at the Rupel Pass for the Metaxas Line. Our fallen were buried in the Heroes' Cemetery at Promachon.

A StuG during the Balkans campaign. Here the protective shields for the headlights can be seen fastened down. Later they were no longer fitted.

The Struma Valley operation was the first for the newly formed Abteilung. Every man of the 191st had learned under the most difficult circumstances what it meant to engage in battle. Every man had extraordinary confidence in the new StuG weapon.

The Abteilung at Thermopylae, 12–26 April 1941

An armistice was not in force in the entire sector of the Metaxas Line. The Abteilung required two days to get its vehicles ready to move. The workshop platoon and repairs detachment had to work flat-out. On Good Friday the StuG batteries interred their dead in Bulgaria, the first painful bloodletting of the fighting units.

On 12 April 1941 the Abteilung set out from Kulata over the wobbly Bistritza bridge and through the Rupel Pass to Sisirokastron, then past Serres south-west over the Struma and on to Ksilopolis, a town in the centre of those mountains which rise between the Struma and Wardar. In the Struma Valley we passed the wrecked and often fire-gutted concrete bunkers and fortification complex.

Unteroffizier Hartwig with his field-pack radio came aboard on the bridge at Klidi to join Major Ens's assault troop operation.

It was cold. We approached Salonika, the capital of Macedonia, drove through the northern suburbs and continued westwards, crossing the Wardar by a pioneer bridge, went along Lake Jiannitza, then over the Aliakmon on course southwards. At Niselion a forced stop was made, the road being blocked and other units having priority. We watched a panzer division rattle by, accompanied by our sister Abteilung, the 190. The column into which we had been threaded now moved laboriously south and by 18 April reached the Aegean, which was totally overcast and dismal. At Litochoron south of Katerini we made bivouac.

Finally the roads seemed free and now the Abteilung formed part of 5 Gebirgs-Div., Group C, and returned northwards via Katerini for the Olympus Pass. The terrible craters in this road, evidence of the activity of the New Zealand Division, required the attentions of the pioneers and forced our column of vehicles to make continual stops. We slept in the vehicles and awoke next morning to the wondrous sight – after so many gloomy days of overcast and rain – of Mount Olympus in shimmering majesty, truly the seat of the gods of Ancient Greece, beneath a cloudless sky. The rainy season was finally over. Our morale now high, we drove up through the Petra Narrows and down to Thessaly, rich in rivers. We had to drive all through the night of 21 April, brakes glowing hot, no headlights, feeling the way dangerously through the darkness, and we would have lost an StuG had it not been for the alertness of its driver and commander halting it at the last second, finding themselves about to go over a cliff-edge on the serpentine road.

At daylight, short of Elason, we found a British provisions compound with huge stocks of tents, biscuits, condensed milk and tins of Fray Bentos corned beef, among other things. Ever since, among veterans of 3 Battery, this has always been known as 'the corned beef time'. Between then and our return to base at Brno in occupied Czechoslovakia it was prepared in every conceivable way, until we could no longer bear to even look at it.

From Elason to Meluna Pass (700 metres) and finally the plain at Larissa. The town had been destroyed by earth tremors and bombing, the former in November 1939 and the latter by Italian air attacks in 1940 and probably some by our Stukas. Henceforth we never fired another round in anger in Greece.

2 Panzer-Div. and StuG Abteilung 190 had cleared the way to Thessaly, breaking through the brave resistance of the New Zealanders at Elason. On

the evening of 24 April we passed the historical battlefield at Pharsalu and next morning in heat and dust our vehicles passed through the Dornokos Pass and the Othrys mountains to the town of Lamia and then Thermopylae, where the unbelievable occurred. On the afternoon of 26 April the Abteilung received a radio message from 12 Armee: 'Return at once to Salonika'.

A difficult 'about turn' on the narrow pass road went off successfully and then we retraced the route we had just come: Larissa, Elason, Olympus Pass, Katerini, coastal road, Nea Agasupolis (bivouac on 28 April), bridges at Alaikmon and Wardar and then through Salonika. At Nai Epivate, the bay to the south of the city, we set up camp on the beach, Mount Olympus being to the west in cloud. In fine weather we would always find our eyes drawn to it.

A field memorial service was held to honour our fallen comrades and after that we had time to reflect. Even now we remember the promenades, the shops and the harbour of Salonika, the remains of the old fortress. No doubt our predecessors in antiquity, who crowned this historical place up to 3,000 years before, did much the same kind of thing.

The Return to Brno in Moravia to Refit, 13 May–15 June 1941

On 13 May 1941 the Abteilung received fresh orders to load aboard railway transports. The journey took us into Yugoslavia, passing through Skopye and Nisch until just before Belgrade we had to unload again on 15 May because the bridges had been blown. This required a temporary stop at a village of the Banat Germans called Nova Pazova before continuing by rail through Agram, Baros, Pressburg, Lundenborg to Brno in Moravia where the entire Abteilung occupied the Laudon barracks. Those men not given leave had to overhaul the vehicles and StuGs.

Oberleutnant Kapp, 2 Battery commander, was transferred out to Jüterbog and replaced by Oberleutnant Möller from Staff Battery. Oberleutnant Brede was appointed to Command Staff Battery.

At a special parade of the Abteilung, our commanding officer, Major Hoffmann-Schoenborn, was decorated with the Knight's Cross. In his address he spoke of the Abteilung's achievements in the campaign in Greece and remembered our fallen. He emphasized that the decoration was not his reward as an individual for we had all fought so bravely and come through the difficult baptism of fire. In that sense, he said, he wore the decoration as our commanding officer with all due modesty.

A ban on leave indicated that the Abteilung would soon be in action once more. The final preparations to make the unit fully operational were made with haste. The batteries received printed buffalo shields in their battery colours as future route markers. It seemed that the route was going to a be a long one.

On 15 June 1941 the Buffalo Abteilung received its orders to move out.

The charging buffalo was the symbol of StuG Abteilung 191, later StuG Brigade 191, on its vehicles from 1940/41. Therefore it accompanied the unit on all its operations from the Balkans campaign of April 1941 until the retreat of the Abteilung in the autumn of 1944.

In April/May 1941 StuG Abteilung 191 transferred out from Germany to Romania and Bulgaria. The photo shows a celebration in a Bulgarian village. Far left in the photo is a StuG.

The Bulgarians were very hospitable. This shows some of the celebration in front of an Abteilung lorry.

Infantry and StuGs advancing to the readiness area.

(left) A donkey being tested by Gefreiter Ossendorf for the transport of men and supplies. Also in the photo is comrade Stich.

(below) The Abteilung at readiness at Strumatal before the operation against the Metaxas Line (the heavily reinforced Greek defensive line).

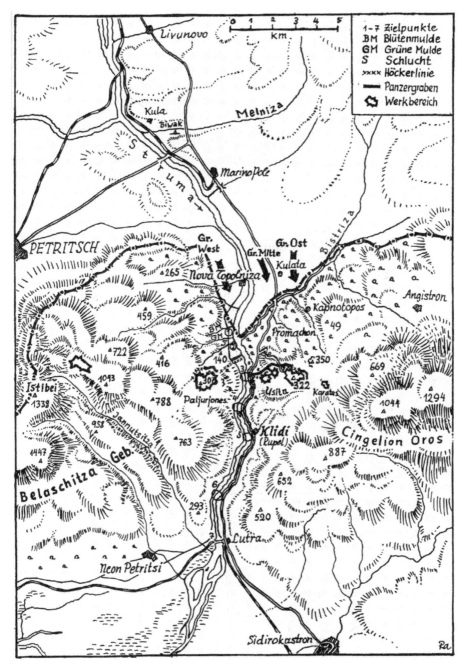

This map of the operational area of StuG Abteilung 191 between 6 and 10 April 1941 shows clearly the dominating narrows of the Struma Valley at the Klidi or Rupel Pass. (Key reads: 1. Zielpunkte, major objectives along Struma river, 2. Blütenmulde, gully of blossoms, 3. Grüne Mulde, green gully, 4. Schlucht, gorge, 5. Höckerlinie, line of dragon-tooth anti-tank obstacles, 6. Panzergraben, anti-tank ditch, 7. Werkbereich, fortified area.)

A StuG III on the way to the operation. This was to be the baptism of fire for the Abteilung. The vehicle is covered with a thick layer of dust. The mornings and evening remained bitterly cold.

Greek bunkers on the Metaxas Line east of the Rupel Pass.

Street scene in Salonika after the fighting in 1941, in the background the 'White Tower', the town's main landmark. StuG Abteilung 191 crossed the town on 14/15 April on the way to Mount Olympus.

Thick mud off the consolidated roads.

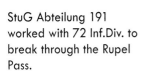

StuG Abteilung 191 worked with 72 Inf.Div. to break through the Rupel Pass.

Arrival at the Aegean Sea!

STURMGESCHÜTZ VOR!

Das Bataillon liegt an den Tafelbergen vor der stark befestigten Felskuppe und der Mondlandschaft fest. Der Feind stört durch starkes Artilleriefeuer und fühlt in die Schlucht nach dem dort verschwundenen Bataillon. In Reihe ziehen 5. und 7. Kompanie durch einen Graben weiter vor. Die schützende Dunkelheit breitet sich über stürmende Männer und blinkende Waffen. Die Spitze der 5. Kompanie erhält beim Vorgehen um die Felsecke Pak- und MG.-Feuer von der Felskuppe her. Ein kurzer Aufschrei! Gerade vor einem helleren Felsen hat das feindliche Infanterie-Geschütz den MG.-Trupp der 6. Gruppe gefasst. Ein Volltreffer schlägt in den gefüllten MG.-Kasten, der völlig auseinander gerissen wird. Die Spitze der 7. Kompanie entgeht knapp einem ähnlichen Schiksal.

Wie ist der Gegner zu erledigen? Die Scharte ist klein. Eine gut gezielte Granate nur kann eine Wirkung erzielen. Pak vor! Ein Geschütz fährt links am Hang trotz stärkstem Feindfeuer in Stellung. Wie glühende Pfeile zischen die Granaten gegen die Scharte. Der Feind schiesst weiter. Die Pak muss Stellungswechsel machen, um dem gezielten Artilleriefeuer zu entgehen. Sturmartillerie vor!

Ein Sturmgeschütz wühlt sich durch Gestrüpp und Unterholz vor. Der Oberleutnant hat sich das Ziel angesehen. Ein Pfiff mit der Trillerpfeife zieht den stählernen Koloss in seine Nähe. Kurze Kommandos werden im Panzer auf Hebel und Geschütz übertragen. Fertig! - Feuer! Ein Feuerschein erhellt den Talgrund. Alles ist auf die Wirkung gespannt. Der Schuss war etwas zu kurz. Schnell werden die Korrekturen gegeben. Wieder bellt der grosse graue Hund. Noch höher! Und dann dröhnt wieder ein Schuss. Getroffen! Der Schuss sass direkt in der etwa 600 m entfernten Scharte. Zwei Schützenkompanien freuen sich über den Erfolg des Sturmgeschützes, das für das Bataillon den Weg freigemacht hat für das weitere Vorgehen gegen das stark befestigte Malianga.

Am nächsten Morgen können wir uns die ganze Arbeit des eisernen Grusses aus nächster Nähe ansehen. Das Infanterie-Geschütz ist ein Trümmerhaufen. Ein Grieche liegt zerfetzt daneben. In der Ecke liegt ein Pak-Geschoss. Das Sturmgeschütz hatte sein Ziel gefunden und dem Bataillon wertvolle Unterstützung gegeben.

Authentic text regarding the baptism of fire of a StuG from the *Balkans Chronicle* of 72 Inf. Div. (*A battalion of 72 Inf.Div. had become pinned down in a gulch. Artillery, anti-tank and machine-gun fire was coming from the crest of a hilltop at one end. An enemy field gun had two companies in its sights. At the other end of the gulch was a narrow gap through which a well-aimed round would resolve the situation. A German anti-tank gun had moved up along the slope, began shooting but had been forced back by fire from the crest.*) The report continues: 'A StuG came up, flattening scrub and undergrowth. The Oberleutnant had identified the target. A blast on the signalling whistle summoned the steel colossus to his vicinity. Short orders were passed into the panzer. 'Ready. Fire!' A glare brightened the valley floor. Everybody had keen interest in the effect. The shell fell short. A correction to the data followed swiftly. The great grey dog barked again. Another round roared out. A hit! It struck directly into the fissure 600 metres distant. Two companies of infantry celebrated the success of the StuG which had now cleared the way for the battalion to advance towards its objective, the heavily fortified Malianga. Next morning we had a look first-hand over the work done by the iron monster. The infantry gun was a heap of twisted metal. A Greek soldier lay dead. In the corner was an anti-tank shell. The StuG had found its target and given the battalion valuable support.'

21 April 1941: a StuG during a pause in the advance. In the background is Mount Olympus shrouded in cloud.

A view over the Domokos Pass towards the Thessalian plain.

27 April 1941: StuGs driving through the town of Lamia received orders there to turn back. Greek resistance everywhere had collapsed and the German Army units were for the most part recalled.

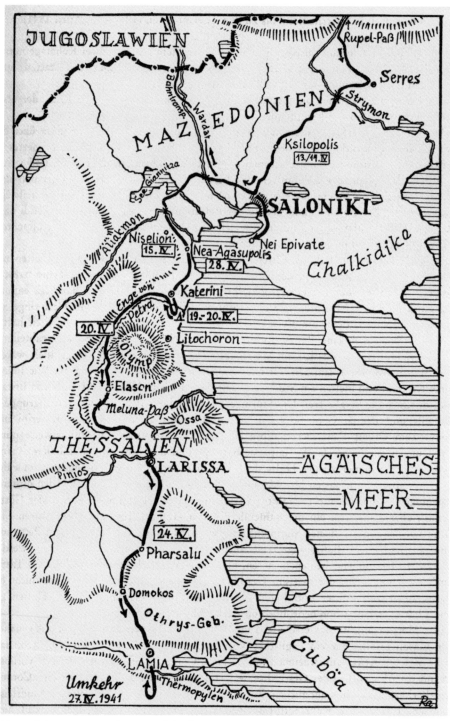

Map of the operational areas of StuG Abteilung 191 during the movement over the Rupel Pass to Lamia, 12 to 26 April 1941.

A railway truck with graffiti painted by members of StuG Abteilung 191. Returning home, the main interest was women!

The StuG Abteilung at Brno for refresher training. Here the Abteilung CO, Major Hoffmann-Schoenborn, seen in the circle of his NCO corps, received the award of the Knight's Cross on 15 May 1941.

StuGs arrayed at Brno for their next operation, not then suspected to be to the east again.

StuG Abteilung 191 took part in the attack on the Soviet Union (22 June 1941) from the first day. Seen here is a StuG of the Abteilung at Wolhynien, early summer 1941.

The burial of comrade Uhl of 3 Battery, Litovka, July 1941.

Downpours transformed tracks into paths of mud, as here at Yampol (Ukraine). The StuG of Oberwachtmeister Bauer has two lorries in tow.

This is how Wehrmacht High Command envisaged StuG operations: infantry and StuGs working together and providing mutual cover.

A StuG at high speed on a good road through a wooded region.

Hauptwachtmeister Bork (left, the author of this book) with Unteroffizier Weber outside their tent in Russia. Bruno Bork began at Staff and was later Spiess (CSM) with 3 Battery.

Map of operational area of the Abteilung in Soviet occupied territories, 22 June to mid-July 1941.

Platoon leader Leutnant Heinrich with his driver, Gefreite Gross, on an Sd.Kfz 253 observation vehicle. The running wheels of the tracks came from various 1-tonne payload towing machines.

Map of the operational area of StuG Abteilung 191 in the Soviet Union from mid-July to October 1941.

July 1941. Oberleutnant Haarberg, commander of 3 Battery, seated on his command vehicle during a situation discussion with Oberleutnant Göring (wearing helmet) and Hauptmann von Schönau. Despatch riders wait nearby for orders.

Leutnant Bingler of 3 Battery captured the important Dnieper bridge intact. He fell on 24 August 1941 at Dnyessna and was awarded the Knight's Cross posthumously.

Abteilung surgeon Dr Schroeder often retrieved the wounded himself while under enemy fire.

This bridge at Gornostaipol was destroyed by Russian bombers on 25 August 1941.

The workshop platoon with foreman Knubben (in uniform) at Yadlovka near Kiev, September 1941. Without capable men in the repairs detachments, a StuG Abteilung would soon have become non-operational.

An aerial leaflet showing the hopeless position in the encirclement at Kiev and urging the Russians to defect.

In the greatest encirclement in history, in September 1941 at Kiev, 665,000 Russian prisoners were taken. This misled Hitler into believing that the Russians were beaten.

A situation conference in woodland: Leutnant Schneemann, Hauptmann von Schönau, Hauptwachtmeister Genz and motor pool intendent, Schirrmeister Wohlt.

The Ukrainian city of Kiev on the Dnieper was a tourist and traffic centre, and also a strategic, financial and military centre of great importance. Stalin had great Party buildings erected everywhere in the city.

A Russian tank transporter has been destroyed by Stukas. Here a KW-1 tank is seen lying on its turret. The T-34 and KW-1 tanks newly arrived at the front were very difficult opponents for StuGs to engage.

Chapter Three

The Russian Campaign

1941: From the Ukraine to the Gates of Moscow

On 16 June 1941, StuG Abteilung 191 was loaded aboard rail transporters at Brno. A day's travel brought us to Chelm/Lublin where we had to unload and bivouac in a wood on the river Bug. This was the demarcation line between the respective German and Soviet zones of power. There seemed no explanation why we had come here. Germany had signed a pact of friendship with Russia in late summer 1939 and traded with the Soviet Union. The fine summer weather did nothing to allay the growing sense of unease.

On 21 June we occupied our readiness positions on the river Bug. Units unknow to us made camp nearby at the edge of the woods. They were equipped with rocket launchers which they called Nebelwerfer. We would soon get to know them. Our CO, Major Hoffmann-Schoenborn, came to see us that evening. He made a speech and then read out the Führer-Directive. The attack on the Soviet Union would be made in the early hours of the following day, Sunday, 22 June. It was said to be a struggle of life and death. We were struck dumb. What was it for? Now we had a war on two fronts.

The Attack as Part of 6 Armee, 22 June–20 July 1941

StuG Abteilung 191 formed part of 298 Inf.Div. for the attack. This division was part of 6 Armee/IV Armeekorps. A last operational conference was held at Division and now we waited for it to begin. An uneasy silence reigned. Our troops had occupied their readiness areas during the night and watched the clock. We wondered if the Russians had noticed anything.

Towards 0300 hrs it began to get light. This was the hour set for the attack. Somebody fired a shot, another followed and then all hell broke loose as the artillery and machine guns joined in. Shells and grenades howled and whistled overhead towards the east. Like glowing balls with fiery tails the Nebelwerfer rockets soared over us too. The sun came up blood red. This inferno affected us deeply. The town of Uscilug on the Russian side of the river went up in flames. We stood trembling near out StuGs and imagined we could already hear heavy fighting through the tumult.

A powerful concentration of fire protected our infantry as they crossed the Bug in rubber boats. Our StuGs covered the pioneers who were quickly erecting a temporary bridge. Within a short time the first vehicles of the division, flak and artillery, crossed this bridge. Our fighting units followed and raced through the burning town of Uscilug towards Voldzimiertz. 298 Inf.Div. had orders to advance to the outskirts of this town and set up a bridgehead so that Panzergruppe Kleist, assembled behind us in the woods, could break through into Russia in the east.

The major part of our Abteilung crossed the river during the course of the day. Russian warplanes attempted to destroy the German bridges but few reached them, most being shot down by flak and German fighters. It was a hot day. We saw the first evidence of atrocities committed against German troops. The Russians attempted to mount counter-attacks but these were easily beaten off. The alarm 'Gas!' came from the fighting front: a false alarm given by motorcycle riders coming from ahead.

A belt of bunkers offered the StuGs and our infantry fairly stubborn resistance. A line of bunkers was destroyed by firing into the shooting ports at close range. The German infantry spread out across the terrain. Communication between them was poor. Fighting continued over wide, open areas towards Vlodzimiertz. 3 Battery was almost without accompanying infantry when it was standing before the burning town. Oberleutnant Haarberg's four StuGs drove through it at top speed and reached the opposite side without firing a shot. Here there was a river with a wooden bridge leading onto a broad road on the other side. No sentries or defences were to be seen. Haarberg sent a couple of pioneers to examine the bridge and they removed some explosive charges.

To build the bridgehead it was necessary to identify and occupy the nearest elevation on the enemy side. Haarberg took three StuGs along the road towards the spot and in doing so received anti-aircraft or anti-tank fire. The CO's usual StuG received a hit to the chassis and took cover on the height itself. Here they had no radio contact with the other two StuGs and later it was concluded that it had been a mistake to withdraw to the height.

Haarberg radioed; 'Bridgehead set up. Spot height 2 km on other side of road.' The message got through. Hoffmann-Schoenborn passed it on, highly pleased. At dusk Panzergruppe Kleist advanced. Oberleutnant Haarberg stood at the roadside and saluted the leading vehicle, commanded by a Leutnant Rall. After reporting on the resistance on the far side of the height, the column moved eastwards despite a brief exchange of shooting. Oberleutnant Haarberg made his report to Hoffmann-Schoenborn and was mentioned later in OKH despatches.

24 June was a rest day for the Abteilung; the day after that the Russians attacked from the north in the hope of cutting off Panzergruppe Kleist during its advance. 3 Battery drove them off with heavy losses. 1 and 2 Batteries advanced with the vanguard of 298 Inf.Div. via Murya to the small river Stochod and set up a bridgehead near Kieslin.

On 26 June, 3 Battery was sent in the Luck–Dubno direction to Wolisa. 1 and 2 Batteries were withdrawn from the bridgehead and headed back to Kieselin via Luck and Dubno. On 29 June two batteries were added from 57 Inf.Div. 2 Battery fought under orders of 114 Inf.Div. south of Dubno and provided security there for LV Armeekorps Staff at Dubno. The other batteries resisted the stubborn Russian attacks south of Dubno–Luck to Brody. On 1 July, 3 Battery destroyed the ten guns of two Russian batteries.

On 2 and 3 July the advance Abteilung of 111 Inf.Div. with some 2 Battery StuGs pursued the fleeing enemy via Krzemieniec to Yampol. Our CO was then able to withdraw the entire Abteilung from the fighting in order to repair guns and vehicles and allow the men some days' rest. The Abteilung made bivouac at Lipovcy. 2 Battery returned from Yampol on 6 July. On 7 July 3 Battery was surprised to be called upon to join the von Auloch Group of LV Armeekorps for a Russenkommando. What this entailed is not known. 3 Battery returned to the Abteilung after the operation.

On 10 July the Abteilung proceeded at full strength via Lipovcy and Yampol to the Gritsev area to join LV Armeekorps at Verbovce. Heavy downpours transformed the roads into mires. Batteries and Staff vehicles which bogged down could only be freed with the assistance of StuGs and heavy towing machines. On 11 July 2 Battery was detached to 75 Inf.Div. south of Krasnopol to act as flank protection for 16 Panzer-Div. until 15 July.

On 12 July the Abteilung distributed the first Sturmabzeichen – Assault Badges. Recipients had to have participated in three attacks in an StuG in which the enemy lines were penetrated.

On 13 July the Abteilung less 2 Battery went to Lyubar to join 75 Inf.Div. We were now in the fertile Ukraine. The only people we saw were women, children and older people. They spoke Polish or Russian and their attitude tended to be suspicious. The terrain was among the most productive regions of the Soviet Union. The soil is black as coal, like garden compost. After the summer rainfall the temperature soars and everything in the ground sprouts. Endless fields of wheat, oats, clover, rape, maize and sunflowers proved the fertility of the land but despite that the people lived in abject poverty. Their villages consisted of huts or cottages with shingle roofs or thatch. Apparently they had no possessions but what they stood up in. Household effects were of the simplest kind and in general we had never seen their like before.

A 'mobile' stove would be found indoors, but for the summer months they had an open fireplace in front of the dwelling. Water came from several draw-wells that were in constant use. The churches were falling into decay and no longer used for religious purposes. There were no independent farmers; all formed part of collectives. Nearly every man and woman capable of labour had to work on one of these collective farms for a small remuneration. Every family was allowed to keep one cow from which 150 litres of milk had to be handed over annually. Pigs and poultry could also be kept, and a garden cultivated, but on a tenant farmer basis involving a relatively high level of taxation. There were no taverns in the villages. The shops were state-owned. The villagers were poorly clothed and few had shoes. Everything of value that they owned had no doubt been hidden away somewhere. Food was scanty, only millet gruel or pancakes, and bread was in short supply. The villagers had little furniture and the women wore no adornment. Strawflowers and simple religious pictures were to be found on the walls of their dwellings. Despite all the anti-religious harassment simple local beliefs had survived. This grim impression was not improved when we entered the Russian Ukraine.

On 15 July the Abteilung was deployed with 75 Inf.Div. south-east of Krasnopol and reached Klitenka south of Berditshev with the advancing infantry. During the fighting at Krasnopol the CO Staff reconnaissance car with Leutnant Barths, Wachtmeister Weindl, the radio operator and driver were surprised by the enemy. Leutnant Barths received a chest wound which saved his life. The Kfz 15 car with the radio equipment and the other three men were captured. We never discovered what became of them.

On 18 July the Abteilung less 1 Battery and workshop advanced via Berditshev–Shitomir–Korostyshev to Tesnovka to join LV Armeekorps. In the Radomyshl area the Abteilung was involved alongside 262 Inf.Div. against Russian stragglers in ambush positions; they often had to be killed off with HE shells or in close-combat situations.

On the evening of 19 July Battle Group Hoffmann-Schoenborn was formed with forces of the infantry division for Operation *Railway*. Freedom of movement in the Pripet March region was severely limited for motorized units so that even our Abteilung had to use the few log roads to reach combat areas. The railway system was used by the Russians to bring up their forces. The plague of mosquitoes in the swamps and woods was a great problem but the infantry came to terms with it.

On 20 July 1941 the battle group began Operation *Railway*. They reached the Korosen–Kiev railway line without opposition, the tracks were blown up by pioneers and the battle group returned to the starting point without casualties.

The Fight for Malin, 21–31 July 1941

On 21 July 1941 the Buffalo Abteilung advanced as part of 262 Inf.Div. towards the town of Malin. The Irsha bridge was down and this brought the division to a standstill. In the evening the infantry crossed the river by means of inflatable rafts under StuG protection.

We captured Malin and set up a bridgehead. The Russians clearly understood its significance for the German south-to-north axis of attack and sent all available troops to the bridgehead in an attempt to force us back across the Irsha. Thus on the evening of 23 July two regiments of infantry (482 right and 486 left) stood north of the Irsha in a hedgehog defensive deployment opposite Malin.

The enemy, strong in infantry, brought up his artillery which, besides light field guns, consisted of two extraordinarily lively and accurate 15-cm batteries which made life very difficult for the German infantry. In support of the latter, at midday on 23 July, 2 Battery was called in. Since it had only five StuGs operational, a platoon of two StuGs was added from 3 Battery. These two guns were commanded by Oberwachtmeisters Piotrowitz and Klose and were the only guns not under repair at 3 Battery after the three-day operation from 19 to 21 July. They set out at 1415 hrs, met up with 2 Battery on the German side of the Malin bridge and were joyfully received.

They remained at readiness until 0300 hrs when they crossed the bridge and went through Malin town to its far outskirts. Here the platoon of Leutnant Vollrath of 2 Battery and the StuG of Klose (3 Battery) received the order to proceed with 11/Inf.Regt 484 and a platoon of pioneers through the next village, Goroditshe, as far as the railway, and set up a hedgehog while the pioneers destroyed the railway tracks.

The StuGs led the infantry to Goroditshe, the town being completely enveloped in smoke laid by the German artillery, and passed through it without contact with the enemy. Not until they were making for the railway did they receive machine-gun and rifle fire from a terrace of houses. After they returned fire, ten Russians emerged and surrendered; others took flight. At the railway tracks the infantry formed the hedgehog and the railway line was destroyed by the pioneers. While all this was going on the enemy artillery targeted the StuGs, since this was where their shelling was concentrated. The StuGs were pulled back at about 1100 hrs and retired to a readiness position at the Malin eastern exit.

Generalkommando LI Armeekorps, Korps HQ, 30 July 1941
From the Commanding General
On 24 July 1941 an assault gun of 1 Battery, StuG Abteilung 191, in the fighting to expand the Malin bridgehead destroyed an enemy motorized 15-cm gun battery. This success was achieved by Wachtmeister Philipp, commander of the StuG and his crew, Unteroffizier Fuchsloch, Gefreiten Klos and Kanonier Kiesewetter, swiftly grasping the situation and reacting in a spirited and resolute manner. In addition, in the fighting over these days, their StuG was involved successfully on a number of occasions and made a decisive contribution to achieving our objective.

Wachtmeister Philipp has been awarded the Iron Cross First Class, Unterofffizier Fuchsloch, Gefreiten Klos and Kanonier Kiesewetter the Iron Cross Second Class.

Moreover I extent to the brave crew of this StuG my especial recognition.
Signed, Reinhard.

Because the situation had deteriorated under the constant Russian counter-attacks, Abteilung ordered another two StuGs (Leutnant Heinrich and Wachtmeister Labusch) from 3 Battery to join 1 Battery. Early on 2 July, Russian infantry, using unknown paths to the right of the highway, broke through to make a sudden appearance from the woods in the artillery limber park. After an exchange of fire involving losses to both sides, the Russians were forced back into the trees. The two 3 Battery StuGs were being driven along the highway to Malin when a flustered artillery Oberleutnant waved them down, explained the situation and requested protection for his force. Labusch was sent to investigate and his appearance resulted in a large number of Russians rising from the undergrowth and attempting to flee. As the StuG of Labusch began shooting, it started to sink in the soft ground of the woods until the hull came to rest on the stump of a tree, with the tracks above ground level. The enemy machine-gun fire now increased. Leutnant Heinrich, summoned by radio, used a hawser to haul the stricken StuG out of its predicament and Labusch was able to continue the mission.

Towards 1500 hrs, when the StuGs were resting in the readiness area, two Russian aircraft attacked and dropped about fifteen fragmentation bombs, scoring hits on the StuG of Oberwachtmeister Klose. One exploded on the roof with a fearsome noise, fumes and fire, others landing very close by. I doubted that the situation was survivable but when the smoke cleared all the crew got out, dazed but unharmed. The only damage to the StuG was a few bolts sprung from the armour plating.

At 1615 hrs the platoon of Leutnant Vollrath (2 Battery) and the StuGs of 3 Battery (Oberwachtmeisters Klose and Piotrowitz) were given the task of escorting two companies of infantry in an attack against the railway tracks to the north. While still en route they received from a despatch rider an order directing them north-west to find that the other two 3 Battery StuGs (Wachtmeisters Labusch and Schoel) had already resolved the problem.

Scarcely had they returned to the readiness position at Malin than came the third operation of the day. A dangerous gap had appeared in the German lines near Goroditshe and had to be closed at once. A 2 Battery StuG and two from 3 Battery protected the gap until a company of infantry arrived to relieve them at 2130 hrs.

At about 1600 hrs the other two StuGs of 3 Battery (Leutnants Heinrich and Labusch) had been called out to a readiness area west of Malin to join 1 Battery, led on this occasion by Oberleutnant Vaerst. The orders were to fend off a dangerous Russian attack coming from the north. One platoon of 1 Battery and the two 3 Battery StuGs advanced in a broad line and found their own infantry dug in on the northern outskirts of Malin. Driving between the trenches, they set course directly for the Russians, who were approaching in hordes. The sudden appearance of the StuGs seemed to come as a surprise, and when the first HE shells fell among them they turned about and began running back to the railway line. Two commissars armed with pistols attempted unsuccessfully to halt the stampede; once the commissars had been killed by the shellfire all resistance vanished. Even after the StuGs had pulled back and ceased fire, 160 Russians came over to surrender. Leutnant Heinrich stayed overnight to bolster the infantry line.

Between 25 and 30 July heavy fighting occurred around the Malin bridgehead. The Russians knew its importance and launched one attack after another in their attempt to overwhelm it. With artillery support we defended it without loss to our StuGs. Heavy shelling by the artillery of both sides transformed the disputed area of Malin into a cratered landscape. The woods ahead of the town looked as though a hurricane had whirled through them. The town itself had been largely destroyed by the Russian artillery. With a few exceptions the population had fled. The Russians had lost many lives and much material around Malin, and our own losses were considerable, especially in infantry. All hell had been let loose at Malin, that was the opinion of the infantry.

To direct the German artillery fire, our observers used moored barrage balloons with great success to spot the Russian batteries. This enabled us to engage the enemy artillery effectively. These balloons were often attacked by Russian warplanes. Although heavily defended by flak, a number of these balloons were shot down in flames. For the frontline infantry this was an interesting and rare sight.

The bridgehead at Malin was expanded and fortified by the planned advances of our infantry. On 30 July one battalion each from of 98 and 113 Infantry Divisions with StuG support headed for the town of Korosten which was captured the next day and cleansed of enemy troops. In this operation Leutnant Vollrath lost his life. 3 Battery, which had been in action frequently in the last few weeks, was now pulled out for rest and maintenance.

The 'Captain'

Our comrade Karsten was known as the 'Captain'. He came from Hamburg, and after serving with a horse-drawn artillery unit eight years previously had gone to sea. He had this habit whenever he spoke of squinting both eyes as if a strong nor'easter were blowing in his face. There was no such wind here in the Ukraine. If he got upset about something he would get muddled and begin to stutter. He was the best kind of comrade and companion. He had the rank of Oberwachtmeister and commanded an StuG. Thus his nickname suited his military position. Later he became Hauptwachtmeister in the same 2 Battery. Whenever the Captain returned from an action, everybody in his battery and the repairs team was always pleased to see him and set to with a will to get his StuG ready for the next sortie for then they would have a chance to hear his personal account of that day's action or of incidents he recalled from his years at sea.

The three men of his StuG crew were Berlin agricultural graduate Schorsch, his driver; Hermann, an East Prussian, who was his NCO gunner; and Sepp, a winegrower from the Tyrol, his gunloader. This gun crew were blood brothers. These three shipmates followed their Captain through thick and thin and he appreciated it. His full story can be read in Wagner's *Buch der Sturmartillerie*, and the episode which follows is taken from pages 91–4 of that volume. The incident happened at Malin and the officer involved was Oberleutnant Vaerst, commander of 1 Battery.

Another report had been received of a Russian attack on the bridgehead. The two StuGs, led by Vaerst, had gone out to support the infantry. On the way the commanders waved to each other as they headed into No Man's Land. It had been agreed that Vaerst would lead and the Captain would stay some distance to his rear to observe and provide fire cover if necessary.

After a while Vaerst's StuG received machine-gun fire from some bushy land. Vaerst fired back. The Captain's gun was approaching a field position from which the Soviets were 'firing like crazy'.

'They're not worth a round from the cannon,' the Captain said, and decided to use the tracks to crush the position. Scarcely had he completed the manoeuvre than he came under rifle fire. The Captain primed a hand grenade, opened the hatch, tossed out the grenade – a dull detonation, and the firing stopped. It was all his crew could do not to applaud.

Meanwhile Vaerst's StuG had reached a spot where the road bore right in a wide, endless arc. A panzer commander had to be vigilant at all times here because some of the road was blind to him.

'We'll go ahead anyway,' Oberleutnant Vaerst decided.

The motor roared, the StuG rattled into the curve. There was a bridge ahead. Suddenly from behind it there came a flash, a powerful blow and the StuG groaned.

'Anti-tank gun!'

Another heavy blow, the cannon jammed. Reverse gear, the StuG rolled back. Another explosion.

'Isn't that a second gun?'

Shell shrapnel flew into the driver's face. Oberleutnant Vaerst received a wound to his hand. Their nerve held. The driver, unable to steer, was lifted into the gunlayer's seat. Still rolling back, the StuG stuck in a sandpit.

Radio message to the companion StuG: 'We need help.'

The Captain and his crew had recognized the dangerous situation. Upon hearing the first explosion they had all thought, 'Mines'. But then Hermann had shouted, 'Burst of fire to the right, heavy anti-tank gun!'

Gunloader Sepp acted quickly. He fired three rounds, all on target. Now they saw the second enemy gun no more than 100 metres dead ahead. The StuG turned to bring the cannon to bear, seconds passed waiting for the anti-tank gun to enter the sights – one round – a hit. Two Soviet heavy anti-tank guns destroyed. Now they could go forward to assist Vaerst's StuG.

Gunloader Sepp volunteered to drive the damaged StuG back. He had never driven an assault gun before but had often watched the way Schorsch handled the levers. And he managed it. On the way, the Captain picked up two wounded infantrymen. By then the counter-attack had been beaten off. At Battery, the repairs team cheered them in and got the Captain to explain all that had happened.

From time to time the Captain carried a walking stick with an ornate head, later he took to wearing a white uniform jacket with polished buttons. This contribution is to his memory.

A Field-Howitzer Battery at Omelyanovka, 7 August 1941

On 6 August 1941, 98 Inf.Div. carried out an advance from Stremigorod to the north-west with the support of Battery Möller. Next day, Leutnant Bingler of 3 Battery was sent to relieve a light field-howitzer battalion of 262 Inf.Div. encircled at Omelyanovka. The following is the report by battery commander Oberleutnant Haarberg.

The officers of 3 Battery were in the readiness area playing cards when a despatch rider from Abteilung roared up and passed the order that one platoon (three StuGs) from 3 Battery was to report to Inf.Regt X. The greatest haste was required.

After a brief reflection I ordered Leutnant Bingler to go. He tossed his cards aside, grabbed his steel helmet and machine pistol, whistled up his platoon and set off. At the regimental command post, the officer received him with the report: 'At Omelyanovka, 3 kilometres ahead of III Battalion sector, a light field-howitzer battery and the remainder of my companies have been encircled. III Battalion made an unsuccessful attempt to free them after other efforts had failed. Now we ask you to help. We must have assault guns. Go at once to III Battalion battle command post. And hurry! Have you any questions?'

Leutnant Bingler shook his head, remounted his StuG and set off. The same story was repeated at III Battalion although here the anxiety was much greater. Everything was quickly explained on a map. Leutnant Bingler asked for infantry support. Battalion refused. Their infantry was so exhausted by the fighting of recent days that a further splintering of the battalion could not be contemplated. Finally after a great hoo-hah he was allowed one man to show him the way.

Leutnant Bingler ordered the platoon's armoured ammunition vehicle to remain behind and provided the commanders of the other two StuGs with an update, after which they both tightened the chin strap of their helmets and placed their machine pistols close at hand.

The route was 2 kilometres through thick woodland vegetation, the worst terrain for StuGs with no infantry support. The transit of the forest did not go too badly. A log path, in places narrower than the width of an StuG, led through the undergrowth. No Russians were seen. After 2 kilometres, when the StuGs emerged from the trees, their gaze fell upon the sorry sight of Omelyanovka. Most of its houses were burning. In the middle stood the four guns of a light-howitzer battery. Even its limbers were on fire. Dead horses lay around, artillerymen and infantry were sheltering in all kinds of cover around the howitzers and shooting – or rather, firing one round now and again. The howitzers had long been out of ammunition and little rifle ammunition remained. The Russians were surrounding them, clearly visible at close-combat distance and poised, when the order was given, to jump up and finish off the survivors.

Upon seeing the three StuGs approaching from the forest, a couple of infantrymen trapped outside the central arena stood up, pointed to the situation in the village and shouted, 'Quick, quick, the Russians!'

The StuGs at once began rapid machine-gun fire on the figures in brown uniform with greenish helmets, who then fled into the woods, and the Russian heavy weapons returned fire with all barrels at the hated StuGs. The encirclement had been broken, however, and the assault guns made for the burning houses. Twenty men and an officer scrambled aboard, the pure joy of salvation on their faces. 'Thank God you came. There wasn't much time left!'

Leaving the StuGs to fire at targets at will, the company commander and Leutnant Bingler discussed what should be done next. They agreed quickly that the three StuGs should drive along the edge of the forest in a semi-circular formation flushing out the Russians from cover ahead of them and so create time for the evacuation. Without it being ordered, every artilleryman and infantryman still able to walk rose up and began shooting, the horror, anxiety and fear of death of the preceding hours now finding their release in their shouts of fury. The StuGs fired and the infantry imitated the Russian shouts of 'Hurra!' in their wild pursuit of the Russians running into the forest for their lives.

From a safe distance the Russians took the village under mortar fire. Quickly, the two still viable howitzers, the still mobile half of an observer car and the troop's flak vehicle were wired to the towing hooks of the StuGs, a number of the seriously wounded loaded on the roof at the rear and then they set off very slowly, for the bends and curves on the log road presented a challenge and the wounded felt every jolt. After a two-hour long and difficult journey through the forest the platoon arrived back at the battalion command post.

The Model Operation, 14 August 1941

From the abundance of StuG operations, an example is provided here to show the versatility of the assault artillery.

6 Armee had ordered an attack to be mounted on 14 August 1941 by elements of LI Armeekorps and XVII Armeekorps to capture the strategically important Height 178 near the village of Medynovaya. The assault on 178 was to be carried out by two groups: 1 and 9 Companies/Inf.Regt 282 (Oberst Garns) with 2 Battery, StuG Abteilung 191, and 5 and 6 Companies/Inf.Regt 282 with 3 Battery, StuG Abteilung 191. The plan was for the two groups to capture Medynovaya first and then proceed to Height 178. This would ease the attack by the neighbouring 56 Inf.Div.

The two groups set out at 0530 hrs, 2 Battery leading with six StuGs as the spearhead. The edge of the village was taken, then by a circumnavigation to the northern side major casualties were inflicted on the two battalions of fleeing enemy troops.

By 0700 hrs the last resistance at Medynovaya had been broken, and the three StuGs of 3 Battery met up with those of the sister battery. 5 Company and StuGs secured the village. During this operation Leutnant Lützow (2 Battery) took twenty Russians prisoner.

At 0855 hrs on account of the artillery fire falling in this sector, Abteilung 191 decided independently to initiate the operation. At 0900 hrs a radio signal was received from Inf.Regt 282: 'Stop 2 Sector, neighbour still at edge of woods of Gorbatchi.' It was not clear in this message, reporting that 56 Inf.Div. had not come up from Gorbatchi, why the assault on Height 178 had to be delayed. Major Hoffmann-Schoenborn raised an energetic protest against the order, and at 0915 hrs he received permission to proceed on the condition that he would have to carry out the operation himself later if he failed the first time.

The nine StuGs led by Oberleutnant Möller had not received the message to hold back until they had almost reached the top of Height 178 by 1000 hrs. They achieved this without infantry, which had remained at Medynovaya under cover on account of heavy mortar and artillery fire. Protected by StuG fire, 5 Company arrived to secure the spot height at 1045 hrs.

Whereas Inf.Regt 282 and StuG Abteilung 191 had attempted to get 98 Inf.Div. to call the right wing of XVII Armeekorps forward into the new positions they could now occupy, and had sent several signals to that effect, the situation regarding the regiment on the other Armeekorps flank was not clear, and the failure of tactical communication left the matter in doubt.

2 Battery commander Oberleutnant Möller understood the situation in his own sector correctly. Leaving 5 Company to secure Height 178, and without waiting for orders, he headed west in order to do what he could to restore radio contact with the nearer Armeekorps.

At 1100 hrs Möller captured the northern exit of Gorbatchi and made the attempt to clear the village in a westerly direction. He was engaged by anti-tank and mortar fire from the south-west of the village for a while but then the Russians pulled back suddenly to the north to avoid encirclement, suspecting that the 56 Inf.Div. spearhead had reached Chodaki. They were intercepted at the Gorbatchi brickworks by five StuGs, where a section was cut off and wiped out or invited to surrender.

The StuGs headed to the south-western part of Gorbatchi and attacked the enemy in the rear. Two StuGs given the task of reconnoitring the wooded area north-east of Gorbatchi effectively halted the retreating Russians fleeing northwards from Kelenskiye.

Oberleutnant Möller left four StuGs behind as security and continued his westward progress, meeting up with a reconnaissance party from 56 Inf.Div. in the southern part of Chodaki, ordering them to occupy that part of the village south-west of the brickworks under the fire protection of the StuGs.

Möller established that another two battalions were deployed between Height 178 and Chodaki but south of the small river. Since there was no possibility of the StuGs crossing, he decided to persist with his attempts to establish contact with Battalion and found a company of the battalion at Soboshchina setting up a defence of the northern side of the village.

Next came an order from the Abteilung CO to Möller to advance his group towards Kalenskiye, and at 1330 hrs in the centre of Gorbatchi, free of Russians except for a few stragglers, he discovered another reconnaissance party from the other battalion.

Meanwhile the Abteilung CO, a little south-east of Height 178, had come across a broken-down StuG with a small assault party from III/Inf.Regt 290 and sent them to Kalenskiye from the east. 5 Company was also sent west to Kalenskiye. The enemy at Kalenskiye was present in about battalion strength, but upon seeing the Germans arriving from various directions realized that they now found themselves in a witch's cauldron and the majority decamped into the woods north of Height 178. There they suffered much bloodletting, and ninety prisoners were taken. The StuGs pursued the enemy until forced to give up for shortage of fuel and ammunition.

The whereabouts of the German infantry was not known precisely and the Abteilung had to hold Height 178 alone. The defence ordered was, to the north: around Height 178, four StuGs and a flak machine gun, leader Oberleutnant Göring; defence to the north-west, northern edge of Kalenskiye: three StuGs and one flak machine gun. The Abteilung command post was here. To resume contact with 56 Inf.Div. an officers' reconnaissance troop was sent ahead to Gorbatchi with a flak machine gun.

At 1745 hrs the first of the neighbouring units arrived at Kalenskiye, this being a bicycle troop from the south, which at 1820 hrs took over the security of Height 178, and a battalion of 56 Inf.Div appeared at the same time at the eastern side of Gorbatchi.

Towards 1930 hrs the order came for the StuGs to return to the departure bivouac site. During this move the Russians attempted to force their way into Medynovaya again but withdrew quickly upon perceiving the unintentional intervention of Leutnant Lützow's StuG with three ammunition-carriers at dusk. The rest of the day passed uneventfully.

The Abteilung considered the 14 August 1941 one of its best operations. It was a big success and its losses, even among the infantry, had been moderate. Furthermore, valuable experience and knowledge had been gained. The important points were that:

(1) An attack at the boundary between two divisions causes difficulties enough for easily moveable heavy weapons, but at the boundary of two corps causes far more.

(2) The technical standard of signals personnel and equipment must be effective or it will cause communication problems between units.

(3) On 14 August the situation and terrain gave all officers new opportunities for independent and far-sighted action which made success possible on the day.

(4) Even a merging of StuGs into a mixed battery is completely possible given ésprit de corps.

(5) Battery leaders and officers of the motorized assault artillery must often act on their own responsibility. This requires tactical training.

The Push to the Dnieper, 22–23 August 1941

After the conclusion of the heavy fighting around the Malin bridgehead, LI Armeekorps regrouped for a major offensive. 111 Inf. Div. had the special role of building a narrow battle strip as the central area for the whole operation and at the same time prepare what was required for the advance of 11 Panzer Division from the same battle strip. StuG Abteilung 191 was assigned to the latter unit.

The commencement of the attack set for 25 August was brought forward to the 23rd and then the 22nd at the last moment, reconnaissance having established beyond doubt that the enemy was pulling back from the front everywhere, apparently to form a new line of resistance further back.

Moreover it had been confirmed that facing LI Armeekorps were between nine and twelve Russian divisions under the command of one motorized and one motorized mechanical Korps. The actual strength of this numerous unit, which also included 'tank crews of foot' and 'paratroops of foot', amounted to the equivalent of two German divisions.

In order to pursue this retiring enemy front, an advance force was set up out of 111 Inf.Div. under Major Hoffmann-Schoenborn, its formation being as follows:

Vanguard

Officer Commanding:	Oberleutnant Haarberg, Commander 3 Battery, StuG Abteilung 191.
Men:	3 Battery, (Haarberg), 3 Pioneer Battery (mot.) 111 (Steinmann), 3 Panzerjäger Abteilung 111 (Hennig), 3/(wheeled vehs) Inf.Regt 50 (Nacke).

Main body

Officer Commanding:	Hauptmann Musculus, Commander Panzerjäger Abteilung 111.
Men:	Panzerjäger Abteilung 111 (Musculus), Staff, StuG Abteilung 111 (Hoffmann-Schoenborn), divisional radio post: 2 Battery, StuG Abteilung 191 (Schneemann), 3/(Wheeled vehs) Inf.Regt 117 (Scharrenberg), 3/(Wheeled vehs) Inf.Regt 70, one 10-cm battery, Art. Regt 285 (Hoppe).

Major Hoffmann-Schoenborn received from 111 Inf.Div. the following order: 'A vanguard commanded by the CO, StuG Abteilung 191, will be prepared to move from Baranovka at 0430 hrs. After 113 Inf.Div. has taken Guska, it will advance to Dukrova, Guska-Nord and Wychev. From there, on the orders of Division, after special instructions further advance to Termachovka, Ivankov.'

This sounds harmless, but the real strategic objective of this vanguard was not stated for security reasons. It was a bold plan, the success of which was very uncertain and a successful outcome unlikely. This vanguard with the striking power of two StuG batteries had not only to break through the Russian lines but then push 120 kilometres deep into enemy territory, reach the Dnieper east of Gornostaipol and capture intact the 2-kilometre bridge there in order to make possible a swift advance to the east by two German Korps. The departure base for the sortie of the spearhead was initially kept secret but would become known at the earliest on the morning of 22 August through an individual 3 Battery operation while attached temporarily to the neighbouring 113 Inf.Div.

The enemy's will to resist had again been underestimated. They defended well but 3 Battery got through to Guska and captured it as per the plan. The vanguard now set off but soon ran into fresh, bitter resistance north of Guska. Excellent camouflage in extensive fields of tall hops with machine-gun nests and anti-tank guns caused problems on the flanks until the StuGs, in cooperation with a company of the neighbouring division, attacked the enemy frontally and from the flanks simultaneously, causing several Russian companies to flee the field. The vanguard then set off again to reach Wychev, the first major objective, at 1500 hrs, after crossing difficult unknow terrain.

From Wychev the vanguard had a 'large new road' identified in an aerial photo which turned out to be a broad sandy path on which the StuGs threw up gigantic clouds of dust. Leutnant Bingler (3 Battery) now commanded the three StuGs of the vanguard. Making their way through the dust, the StuGs fired at anything in their way until they reached Krassilovka. In a brief fight, a hundred enemy infantry fled into a nearby wood, leaving twenty dead and wounded behind. The wheeled vehicles summoned forward cleansed the wood under StuG protection and captured two dozen prisoners. As they moved on, a cavalry unit appeared and attacked with great bravery. This elegant attack broke up the fire of the panzers but cost the vanguard one StuG which was ambushed in the pursuit. Driver Sippelt was killed and gunlayer Lauterbach wounded. The StuG burned out.

A horse-drawn enemy battery drove up an elevation as if on the exercise ground and took the vanguard under fire, managing to get off a few rounds before being wiped out by the StuGs. The aim of reaching Termachovka by the evening of the first day had to be abandoned when Leutnant Bingler's leading StuG broke through a wooden bridge at Ssidorevitch. It was not possible to pass it; there was no enemy presence and some units of the vanguard would have been able to get across on the second carriageway but not the 2 Battery StuGs and the 10-cm battery of Art.Regt 285. Accordingly Major Hoffmann-Schoenborn decided to wait until pioneers repaired the bridge. This was undoubtedly correct for the risk of other parts of the bridge breaking was too great, and in any case the primary objective of the vanguard could only be achieved for certain by using all available forces, especially all StuGs. In addition, night was falling and so a hedgehog defence was set up either side of the bridge by the vanguard and main body. The pioneers set to work, Bingler's StuG was extracted and the infantry slept where they dropped.

That afternoon the vanguard lost Oberwachtmeister Töpfer to a sniper. He had been standing up in the hatch of his StuG while passing Russian stragglers from a convoy. Wachtmeister Nietert took over his StuG. The vanguard continued to come into close contact with Russian vehicles and small military units. A more serious obstruction was encountered at Obuchovitchi, where the bridge had been coated with petrol and set alight. The pioneers carried on the StuGs were just able to save it, and the same occurred at the Stavok bridge.

Ivanov was taken after overcoming light resistance, then to our astonishment we made the first crossing of the Teterev without a fight and reached Pirotsovitshi towards 1100 hrs. From here the resistance was stronger with heavy defensive weapons. Approaching Priborsk, we put two 7.6-cm long-barrel anti-tank guns out of action during a brief exchange.

In this increasingly dangerous situation, the vanguard now became involved in an almost unbelievable calamity that claimed many lives.

We had recognized the aircraft early on as Luftwaffe bombers, and Oberleutnant Haarberg, commander of the vanguard, ordered at once, and early enough, that the German swastika warflag should be spread on all vehicles. The flight leader must have had his doubts, for the aircraft circled and then there was a long pause, perhaps while he asked his airfield for guidance: 'What are German panzers doing 100 kilometres behind the Russian front?' Probably believing that we were a Russian false flag operation, he dropped his bombs. Six dead and six wounded was the result. One StuG took a direct hit and became a write-off. (In this StuG, the Abteilung paymaster was seriously wounded. Although he was married and had children, he had kept up pressure to be allowed to take part in 'respectable' activity for a warrior. He was overjoyed when his request was granted and he proved himself worthy.)

The advance was only briefly delayed, the aircraft were cursed and we went ahead, unstoppable. When the vanguard reached the village of Stracholessye, the 120-kilometre push had achieved its objective. Now we confronted the greater and far more dangerous task: to capture the bridge over the Dnieper.

We could not have had a young officer better suited to lead such a suicidal task force than Leutnant Bingler of 3 Battery. The old experienced hands Wachtmeisters Labusch and Nietert commanded 2 and 3 Battery StuGs and showed their circumspection and resolve. While the main body of the Abteilung had difficulty in keeping up with the spearhead, these two men were scarcely to be restrained despite the new dangers they had to overcome. On the way to the Dnieper a small cavalry unit suddenly appeared in the path of the vanguard. The StuGs ignored them, the riders galloped to the right and left and made off.

'That settlement ahead could be the village of Gornostaipol!' Nothing moved; they carried on. A lorry came from around a corner, stopped, soldiers jumped down and sprinted for cover.

The pioneers on Bingler's StuG called on them to surrender, at which the lorry moved back. A grenade was thrown, exploded in its centre and the lorry collapsed. Immediately the Russians stood up with arms raised. Bingler asked how far it was to the Dnieper: the Russians said 3 kilometres.

The village seemed devoid of enemy troops. The road led to a wooden bridge at the far end. A Russian soldier ran towards it, holding something in his hand: Bingler stopped. One of the pioneers disarmed the Russian, another cut the fuse wire to an explosive charge.

Another wooden bridge, then a sandy track, then cobblestones. The StuGs rattled on. Ahead were a couple of overturned horse-drawn carts ('panjewagen'), the cargo strewn across the roadway. Bingler halted. He did not want to risk running over landmines and ammunition. Pioneers jumped down to examine the boxes. Just provisions. Let's go!

Coming round a bend in the road, Bingler saw the shimmering ribbon of a large river. The road ahead was blockaded and behind it was another of the damned wooden bridges. Two panjewagen were galloping towards it but Bingler's StuG was faster; the right-side track struck the leading cart and hurled it aside. He went around the blockade but stopped before the long bridge over a broad expanse of water.

'That cannot be the Dnieper,' he said out loud. 'How the devil is one to know the name of each of these rivers and swamps?' By now he had lost contact with Labusch and the other two StuGs and, though inclined to await their arrival, decided to proceed and crossed the bridge without incident. As he looked back he saw the other two StuGs coming up in the far distance, veiled in a cloud of dust.

He had gone scarcely 100 metres further when he saw flashes from the scrub to his right and shells exploding in his vicinity. Bingler sought the nearest cover and radioed Labusch, 'Enemy anti-tank or flak, right side of the road, destroy and follow.' Labusch acknowledged, Bingler continued and shortly afterwards he heard shooting and shelling as Labusch and Nietert got to work. He accelerated and after a few minutes a long row of bridge arches came into sight, curving across a huge broad river. 'That is the Dnieper. And that is the bridge in question.'

As he slackened speed he came across a tumult of fleeing vehicles and people. He also thought that he saw bunkers and field positions. Bingler wasted no more time. His orders were to build a bridgehead, and that meant on the far bank. Who and what was crushed as he crossed that bridge cannot be accurately described. Stubborn farmers were run down in their vehicles before they understood what was afoot. Courageous Russians simply climbed the safety rails and jumped into the swamp or river. Somebody pulled out a pistol and fired at the StuG, seriously wounding a pioneer aboard. A heavy lorry came towards them, occupying at least half the carriageway; the collision was of such a force that the StuG crew fell from their seats but remained unhurt. How the pioneers came through all this unharmed, perched on the hulls, is a mystery although they surrounded themselves with constant and indiscriminate fire.

The drive through hell came to an abrupt end. The wreckage of the aforementioned lorry lay across the carriageway and Bingler's StuG slid over it to the right-hand side of the bridge. With great presence of mind the driver, Pfeiffer, applied both handbrakes to bring the panzer to a halt but the nose had gone through the bridge railings and the right-side track hung over the abyss. Radio operator Postler received a bullet through the arm as he opened the exit hatch. The pioneers had jumped down from the panzer seconds before the collision and took cover in the wreckage of the lorry. Bingler and his crew, except the wounded Postler, climbed out gingerly so as not to cause any untoward movement that might tip it into the river. No sooner were they under cover than they received fire from the field positions on the far bank but they refrained from responding and the shooting soon stopped. Despite his wound, Postler continued to relay the order, 'Bingler to everybody. Buffalo forward at once!' After a few minutes he received a reply, 'Labusch here: we are coming!' Alighting with caution from the StuG that was lying at an angle on its side, he let gunlayer Sablatnik dress his wound.

Prior to this misadventure, Labusch and Nietert exchanged fire with the Russian battery, pressed ahead at full speed and soon reached the Dnieper bridge, where they were sprayed with machine-gun fire from the field positions. Nietert arrived before Labusch; suddenly a great flame came up out of the ground and the StuG disappeared in a cascade of earth, stones and smoke. He and his gunlayer clambered out, bleeding and dazed, and the two of them pulled the radio operator through the hatch.

Labusch, who had inferred from Bingler's radio message sent by Postler that he was needed urgently, steered his StuG coolly along the edge of the crater, ignoring the machine-gun and infantry fire aimed at the bridge, and headed for it – despite fire coming from his left and right from the riverbank. Ahead of him to one side was an earth bunker from which an anti-tank gun was shooting across the roadway. Labusch remained calm, waited, fired two 3-inch rounds into the position which gunlayer Sablatnik had identified and silenced the gun.

By now, Labusch could see Bingler's StuG and the wreckage of the lorry ahead but had begun to receive fire, apparently from a heavy anti-aircraft gun on the far bank. He increased speed but this did not disturb the gunner's accuracy, and would begin to threaten Bingler and his crew as the range shortened. As he approached, everybody shouted to him, 'Drive on! To the end of the bridge!' Labusch understood at once, accelerated sharply, and this got him out of the maximum depression of the anti-aircraft gun. Labusch was therefore the first man to reach the other side of the Dnieper. He engaged and destroyed the anti-aircraft gun and was down to his last two rounds of armoured shells.

Meanwhile, the vanguard under Oberleutnant Haarberg had reached the western side of the Dnieper. Here the situation was not clear because the Russians seemed to be defending from behind every bush. The German infantry soon put an end to the earth bunkers, protected by the remaining 3 Battery StuGs, while the pioneers retrieved Nietert's panzer from the crater and got the road passable again.

Although the situation continued to improve, Bingler and Labusch were not yet out of the woods, so to speak. The could see through binoculars that Russian troops were moving between the iron arches of the bridge. 'Are they going to demolish the bridge?' Labusch drove back to Bingler with his observation. Now he had to make a difficult decision. If the Russians blew up even only one arch of the bridge it would stop the entire advance. Labusch had two rounds of 3-inch left which were not much use but the demolition teams could be driven off by the pioneers. Bingler crammed Labusch's StuGs with pioneers inside the vehicle and on the hull. As it approached the western end of the bridge, half a dozen Russians scattered in all directions, jumping off the bridge or waiting to be disarmed by the pioneers.

Bingler and his squad of pioneers arrived back at the west end of the bridge as the hawser attached to Nietert's StuG tensed. The 'bush war' was not yet at its conclusion: Postler was wounded a second time (a bullet through his right hand) and even Labusch had a bullet graze his forehead. Infantry, pioneers and StuG crewmen formed a human chain from the ammunition truck to the panzer to refuel it and replenish its ammunition while Bingler made his report to Oberleutnant Haarberg, and also to Major Hoffmann-Schoenborn who had just arrived, having hurried ahead of the main body to receive precise information. He had not been aware that Bingler and Labusch were on the far bank but approved their decisions. He insisted that everything had to be done to hold the bridge. Bingler's request to lead the spearhead was approved after a short consideration. He took over the StuG of Labusch, was given a platoon from 3 Battery to ride with him and set off. The pioneers had meanwhile cleared the explosion site.

Scarcely had the StuG reached the bridge approach road than Russian fighters and ground-attack aircraft made low-level attacks. They did no damage and none of the infantry on the roof of the panzer was harmed. Against all expectations they crossed to the other side without incident and were then briefed by Bingler regarding the selected terrain for the bridgehead.

The creation and expansion of the bridgehead was soon under way on the east bank. First, all the remaining StuGs, Command Staffs and Abteilung fighting vehicles crossed the river, joining units of the vanguard. German infantry occupied field positions on both sides of the Dnieper, the pioneers checked the bridge structure for explosive devices and cleared the carriageway of wreckage and dead bodies. Major Hoffmann-Schoenborn took command of the bridgehead on the eastern side. A company of assault pioneers (1 Stu.Pi. 51) then secured the bridge technically, with the first units of 11 Panzer Division being due to reach the Dnieper in the early hours in order to further reinforce the bridgehead. By nightfall sentries and field outposts had been arranged and reinforced by StuGs. Anybody else could sleep. Despite sound of motors and shooting in the distance the night passed quietly bar one incident. A Russian fuel lorry, apparently unaware that the bridge was in German hands, drove close to a StuG. A single round was fired into the cargo. The burning canisters acted like rockets and came back to earth with a fiery tail. After the pyrotechnic display ended everybody went back to sleep.

The Push to the Dnyessna, 2 August 1941

In the early hours of 24 August, the Abteilung, fresh from its great success at the Dnieper, set out to force a crossing of the Dnyessna at Oster. The vanguard was augmented by II Battalion/Schützen-Regt 110, whose commander Hauptmann Jung took over the vanguard. Also newly added was 5 Art.Regt 115. The Abteilung CO made known the latest orders, then the StuGs rolled out with infantry and pioneers seated on the upper structure, Leutnant Bingler leading 3 Battery on the right; 200 metres back on the left was 2 Battery. The direction of travel was Sstaro, Lukashovka Guta, Karpilovka. On this last stretch 3 Battery StuGs carrying infantry were attacked with hand grenades from between two sand dunes. There were no German casualties and the event would not have been worth mentioning if the leader of these 'desperadoes' had not been a young woman wearing the uniform of a Russian lieutenant. She had a clean through-and-through wound to the upper thigh. This was dressed and the Maid of the Battles was sent home.

The advance continued on an excellent road surface but through difficult dense woodland. Numerous fleeing enemy ammunition lorries were intercepted and destroyed. Attacks by Russian aircraft of all descriptions were incessant all day, each attack coming hot on the heels of the previous one. At 0450 hrs our flak gun shot down a Rata fighter.

An hour after sunset we saw the first houses on the horizon at Sstaro. We came under fire from a battery situated on a low elevation. The area of the shell impacts was a small wood into which our Command Staff had driven shortly before. Leutnant Bingler acted at once. The StuGs moved along a track at the side of the highway and quickly identified the firing positions at the edge of another wood. We terminated the resistance of these batteries.

The nearer we came to the village the stronger we found the resistance to be. The enemy had set up an interception point here. Leutnant Bingler's StuGs had not yet reached the edge of the woods on the eastern side when Russian batteries began to shoot. The StuGs advanced to visual range and returned fire. They silenced all the heavy weapons on the eastern edge, leaving only the enemy battery east of the village still shooting. The StuGs and vehicles of the Command Staff now attempted to advance below the curtain of fire. At high speed and widely spaced, it was still a matter of life and death because the enemy soon dropped the range: an StuG received a direct hit at the rear which set the motor alight. The crew got out and ran behind the advancing vehicles towards the village.

Now the hour had arrived for the infantry and pioneers. In house-to-house fighting they cleared Lukashova Guta of the enemy, who made a very determined stand. The enemy artillery now decided to set the houses on fire, shooting from Morovsk. The CO ordered the StuGs to storm Morovsk and engage the enemy artillery positions until it was safe for the remaining StuGs to drive through unscathed. The vanguard should spend as little time as possible on this task.

Since there was no radio contact with the Abteilung at this time, despatch rider Gefreiter Schanner was sent with orders from the Abteilung CO to Leutnant Bingler: 'Bingler proceed with 1 Platoon from Guta in direction ESE to Oster, capture the bridge and set up bridgehead. 2 Battery is to follow Bingler's platoon and cross the bridge as soon as Bingler is over it. 3 Battery advance NE, join up with Command Staff and if necessary engage enemy artillery.'

The action of the despatch rider which follows should serve as an example for everybody who has to carry out an order without fail under very difficult conditions.

Franzl Schanner set off on his heavy machine to find the way through to Leutnant Bingler. Towards the edge of a birchwood he saw Russians 60 metres ahead. Zig-zagging to avoid their bursts of machine-pistol fire, he slewed the machine among the trees. After resuming his journey, he followed a log road through swampy terrain and reached open meadowland. At that moment the Russian artillery began shelling the route along which he had to travel to his destination. Suddenly his machine bogged down, the rear wheel burrowing ever deeper into the morass. He got off, pushed and pulled in vain. As the machine sank ever deeper he came under machine-pistol fire again, threw himself down and reached for his carbine.

When the enemy fire ceased, he resumed his struggle to free the rear wheel, and was finally able to drag the machine to firm ground. He spotted StuGs in the cover of bushes and rode towards them. In his haste he had failed to notice the shell crater on the road. Franzl tried to avoid it, but too late. The motorcycle rolled into the crater, overturned and fell on top of him. Despite the pain in his thigh, knee and one foot, his only thoughts were for the despatch. Gasping for breath, blood trickling through his torn clothing, he pulled himself to his feet and staggered to the bushes at the roadside.

Two men came running from the StuGs and hooked his arms round them. At 3 Battery he tore the despatch from his message pouch and gave it to a crewman who ran with it to the battery commander. Franzl had his wounds treated and dressed, and then he was driven to the nearest main dressing station.

Battery commander Oberleutnant Haarberg forwarded the order from the Abteilung CO by radio to Leutnant Bingler, and the 3 Battery StuGs headed out for the nearby woods en route for Morovsk. First they put down Stalin-organ fire [Katyusha rockets] coming from the edges of the woods and then quickly silenced two Russian artillery batteries. The enemy resistance slackened and our infantry finished off what remained. Having eliminated the threats to the flanks of the vanguard from the north, our CO turned the battle group to the east.

It now seemed peaceful. The sky was clear and the sun shone: another hot day was promised. Suddenly a couple of enemy flak rounds exploded in the swampy vegetation to the right of the road. The three StuGs halted, and identified the position of the gun dominating the road. Bingler discussed the situation with the other two commanders using a map, then the panzers rolled back from the edge of the swampy land to the road, crossed it hurriedly and disappeared into the bushes. They followed the depression alongside the road, which became gradually steeper, and then fired up at the flak battery without it being able to return fire. The mad scramble of cars and lorries attempting to escape eastwards were easy targets for the StuGs while pioneers finished off the last enemy resistance in the earth bunkers and other positions of cover.

After a short rest, Leutnant Bingler's platoon headed for the village of Karpilovka. It was defended by field positions, artillery, anti-tank obstacles and ditches but these presented little problem since the enemy quickly abandoned the position en masse and at 0830 hrs the three StuGs drove through the long village without meeting resistance. Passing a belt of swamps south of it, they crossed a wooden bridge and noticed Russian tanks lurking in the bushy terrain beyond. After a brief duel, three tanks were destroyed, the others turned away and made off at speed into a cornfield. The StuGs returned to the road and continued towards Dnyessna.

By 0945 hrs the spearhead platoon stood 1 kilometre short of the Dnyessna bridges. As they moved up to survey the bridge defences, they were met by mortar fire from the left and right of the main bridge. While the two subordinate StuGs gave covering fire, Leutnant Bingler drove up to the first bridge, to which the enemy had already set fire, and succeeded in crossing the burning section. Pioneers extinguished the flames after a short while.

Towards the end of the battle for the first Dnyessna bridge, when the StuGs were already across, as Leutnant Bingler was taking a quick look from the access hatch of his panzer at the road ahead, a sniper's bullet passed through his steel helmet. Pioneers on the hull attempted to hold him as he tipped backwards and then collapsed. At that moment driver Ippich halted the vehicle at the warning given by gunlayer NCO Woldenge that he could see Russians ahead laying landmines, and fired a shell among them. It was only then, when Leutnant Bingler's crew received no more orders from him that they realized with horror that he had been killed. The other StuGs were advised of his death by radio. A short while afterwards he was awarded the Knight's Cross posthumously and his name was entered in the Honour Scroll of the German Army.

Although the bridge over the Dnyessna had been rendered impassable by the fire, our CO Major Hoffmann-Schoenborn was determined to cross the river before nightfall and get at least some of the minor elements to the other side of the river. During these efforts, the commander of VIII Battalion/ Schützen-Regt 111 was killed and all requests to Division for infantry, pioneers and inflatable boats were rejected. Division would also not give approval for his proposal to lead personally all available forces in the attempt. This ended the advance and we went over to defence. It was a bitter blow for all the StuG men that our most daring officer had had to lay down his life before the end of the three great, significant days of battle. His body was driven back at dusk laid out on his StuG.

At the same time as the vanguard was on the way to the Dnyessna bridge, the first elements of 11 Panzer Division reached the Dnieper at the previous bridge near Gornostaipol that had been taken a day earlier. A fast squadron crossed the river, then the first panzer battalion, covering the long stretch to the bridge at high speed, crossed it in order to keep in check the scattered defenders on the other side.

This wooden Dnieper bridge, 2.5 kilometres in length, was attacked in the afternoon by Russian aircraft which kept to a very high altitude. Even so they were put off by our flak and their bombs missed the priority target, the bridge, but left four vehicles of the panzer battalion burning like torches by the roadside. Thus ended the prelude.

Ten minutes later the bridge came under attack by Il-2 ground-attack aircraft, immediately followed by a formation of Boston bombers. The bridge was hit, and flames licked up from the wooden columns at the eastern end, but it remained intact. A stream of our vehicles stood waiting on the western side of the bridge for the opportunity to cross. During these two air attacks panzers and infantry carriers had hastily scattered in all directions. An Opel Blitz lorry in open country was blown apart by a direct hit, killing ten panzer grenadiers.

After a while our flak on the west bank began shooting to the south in the direction of Kiev. Illuminated by the evening sun, a number of gunboats appeared from behind the bend in the river. When all were in position they opened fire at the bridge. The German flak offered blistering defensive fire while panzers of 11 Panzer Division also became involved. A unique duel began. One of the gunboats was hit amidships by armour-piercing shells. The violent explosion tossed the superstructure into the air, the boat broke apart at the centre and sank. This made no impression on the little flotilla, which fought on.

Suddenly the bridge was shaken by three hits, one at the wooden support column near the wrecks of the lorry and Bingler's StuG. The railings broke away, the front of the gun rose up and then tipped over to land in the swamp below. The gun crew arrived too late to assist in the recovery operation. Gunner Hugo Preiss lost his life when he went inside the StuG to retrieve a machine pistol he had forgotten.

Meanwhile the German flak had sunk several more of the river gunboats; enemy bombers now made a fresh attack against the bridge and scored a hit exactly halfway along it, causing it to collapse into the water with a mighty crack. Our flak shot down three enemy aircraft but the Soviets had finally achieved what they set out to do: the great bridge over the Dnieper at Gornostaipol had been destroyed. The greater part of 11 Panzer Division on the west side of the river could no longer cross. Only advance elements of the division had managed to reach the eastern bank, together with the spearhead led by Major Hoffmann-Schoenborn.

Fighting between the Dnieper and Dnyessna, 25 August–8 September 1941

Following the three days of the Dnieper operation, StuG Abteilung 191 spent the next three days differently. On the evening of 25 August 1941, news was received that the Gornostaipol bridge had been destroyed by the enemy air force. Hoffmann-Schoenborn's spearhead was ordered to assess this change in the situation and other orders then came very swiftly from 111 Inf.Div. The division had transferred command to Oberst Behlmann, commanding officer of an infantry regiment attached to 11 Panzer Division, over all its forces deployed to the east. The spearhead was abolished but its units, strengthened by units from Inf.Regt 111 and Artillery Abteilung 852, were grouped up for the defence to the east and north. Major Hoffmann-Schoenborn was given command of this battle group.

The defensive measures were quickly coordinated and set down. The supply of ammunition and provisions had to be guaranteed, the damaged vehicles and StuGs repaired on the spot and every available man was to be used, whether directly involved or not.

On 24 August the Anacker Battery of Abteilung 191 ejected the enemy occupying Kovopye and relieved the Divisional Staff of the immediate threat. The StuGs of the Abteilung could now be stood down as an operational reserve but were called upon at once to assist the units led by Oberst Behlmann.

On the afternoon of 25 August, the Russians had recaptured the fortifications at Sstaro and Lukashova Guta and had encircled the units of the infantry regiment at the village. A StuG platoon led by Leutnant Pantel saved the situation and on 26 August the remnants of Anacker Battery cleared the village of Russian troops and reopened the road.

In the east, enemy air attacks had to be beaten off constantly and we had to be very alert for attempts by the Russians to cross the Dnyessna to our side of the river using small companies and reconnaissance troops. In the west, contact to the Dnieper was often broken and had to be regained. To set up a uniform bridgehead capable of being successfully defended – which would be indispensable as a springboard for new operations and shortening the supply lines – the order came that evening to break off contact with the enemy and pull back to a new bridgehead position, Sstaro, but above all Lukashova Guta, as important places within this bridgehead which had to be held at all costs. Major Hoffmann-Schoenborn passed this order to the officers of his battle group in the Abteilung command bunker at Karpilovka, which had been made into a model command centre equipped with a telephone exchange and radio. Disengagement from the enemy went off without incident. No equipment was left behind. The CO led and supervised the operation personally and returned in the last vehicle at daybreak on 27 August. Two hours later the enemy had still not set foot in Karpilovka. In the dune-and-scrub terrain west of the village the Abteilung prepared its readiness area.

The enemy had settled in the woods south of the road of advance. Around midday on 27 August they launched a wild attack against this section of the new shortened bridgehead. Those personnel not involved in the immediate defence, namely medics, Staff and parts of the Tross had prepared themselves and occupied some dune-like hills north of the road. When the Russians appeared at the edges of the wood south of the road, they were met with withering fire from all barrels. The crews of the four flak guns set up on the dunes by the CO personally distinguished themselves quite spectacularly by their versatility and effect.

Commanding a StuG which engaged the enemy on the first attack, Leutnant Fuchs in the thickest wooded area was the target of a 'Molotov cocktail' assault. This weapon was thrown by hand and had not been seen by us before. Leutnant Fuchs's panzer was destroyed and the crew received severe burns. This resulted in the order that in future whenever possible no operations by StuGs should be carried out without supporting infantry.

The Abteilung maintained its position in the dune terrain. Its situation became serious when the shortage of ammunition and provisions for the fighting units in the bridgehead became acute and supplies were arriving only sparingly. This led to an increased use of rubber boats and assault craft to bring ammunition and provisions across the river from the west bank of the Dnieper, returning with the wounded. Transport aircraft were also used, a Staffel (twelve machines) of Ju 52s dropped supplies 'bombs' and ammunition containers at indicated sites within the bridgehead, and these were quickly gathered up by the German units. The emergency war bridge over the Dnieper was completed in four days, enabling 11 Panzer Division and LI Armeekorps to flow into the bridgehead and reinforce it. Thus on 28/29 August the bridgehead was extended to the north and south by 111 Inf.Div. and on 30/31 August the route of advance as far as Dnyessna. Supplies could now roll to where they were needed.

In order to be able to make an effective push to the east from the Dnieper bridge at Dnyessna, LI Armeekorps' base had to be broadened, and our Abteilung now came under 113 Inf.Div. and Inf.Regt 260. The regiment's plan was for Nebelwerfer rockets and the artillery to soften up Height 112 south of Oshitki, after which III Battalion would advance to the height from Oshitki and capture it. Once the height was occupied, II Battalion would proceed along the same path through the swampy area and then turn south to take Height 125. This line between Heights 112 and 125 would be the new line of resistance. I Battalion in reserve would then insert itself between the other two battalions to defend the gain in territory.

Although the Abteilung was at readiness from the early hours, the attack was postponed hourly; apparently it was reckoned that success could be achieved more cheaply after the appearance of the neighbouring regiments.

At the Inf.Regt 260 command post, which was difficult to find in the region of the Dnieper swamps, peace and quiet reigned. At 1140 hrs, Generalleutnant Stapf, divisional commander of 111 Inf.Div. detailed on his own responsibility the deployment of the Abteilung for operations against Lukashova Guta. Three StuGs still under repair were placed with Oberleutnant Göring at the disposal of 111 Inf.Div. The Generalleutnant remained at the Inf.Regt 260 command post from where he issued the order 'Paula 160', which meant that the operation was to commence at 1240 hrs.

Anacker Battery was in reserve, and Möller Battery with four StuGs rolled out to give battle. Although it was ascertained that the Nebelwerfer rockets had performed well, at 1355 hrs the enemy embarked on a spirited counter-attack. Characteristic of the Russian manner of fighting at this time was its pronounced wildness and aggression. In this swampy, bushy vegetation, totally impossible to survey from the ground, the Russian fought fanatically, one might even say he seemed to be in his element.

Finally at 1400 hrs the spearhead company with the StuGs reported that 'Buffalo Point 2' on the road 2 kilometres south-east of Oshitki had been taken. At 1410 hrs, however, two StuGs of Möller's Battery of four broke down, at which point the infantry would go no further and stopped where they were and asked for reinforcements.

The enemy had inveigled himself in the unbelievably tangled terrain south-east of 'Buffalo Point 2', sending out occasional small feelers until at 1500 hrs they made a counter-attack of battalion size, running towards the Germans at the double, faster than the StuGs. The panzers kept shooting until they were as close as 25 metres, then turned about to keep the cannon trained. It was only through their resolve that the enemy advance was brought to a standstill. Leutnant Lützow was seriously wounded during the encounter.

At 1520 hrs Oberleutnant Möller reported that the third StuG had broken down and the infantry could not proceed. Upon hearing that, Anacker Battery moved in and under the overall leadership of Möller, Height 112 was finally captured after skirmishes with hand grenades. It was already dusk when the Tenner Platoon destroyed with two rounds two anti-tank guns which had just been unlimbered. The limber succeeded in escaping into the darkness.

Despite the failing light, the advance went ahead with the infantry seated on the vehicles. In full darkness the leading StuG slipped into a ditch and needed a lot of effort to be freed. During this recovery a number of Russians crossed the road no more than 30 metres away. When the assault group resumed there was a sudden flash: the report of the gun and impact were heard at the same instant. Leutnant Tenner's StuG had been taken under fire at a range of 80 metres by a 7.62-cm anti-tank gun. On the loading side a large hole gaped in the armour near the barrel. The gunloader, Gefreiter Hopfensberger, a very reliable man, died at once from a piece of shrapnel to the heart. The Russian gun was destroyed by Oberwachtmeister Piotrowitz. The progress of the StuGs was blocked by a barrier of tree trunks, and landmines were avoided with skill and luck. Orientation in this vile terrain became ever more difficult. Finally the assault group moved in a straight east-to-west line towards Height 125, and therefore through the centre of the Russian units, an operation which was no longer justifiable. Our CO therefore sent signals calling it off, and the assault group returned to the departure point. All elements of the Abteilung reunited around 2230 hrs at the Okuninovo bivouac.

On 5 September, in the StuG operation with 113 Inf.Div. against the villages of Lukashova Guta and Karpilovka, the Russians troops were ejected and pursued to the villages of Lutava and Vypolsovo. Meanwhile the remnants of 3 Battery had been pulled back to Lytovka near Gornostaipol, where all Abteilung rearward services were to be found. On 8 September the still-operational StuGs of the Abteilung in the north between the Dnieper and Dnyessna were attached to 98 Inf.Div., which for some days had been in a peculiar situation.

2 Armee was exerting pressure with 17 Inf.Div. from the north against Russian units still present in the sharp angle where the rivers Dnieper and Dnyessna met and against which we had fought at Malin. It was the task of 17 Inf.Div. to eliminate the threat to our flanks which these units, now battleworthy, represented.

Inf.Regt 290 was securing the front of the division to the east and had occupied Shevedy and a line running south from there. Inf.Regt 282 under its CO Oberst Gareis, highly esteemed by our Abteilung, was building several hedgehog defences towards the east. Russian prisoners had provided information that their encircled compatriots had the job of escaping from the German pocket via the Dnyessna bridge at Maksin and Sokolovka. Our StuGs were then readied for action with the still mobile Inf.Regt 289 (Oberst Geiger).

The operational order of the Korps did not arrive until 1900 hrs on 8 September. The advance then went ahead for the whole night along the most difficult tracks and paths. More than once the entire endeavour was brought into question by fragile bridges, diversions caused by swamps, breakdowns and the like. Only the endless patience and restless energy of our CO enabled the Abteilung to reach its destination at Ssaponovo Guta after travelling from Okuninovo via Sstar, Glybov-Nov and Glybov-Ssoro Kotichi.

Upon receiving news that elements of 17 Inf.Div. had reached the town of Andreyevka, 98 Inf.Div. gave our CO the target, with two StuG batteries and one company of the Tröger Battalion, of capturing the village of Shidinichi south of Kolpyta in order to relieve the pressure from the north and to eliminate the enemy artillery operating from there.

The CO urged Division that Garais's Regiment should make a simultaneous thrust from the south against Revunov-Krug, and reported minutes later that there was no way that the force for Shidinichi intended by Division would be sufficient. He repeated the warning an hour later. He asked once more for infantry reinforcements and artillery fire on Shidinichi and the southern edge of Kolpyta from where the Russian fire was being directed.

When the StuGs had worked their way forwards to within 2 kilometres of the village the infantry dismounted and started to advance but were forced back by heavy defensive fire. Ahead of the village there were three batteries in position and a lot of anti-tank weaponry and mortars were sited at the edge of the village. Even the woods south of the village where the Abteilung command post was located came under systematic artillery fire.

The StuGs bore the brunt of the fighting and approached very close to the village but with great expenditure of ammunition. Without infantry they could not enter. Russian foot soldiers estimated that the strength in the village was a regiment, later confirmed as correct by prisoners. Up to this phase of the battle the StuGs had lost one light battery and two StuGs to anti-tank gunfire. An enemy battery shooting by indirect fire from a concealed position to the north hit the leading StuG of 1 Battery. The crew were wounded, the commander Oberwachtmeister Jäger was blinded and lost an arm. His StuG had received a direct hit to the rear and burned out completely.

Following the submission of another situation report, it was maybe clear to somebody that the operation should not have gone ahead with the totally inadequate forces made available and it was now called off. The StuGs took aboard the wounded, arranged to pick up the infantry and then searched the terrain for the last stragglers before setting off as the last rearguard. The enemy fire died down as soon as we withdrew. The reinforced company of Tröger's Battalion had six dead and twenty-two seriously wounded, and these latter were immediately taken by our ammunition truck to the main dressing station.

In the view of Division the value of the operation, which terminated at 1430 hrs, was the aimed-for reconnaissance results and subjecting the enemy to pressure to make him recognize that he ought to be preparing to surrender without a fight. Our Abteilung requested in conclusion that more artillery protection be made available and to have a say in how things were done, in accordance with its knowledge of the situation.

An Unsuccessful Attempt at Encirclement at Koserogi, September 1941

After reconnoitring the situation in the triangle between the Dnieper and Dnyessna, Army High Command decided it was time to roll up the groggy Russian forces and compel them to surrender by encirclement. The approach of 17 Inf.Div. from the north cleared the way for 98 Inf.Div. to form the encirclement, and this was taken in hand at once.

17 Inf.Div. had taken Andreyevka and Sslabino that morning of 9 September. 98 Inf.Div. held Sholino and Shevedy, while a third division to the west was erecting a closed defensive front. This left a yawning gap between Sslabino and Koserogi which had to be sealed urgently. StuG Abteilung 191 was brought up to support this measure, cooperating with Battalion Clotz (1/290). Koserogi in the southern part of the encirclement was to be taken first.

After 5 kilometres of rapid advance the leading StuG reported that it had met elements of I/Inf.Regt 55. It had come from the north with 17 Inf.Div., was involved in setting up the encirclement and had occupied the heights east and west of the road. A despatch rider halted the advance of the battalion, which turned about, occupied accommodations in Koserogi and set up a hedgehog defence. The StuGs secured the entrance to the town.

Shortly after nightfall heavy artillery and mortar fire commenced from the north. The heavy-calibre shelling of the southern end of the town ceased after a few rounds but the mortar fire persisted on and off for hours. The Russians began shooting into Koserogi from the south-east. A heavy shell landed close to the Abteilung command post, shattered all its windows and created confusion inside. The shrapnel all struck an StuG which had been parked by chance against the wall of the house. Gefreiter Kaul who had sought shelter beneath this StuG was killed and the gunlayer Jäger seriously wounded. After this warning and during the nuisance fire which followed, the Russians attempted to break out of the encirclement through Koserogi. The dark night was lit up by burning houses and lorries while machine guns had been set up on the access roads into town from the north, east and west.

Our StuGs fired into the night blindly at all engine noises. Battalion Schnedler, which had arrived at Koserogi in the course of the evening, was given the task of close-combat defence.

At daybreak a surprising sight met the eyes of the StuG crews. Lorries destroyed during the night were strewn across the town entrances. The StuGs at the western end had been particularly successful and claimed many victims. At the eastern end the wrecked Staff vehicles of a Russian division were found to contain maps and files. Particularly noteworthy was the material of German origin in the possession of this Staff consisting of machine-pistol cartridge clips, NCO's tassels and similar minor items. A Russian colonel, a divisional commander, was found shot dead. It had been he who on 27 August had given the order by radio that the men of 111 Inf.Div. cut off between the Dnieper and Dnyessna were to be wiped out by a concentrated attack. Women in military uniform were also found dead or seriously wounded.

During the morning the situation seemed calmer but was not yet clear. Therefore the two COs decided to send one platoon of StuGs led by Oberleutnant Göring and a reinforced infantry platoon from the battalion to reconnoitre to the west. This party headed north-west of the road to the north in order to take the high ground north of Koserogi.

Scarcely 800 metres after leaving the town the leading vehicles ran into withering fire from all calibres. While the infantry ducked low and Piotrowitz's StuG reversed to secure to the right, Oberleutnant Göring proceeded ahead alone and from cover engaged the enemy artillery. Despite coming under fire himself, he worked his way forwards, which seemed to sow confusion among the Russians. The skirmish was short-lived and ended with a success which exceeded all expectations. About thirty guns of all calibres, including anti-tank guns and a heavy anti-aircraft gun stood abandoned in field positions, wheels dug in and ready to fire. In the folds of terrain behind were some 160 vehicles, mostly lorries, all loaded with ammunition or provisions, but among them

tractors of the heaviest kind. From the midst of this enormous field of booty –
all the result of the determination of a single StuG commander – the infantry
also took 200 prisoners. Battalion Clotz took charge of the booty and occupied
the height.

Meanwhile a signal had come from Division which, in view of the five StuGs
available, caused amusement by ordering one battery of Hoffmann-Schoenborn's
Abteilung to support Battalion Clotz with two batteries at Shevedy for a new
operation. Interpreting the text of the order literally, all sections went at once to
Shevedy, where at the command post of Inf.Regt 290 Oberst Geiger explained
the new situation.

The problem was that despite all the regroupings and the encirclement
there was no sign of the expected hordes of enemy troops and equipment. In
the opinion of Division, the encircled elements of the Red Army must have
withdrawn into the woods north of Koserogi, and several battalions would be
forming a ring for the purpose of clearing them out of there.

These battalions had not arrived and the StuGs set out for the woods in
question during the late afternoon with Battalion Tronnier, with which they
were to work closely in the suspected woods. The advance was led again from
the east by Oberleutnant Möller.

All around the woodland were elements of the division's infantry regiments,
either inactive or moving about the terrain, and also vehicles of StuG Abteilung
243. Although it had been made plain that the StuGs were to remain outside
and not penetrate the forest, the lack of men made it necessary.

Accordingly the woods were crossed and searched twice in full line abreast
and eleven prisoners were taken. No equipment was found. It appeared that
the Russians had known how to escape from the trap, taking their material
and belongings with them. The only valuable and tangible result of this two-
day operation by 98 Inf.Div. was the booty which Oberleutnant Göring's
StuG had captured. On the other hand all German units used to set up this
encirclement suffered casualties. Besides Gefreiter Kaul, StuG Abteilung 191
lost Gefreiter Rennert, gunloader on Piotrowitz's StuG, who was hit in the
neck by rifle fire.

On 12 September 1941 the entire Abteilung Tross was moved from Lytovka
near Gornostaipol to Lutava, 50 kilometres eastwards, led by Oberleutnant
Haarberg. 1 Battery received seven new StuGs and was thus restored to full
operational status. The other panzers were held as reserves at the bivouac site.

On 13 September, the CO's Staff and 1 Battery moved out as part of 79 Inf.Div. During this movement, Leutnant Nordhoff, Staff Reconnaissance Officer, was killed by a burst of machine-gun fire. His despatch rider was taken prisoner by the Soviets and later found murdered.

The Battle of Kiev, 15–23 September 1941

The Battle of Kiev was a pincer operation by two reinforced panzer armies, those of Guderian from the north, and Kleist from the south. While the Russians were involved defending in the bend of the Dnieper, the motorized troops prepared the trap behind them. The cleansing actions between the Dnieper and Dnyessna ended on 13 September. Now the time had come to force the enemy from the north-west to the south where the surrounded Russian armies would be disarmed.

On 15 September, 1 Battery crossed the Dnyessna at Oster and advanced via Koselets to Kobyshchi as part of 79 Inf.Div. On 17 September, 1 Battery went into action with 262 Inf.Div. in the Pustotin area. The Russian resistance was becoming weaker. Large quantities of material and countless prisoners were taken. The division's direction of advance lay south-east of Kiev. The Abteilung Tross had to follow and on 18 September, after proceeding 110 kilometres, arrived at Novy Bykov, 180 kilometres east of Kiev.

The 3 Battery StuGs were formed into a battle unit with the remnants of 2 Battery led by Oberleutnant Möller, then headed at full speed south-west towards Kiev to attach to 298 Inf.Div. The panzer groups of Kleist and Guderian closed the ring around Kiev about 200 kilometres further east. It was now the task of the infantry divisions to enter the great encirclement and break it down into smaller pockets.

Prisoners had to be taken, and for the purpose the Luftwaffe dropped leaflets everywhere over the encirclement. Much use was made of these leaflets by Russian soldiers as their document of surrender.

On 19 September the entire Abteilung was involved, some with supporting infantry, partly as a vanguard in the area Brovary–Borispol–Baryshevka–Rogosov and Ivanko. The Russian units were in total disorder. Gigantic quantities of material were captured. Large heaps of broken guns of all calibres and huge stocks of ammunition were found. We seized Russian lorries complete with driver for the work. Transport vehicles were very important for our supply lines.

On 22 September, Oberleutnant Möller (commanding 2 Battery) fell in action. He was one of the best officers in the Abteilung. He had previously received the Knight's Cross for his personal service at Malin on 14 June.

On 23 September the Great Encirclement Battle at Kiev ended for the Buffalo Abteilung. Our next bivouac was at Yadlovka, 60 kilometres east of Kiev. The StuG contributed to this unique success with great achievements.

Abteilung Order No. 77 published by Major Hoffmann-Schoenborn on 1 October 1941 on the occasion of the first anniversary of the formation of the Abteilung contains statements by Russian generals regarding its effectiveness:

On 26 September, the Commanding General XXVII Russian Army Corps was taken prisoner. He stated, 'We know and fear Abteilung 191. Every time they appeared, panic would break out. All we could do was wait for evening to collect our companies together.'

The C-in-C 5th Russian Army confirmed these details in conversation with Generalfeldmarschall von Reichenau. He stated that the Russians would certainly have defeated the Germans at Malin if the latter had not brought their 'infantry panzers' (StuGs) so devastatingly into the action.

Major decorations and honours crowned the success of the proud Abteilung: on 31 December 1941, Major Hoffmann-Schoenborn, the forty-ninth soldier of the German Wehrmacht to be so honoured, was awarded the Oak Leaves to his Knight's Cross for his personal involvement and often tactically decisive leadership. He himself stated, 'I did no more than my capable StuG men, irrespective of rank. Let us mention as an example the service of Leutnant Bingler. He fell at the Dnyessna, and he was a brave officer.'

On 24 September the entire Tross and rearward services of the Abteilung removed to Yadlovka where the fighting Staffs had their bivouacs. During these quiet days the vehicles and StuGs were overhauled ready for new missions. Because of the shortage of spare parts a lorry had to be sent to the Reich with a list. On 1 October we celebrated the first anniversary with a rifle-shooting competition, a grand Abteilung roll call and march past, address by Oberleutnant Haarberg in the church, a banquet at midday, skat (card game) competitions, then came the evening meal and after-celebration, all followed by a film. To celebrate the day, every member of the Abteilung received a mimeographed chronology of the historical events of the Abteilung.

The Advance on Moscow, 5–30 October 1941

After resting at Yadlovka near Kiev, the CO received orders from 4 Armee to head for Moscow. Oberleutnant Anacker now commanded 2 Battery and Leutnant Tenner the Staff Battery. An advance party went ahead to mark the route with very useful 'Buffalo' shields to direct broken-down vehicles and the Abteilung supply lines to the whereabouts of the Abteilung or a particular battery.

On 5 October the Abteilung set out from Yadlovka via Koselets to Olishevka (151 kilometres) on a cobble-stone road which enabled all batteries to make good progress. We often saw rest huts on the way intended for nomadic Russians, or so we were told by a road maintenance official. Each hut had a Soviet star on the roof and a bench for repose inside. Resthouses were to be found along this road, each with a plaster monument to Lenin or Stalin, often with the inscription 'Long Live Stalin'. Many of these figures had been overturned.

The second day of travel took us from Olishevka via Tchernigov and Gomel to Kosyukovka (175 kilometres), a praiseworthy effort by our drivers. It was a tiring journey and the quarters made available to us provided a good night's sleep.

The third day, 7 October 1941, from Kostyukovka to Propoisk (130 kilometres), was swift and trouble-free. Here we left the Ukraine for White Russia. We thought we might be about to get to know the Soviet paradise but found the houses and villages just as uncared for as they had been in the Ukraine.

The number of block houses was striking. The rooms were all the same as the others we had stayed in. Filth and vermin everywhere. The people were poorly clad and the shortage of food here worse than anywhere else we had seen. In brief, the vaunted glorious life in the Soviet Union could not be found. This experience was the best cure for those of our men keen on Bolshevism.

On 8 October the Abteilung left Propoisk for the area of Roslavl, 80 kilometres north-east. 3 Battery was given quarters at Krapivna. Three days were set aside to get the vehicles fully roadworthy. Meanwhile it had begun to snow and become cold. On 12 October the fighting units arrived in the battle area via Medyn, about 40 kilometres behind the front. 3 Battery occupied quarters at Doshina on the military road to Moscow. Snow and cold promised a harsh winter. Our vehicles received their winter oil and anti-freeze. Speed was now important!

On 18 October the Abteilung received its first operational orders since the advance had begun. The battleworthy StuGs of the three batteries were assembled as 'Battery Haarberg' for the relief of Borovsk, where the foremost elements of 3 Inf.Div. (mot.) were nearly totally encircled. Battery Haarberg rolled out almost at once from Medyn and headed for Borovsk by road. Contact with the enemy was made outside the town. The encirclement was forced open, the StuGs joined up with those trapped inside and all attacks by Russian forces rushed to the area were beaten off. For the first time our StuGs had the chance to prove themselves in a night action.

On 20 October the battery set off again and the advance flowed but only very sluggishly. The persistent rain transformed the roads and tracks into bottomless mud. The advance was halted partially because supplies of ammunition and provisions could not get through. Now we found out what a thaw in the Russian winter meant for fighting troops and their supply lines. On 22 October: the entire Abteilung pushed forward to Balobanovo, 60 kilometres south-west of Moscow. It was a very difficult drive to these new quarters. Vehicles which bogged down were pulled free by our towing machines and some taken in tow. The battery repairs detachment and Abteilung workshop had their hands full getting broken-down vehicles driveable. During the next few days frost set in and the thermometer fell to −20 degrees Celsius. The weather conditions brought the advance of all our troops to a standstill. The infantry dug in.

On 29 and 30 October a number of StuGs went into action at Rochestvenskoye in order to get the advance restarted. At Balabanovo Hauptmann von Schönau left 1 Battery and was replaced by Oberleutnant Vaerst.

The Battle in Front of Moscow against Cold and the Enemy

On 11 November the fighting Staffs of the three batteries were moved forwards to Redkino, 8 kilometres west of Naro-Fominsk. (The following description of the operation involving Abteilung 191 in the attack on Moscow is based on the experiences of the men involved and especially on files of 258 Inf.Div., to which we were attached, placed at our disposal by Oberst (General Staff, ret'd Dr Pflanz).)

Redkino lay 6 kilometres behind the foremost German line, namely the south bank of the Nara. The quarters there, though very narrow, were warm. The Tross was further back at Klin, west of Redkino. Without doubt, Army High Command wanted a demonstratively good conclusion to the year 1941 and planned the assault on Moscow accordingly. We had given careful consideration to our preparations, the StuGs were painted white and attempts were made to fit cleats to the tracks. The crew organized snow shirts and padded jackets for the worst possible weather.

The attack scheduled for 20 November was aborted, so it seemed to us, because of the low temperatures and the Abteilung taking up provisional quarters at Klin. Only 3 Battery remained in the readiness area at Redkino. Its commander, Oberleutnant Haarberg, made contact with the infantry in position at Nara. He described how it looked there in the following report:

A few kilometres ahead the infantry occupied small open holes in the ground. Apart from greatcoat, headwarmers and a blanket, they had nothing else to protect them against the cold. Those who did not absolutely have to be in the foremost holes created some small dugouts a little way back, tiny rooms covered with boards, beams and tree trunks. Access was by crawling through the small entrance, covered by an old blanket. Inside, the floor had a covering of straw or hay and in a nook on one side would be a small open fire, the smoke from which rose lazily through the hole in the blanket. That was how those poor infantrymen lived at the foremost front. It was amazing that they tolerated this life with such self-possession and patience.

Meanwhile the readiness area had been formed into a gigantic encircling action, and for the advance on Moscow in general, StuG Abteilung 191 formed part of XX Korps/4 Armee. 1 Battery was with 3 Inf.Div. (mot.), 2 and 3 Batteries with 258 Inf.Div, and Pomeranian Inf.Regt 478 was also attached. The Abteilung assembled once more at Redkino.

The orders were as follows: '1 Battery is assigned to 3 Inf.Div. (mot.) until reaching the first objective when it will return to Abteilung. 2 and 3 Batteries are completely at the disposal of 258 Inf.Div., will cross the Nara at Tashirovo with Inf.Regt 478 and then advance with that force for approximately 25 kilometres north-east to capture the bridges over the Desna at Yushkovo-Burtzevo.'

The additional information in the order put the enemy strength faced by 258 Inf.Div. as being elements of 1 Moscow Guard Rifle Division and 222 Inf. Div. with three regiments of infantry, three artillery regiments, one battery of army artillery, one pioneer battalion and armoured units of unknown strength. Two rocket positions had also been identified and a large number of staggered fighting positions in the field. The fighting value of the enemy, in the opinion of Division, would be slight after heavy losses and by nature of the conditions.

X-Day was 1 December at 0650 hrs and began with the usual exchange of fire at the Nara bridge. It passed off relatively quickly and smoothly, and even a not very deep zone of bunkers was eclipsed after a short, violent battle. The fighting spirit of the Russian infantry was not broken, only a few bunker crews gave in without a fight and most of them defended resolutely to the end (as per the report of 258 Inf.Div.).

The advance now got under way. The StuG encountered no problems up to a certain point. The Division reported:

> Thanks to the rapid pace of the StuGs, our foremost elements reached the village of Malyic Sxemyonychi by 1045 hrs. Up to that point we had only stopped once when some heavy tanks appeared east of the village and attempted to halt our advance. With the special assistance of the StuGs we succeeded in destroying three tanks including a T-34 without loss to ourselves. The T-34 resisted until hit by the eighteenth round of AP fired by the StuGs.

The T-34s, which we were meeting in action for the first time, were superior to the StuG in firepower, radius of action and armour. Nevertheless the StuGs engaged them bravely and put many of them out of action. During the enforced stop and subsequent pause to group up, 2 Battery moved up to combine with 3 Battery and provide the infantry with a very welcome, powerful spearhead. The advance resumed and soon there occurred another less serious skirmish. From the 258 Inf.Div. report: 'A T-34 approaching the StuGs was so badly damaged by the first round fired by 3 Battery (Oberleutnant Göring) that the cover of the gun structure flew off, with the result that the tank turned away at once and fled'.

At midday the spearhead reached a snowed-in tank exercise yard of the Moscow garrison. Here the infantry and StuGs occupied a commanding height but the men spent a cheerless night, some in the vehicles, others huddling close together for warmth on the motor covers of the StuGs, and a number in ice-cold bunkers.

During the night there was some wild shooting in the nearby woods. The cause was unknown, the StuGs had no reason to become involved and it was put down to nuisance fire. By daybreak the crew had not slept well, but had not experienced the biting cold and sharp wind as much as the infantry. It was amazing what the Pomeranian grenadiers had put up with, and their readiness to get stuck in at daylight. According to the 258 Inf.Div. report: 'One must remember that Inf.Regt 478 had had to come up during the night of 30 November 22 kilometres from the rearward billets to the readiness positions. Even here there was no warm night rest for them and so no quarters were on hand. When the attack began the infantry were not rested and frozen through.'

Nevertheless the advance continued. The orders had specified the Desna bridges, III/Inf.Regt 178 with 2 StuG Battery was to head for Yushkovo, and II Battalion with 3 Battery to head for Bertsevo.

An 'Advanced Abteilung Major Bracht', a reconnaissance sub-battalion reinforced with anti-tank units and flak, was to make a surprise attack on the Yushkovo bridge and build a bridgehead there. The bridge was found to be intact at 1300 hrs, and shortly afterwards 2 Battery StuGs arrived carrying grenadiers, and III/Inf.Regt 478 brought up the rear. The units formed a hedgehog as the bridgehead and occupied the bridge and village without resistance. After making security arrangements, the frozen infantry had the chance to warm up by the stove of a local house and sleep. Many who had to go out to take their turn to relieve the sentries carried hot stones wrapped in rags.

During the late afternoon, T-34s opened fire at Burtsevo from long range, setting fire to several houses, and at 2200 hrs Russian tanks entered the village. Those who experienced this ghastly scene will never forget it. The tanks fired particularly at the burning houses, but not much into the darkness. Our CO, Major Hoffmann-Schoenborn, received two machine-gun bullets to the arm and stood down, being replaced by Oberleutnant Haarberg. 2 Battery at Yushkovo had a much worse experience. A Russian tank attack unleashed at 1700 hrs from the north-east and south caused total chaos.

The report 258 Inf.Div. related:

All anti-tank guns fired round after round against the oncoming brown monsters of steel and iron which paused only to shoot. The tanks received hit after hit but the projectiles bounced off their armour with a clang, and either shot up in the air or were deflected to one side in a great arc, causing more danger to our own people than to the tanks. Our infantry, crouching in cover whenever the opportunity arose, observed with hopeless rage that our Pak guns were ineffective against these giant tanks. Now the tanks went after the StuGs in the village. Though firing with all barrels without visible success against the StuGs, they did set alight numerous houses and the regimental command post which had been set up in one of the houses was destroyed by three direct hits. The Russian tanks drove around the village as suited themselves, behaving as if they were invulnerable. Now the last reserves of StuGs were thrown into the battle and set two tanks burning with a couple of lucky hits. At that the others turned away at once.

These attacks were repeated on five occasions that night but by morning the Russians had still not managed to take control of Yushkovo.

Although an order given by Inf.Regt 478 on the late afternoon of the previous day had ordered that Yushkovo and Burtsevo be held at all cost and a hedgehog formed, at 1415 hrs on 3 December the order came from Korps for all elements to withdraw to the readiness positions on the other side of the Nara.

The Inf.Regt 478 convoy was 24 kilometres in length. Korps reserves and units present to protect the supply route made great efforts and took substantial losses to prevent the fighting units at the Desna from being totally cut off by Russian attacks on the flanks.

Before 2 StuG Battery could begin to turn back, it had to defend against a large squadron of T-34s at Burtsevo. Outside the town both sides engaged in a long, bitter battle in which we suffered very regrettable losses. The commander of 2 Battery, Oberleutnant Anacker, Leutnants Hälbig and Runge, six StuG crewmen and the driver of the CO's command vehicle were all killed.

The 258 Inf.Div. report stated: 'In this uneven but nevertheless resolutely fought battle against an enemy superior in numbers and weapons technology, we were given invaluable support by an 8.8-cm flak gun which thanks to the much greater penetrative power of its armour-piercing shells could shoot through the wooden houses behind which the T-34s continually sought cover.'

Those elements which had not evacuated Burtsevo completely won time to pull out by means of this delaying action. Abteilung surgeon Dr Sievers managed to despatch all wounded StuG men and infantry delivered to his dressing station on lorries or horse-drawn sledges; a heavy flak towing vehicle brought out the serious cases.

What had been the vanguard on the first day now became the rearguard and consisted of 2 and 3 Batteries and one company, at first of III, and then of II Battalion of Inf.Regt 458. They did not leave Burtsevo until the main body had got a sufficient distance away. Without excitement and swiftly the rearguard evaded the cautiously pursuing enemy. Occasionally Russian tanks would be seen but the StuGs kept them out of range.

In the fighting during this retreat the 'Captain' (Oberwachtmeister Karsten, 2 Battery) destroyed two T-34s with hollow-charge ammunition. Each hit had full effect immediately, even on the other tanks, which then pulled back at once. The hollow-charge shells had been delivered to the Abteilung before the attack on Moscow but – as was stated, by order of the Führer – had had to be given back shortly before X-Day. (The effect of the shell is based on the hollow-charge principle. The head of the shell, with a mantle of a soft metal cap, has a conical or bullet-shaped hollow space which at detonation gives it a greater explosive or penetrative effect.) Our 'Captain' had returned three other shells but kept the hollow-charge ones.

'That was what gave you the pyrotechnical display when I fired into the Russian tank formation,' the Captain remarked when telling the story later.

If the situation permitted, infantry sat on the superstructure of the panzer. When danger threatened they would seek cover at once and wait until the air was clear, always ready to provide the StuGs with the necessary protection in close-combat situations. An outstanding brotherhood-in-arms therefore developed through experience and trust.

According to the report of 258 Inf.Div. the units returned in columns several kilometres long, prey to many interruptions. Extraordinary difficulties were caused by the cold weather, poor roads and tracks, the exhaustion of men and horses, lack of rations, unsuitable vehicles in use as ambulances for the wounded and frostbite cases. The enemy held back and had little chance of causing much real damage.

The battle report of the division recognized the role of the StuGs during this retreat: 'Once again worthy of mention is the unselfish and self-sacrificing devotion of the StuG crews whose "Buffalos" covered the retreat to the end, warded off pursuing enemy forces and were constantly the last men facing the enemy.'

1 Battery, assigned to 3 Inf.Div. (mot.) had extremely bad luck on the first day of the advance and lost an StuG during the crossing of the Nara when it broke through the ice and had to be destroyed later by explosives. Then leaving Tashirov to the south-east to reach 3 Inf.Div. the battery ran into a large minefield where four StuGs were seriously damaged. The transfer to 3 Inf.Div. was then cancelled and the battery placed at the disposal of 258 Inf.Div. The repaired StuGs were placed in reserve and brought to Golovenkino, 5 kilometres north of Tashirov,

in readiness. The division had removed its command post there on 2 December. The following day 1 Battery was put to the test when two battalions of Russian infantry descended on the village and the Divisional Staff had to be extracted from the danger. The attack broke up the fire of the StuGs.

The losses of the Abteilung in the advance to Moscow were considerable. Over the three days, eight of the twenty-one StuGs and a number of other fighting vehicles were lost. Three officers and seven men lost their lives, many were wounded. Frostbitten feet accounted for a number of the latter and were also treated at the field dressing stations.

The ten fallen in the advance to Moscow from 1 to 3 December 1941 were the three officers, Anacker, Hälbig and Runge mentioned above; NCOs Wachtmeisters Lehmann, Gabel and Müller; and Gefreiters Kumpitsch, Schulz, Borris and Gruss, all from 2 Battery except Gefreiter Gruss, who was from 3 Battery. The CO, Major Hoffmann-Schoenborn, two officers, six NCOs and seven other ranks were wounded.

Two Russian reports on the attack towards Moscow fell into German hands and provide information on how the other side experienced the events and what conclusion they drew. What interested us mainly was what the Russian commanders had to say about German StuGs, and some is repeated here. The term Sturmgeschütz – assault gun – was not colloquial for the Russians even in translation, they referred to all armoured tracked vehicles as 'panzers' but nevertheless it is obvious when StuGs are meant. On 3 December 1941 the Operations Group of 33 Army Staff stated in its battle report:

In the enemy advance on 1 December 1941 from Tashirov towards Noraya, our foremost line was penetrated in a powerful attack by the enemy in regiment strength supported by fifteen to twenty panzers. Without stopping, the panzers quickly entered the Noraya sector, each panzer having four to five 'landing troops' armed with machine pistols.

From a 'Report of the Operational Division of the West Front Staff' dated 8 December 1941 on the German breakthrough and halting it in the sector of 33 Army of the West Front (1 to 4 December 1941):

On 2 December 1941 enemy infantry of unknown strength and a group of eight to ten panzers occupied the towns of Yushkovo and Burtsev. The enemy did not advance in a uniform frontal attack but in groups led by a single panzer, or small groups of them. This is the usual attack tactic of German troops, forming 'spearheads' and joining them all up once behind the enemy's rear.

The report recommended that the best counter-measure was to strike at the flanks and in the back of the enemy once they had broken through. The Russians had done this repeatedly during the attack on Moscow and had caused serious losses among German rearward units.

When the rearguard had crossed the Nara again, the two dozen infantrymen returned to their units and reoccupied the slit trenches and accommodations dug into the ground in the old readiness area, and anything else which had four walls and a roof. In accordance with the order from Korps, the StuGs were withdrawn from the front and sent back to Klin, the Abteilung's supply centre, for repair and for the crews to occupy quarters there.

What had actually happened on the Moscow front? By 5 December 1941 the German spearheads had reached as far as the suburbs of the Soviet capital from the north and west. In the north, the divisions of Panzer Group 3 had formed an arc 1,000 kilometres in length and reached the Moscow–Volga Canal. To their south were the foremost units of XXXXI Panzerkorps which had fought through to the crossings over the canal at Lonya.

Panzer Group 4 ran from Krasnaya Polyana to Svenigorod, and the spearhead of 2 Panzer Division had reached the outermost terminus of the Moscow tram lines, 6 kilometres from the city ring road. Attached to Panzer Group 4 to the south were seven infantry divisions, two panzer divisions and the motorized SS-Division 'Das Reich'. Then came 4 Armee of which our Abteilung formed part. At the southernmost point of the arc before the capital was 4 Panzerarmee (Generaloberst Guderian).

A thousand kilometres of front! They were frozen in and stuck in the true sense. A temperature of –50 degrees Celsius embraced man, animal and equipment. Officers and men lacked adequate winter clothing. The infantry wore what they could find. One often saw the most exotic apparel. It was not only just the frost; there was hunger too. Bread and butter resembled lumps of ice. The ice-cold rations caused serious digestion problems; they were responsible for more field hospital admissions than the fighting. Frostbite reduced some companies to half their complement within a few weeks. The horse-drawn units suffered no less from the frost. Fodder for the horses no longer got through. Frozen hay and straw made them ill. Mange and colic finished many of them off. There was insufficient anti-freeze available. Water froze in the radiators, engine blocks cracked apart. The troops had to stay where they were. Weapons failed because the oil froze in the breech. Nobody had thought of winter oil. It was supposed to have been another Blitzkrieg.

What action did the Russian High Command take? From across the Soviet landmass troops came to Moscow as if as the result of a gigantic mobilization. Siberian divisions accustomed to the cold and well equipped for winter warfare came to save Moscow. The ratio of the forces now favoured the Soviets.

At Klin, StuGs and vehicles were repaired insofar as it was possible. Quarters were improved for over-wintering. The men made themselves as comfortable as possible in the houses and shacks, built wooden bunk systems to accommodate more men. The fug and stink was often intolerable but had to be got used to. When one entered a room from outside 'it took your breath away'. The Russian family nearly always dominated the stove. They wore blankets and furs. Their sustenance consisted of potatoes, cabbage and buckwheat accompanied by onions and garlic. Their meals were ladled from an iron pot or earthenware crockery. Whatever we could spare from our rations we fed to their small horses and this was repaid by access to the potato stocks hidden in the ground.

Yet a Russian winter with its horrors could not totally deaden an infantry-man's sense of humour. This true event occurred in the last days before the advance over the Nara when the fighting units were still at Redkino. A rumour had spread through the quarters that the men of 2 Battery had discovered a Russian provisions compound somewhere on the Nara and had seized the finest salads and cooking oil. All requests from comrades of the other batteries for a share had been rejected out of hand. The irritation grew when during the evening their whole nest reeked of potato pancakes and baked potatoes as they celebrated an eating orgy. Next morning, however, they reported sick in droves. Word got around that they had spent much of the night in the open in the bitter cold with a biting north-east wind with super-diarrhoea. The cause of all this suffering was a mistranslation of the Russian label 'Rata Aircraft Motor Oil' as 'finest salad oil'.

Finally the Abteilung received the long-awaited order to move out, and preparations were taken in hand very quickly. An advance group was despatched to Spass-Demenskoye 90 kilometres north-east of Roslavl.

On 17 December 191 in snow and cold the Abteilung moved out in daylight to the area mentioned, the total distance involved being 350 kilometres. Proceeding with so many damaged vehicles was laborious. The Staff and Staff Battery were allocated quarters in the town, 1 Battery was lodged in the neighbouring village, 2 and 3 Batteries in accommodation at Lyeskov.

Over-Wintering in Spass-Demenskoye, Christmas 1941–21 March 1942

The quarters for the batteries to over-winter were soon set up for Christmas. A convoy of vehicles led by Oberleutnant Pantel had arrived from Germany with 650 much-anticipated parcels, Army stores and spare parts. The Christmas preparations included Advent wreaths for the rooms, small fir trees with tinsel and candles and other decorations. The harsh winter, though seasonal, set the mood.

Staff Battery had taken over a former hall in the town, decorated it fittingly and from 1700 hrs celebrated with carols, a reading of the Christmas gospel by Paymaster Schulze, and an address by battery commander Oberleutnant Tenner, and then the distribution of gifts.

The Abteilung CO, Oberleutnant Haarberg, was present. He also visited the outlying batteries by horse-drawn sled. In the moonlight and deep snow it was a fitting form of transport. In the marketplace at Leskov (which had not known religious celebrations since the Soviets took power in 1917), a large Christmas tree with electric bulbs had been erected as if to convey the message of Christmas.

Oberleutnant Haarberg distributed decorations and announced promotions. His determination, thinking and acting as CO helped deepen and consolidate the *ésprit de corps* of the Buffalo Abteilung. It was a stirring Christmas far from home. Many of the men said it was the best Christmas they had ever had. We had no interruptions and after all we had gone through we could even relax. The sentries had the worst of it in the bitter cold; it never stopped snowing and the snow lay 1 metre thick, the roads and access paths to the quarters had to be continually shovelled clear. The prevailing temperature day and night was –45 degrees Celsius. The dressing stations were full of frostbite cases, some of them even from our own Abteilung.

Partisan activity behind the German lines had become very worrisome, On 30 December 1941 the Abteilung had to place three 1 Battery StuGs led by Oberleutnant Kollblöck with men transferred in from 3 Battery as infantry for protection duty along the Yuchnov–Roslavl road. They were deployed there until recalled on 14 February 1942. Most of their casualties were from frostbite. Partisans were also reported in the Yelnya area. To protect the units behind the front line, all occupied villages were built up into strongpoints, and those not occupied were searched thoroughly by specially trained teams. Our Abteilung provided some of these, accompanied by StuGs, but they had little to do in the Spass-Demenskoye area.

On 31 December 1941 Oberleutnant Haarberg issued the following 'New Year's Order of the Day':

The year 1941 is over. For StuG Abteilung 191 it was a year of heavy fighting. In Greece and Russia it has been outstanding. There has been much repeated recognition of the crews at the higher levels of command. This is reflected in the large number of important decorations awarded. In the Abteilung:

3 Knight's Crosses

3 German Crosses in Gold

4 Mentions in the Honour Roll of the German Army

5 Certificates of Recognition by Army High Command

29 Iron Crosses, First Class

120 Iron Crosses, Second Class and 1 Clasp

37 War Service Crosses, 2nd Class

205 Assault Badges

121 men received the Wound Badge in Black (and 7 in Silver).

The military successes were stunning. As we can confirm with pride, the Abteilung was often involved decisively in the success of large battles. An excellent reputation based on that precedes you and smooths the way at all military centres.

The sacrifices were also large for the Abteilung on the field of honour. It lost 11 officers, 40 NCOs and men dead; 28 officers, 142 NCOs and men wounded; and 8 officers, 144 NCOs and men afflicted by a medical condition.

Every man should know that these sacrifices were not made in vain. The year 1942 lies ahead. Today at the turn of the year we stand battle-weary in the rearward Army area. It is obvious, however, that in the coming days we will be sent into combat again for StuG Abteilung 191 cannot remain inactive when danger threatens. In the weeks and months ahead we shall prepare thoroughly for more fighting engagements. There is only one goal. Beginning with the spring offensive, the Abteilung must be fully battle-ready and equipped in the best possible way. Then, true to its great tradition, corresponding to its outstanding reputation, it will stand in the foremost front line against the enemy, the most loyal friend and best help for the infantry and then be decisive once more in obtaining great victories and mighty successes.

May the year 1942 bring us final victory. Then may StuG Abteilung 191 march proud and victorious into the Homeland.

> Haarberg, Oberleutnant and Abteilung Commanding Officer.

As a result of the increase in partisan activity in rearward areas, ultimately all available StuGs, field sentry posts and security measures were employed by the Abteilung for anti-partisan work. This is how the front situation was depicted in our sector at that time:

The fighting here has taken on a a quite peculiar character never previously seen. At the moment we do not have a fixed front. At best it is described as a line which theoretically separates friend from foe. We occupy the villages on one side of this line, on the other side it is the Russians. The villages have been developed into strongpoints wherever possible. Trenches have been dug in the snow, machine-gun nests built into them, rifle ports cut into the walls of the houses and heavy weapons brought up, all ready for the enemy.

Between the scattered villages are woods and fields better described as a snowy desert. The snow is about 1 metre deep. The fighting now is for these villages. Some of the inhabitants are still there, some were evacuated, those who remain lead active lives, though in the event of fighting they withdraw into the innermost corner of their dwellings.

The Red Army attacks continually, today here, tomorrow there, with forces of increasingly greater size, often in hordes. They surround the German-occupied villages, then attack from all sides. We take up arms; if we get into dire straits other troops in the vicinity come to our aid but if that doesn't work then they finish us off.

The inhabitants of a small town in the vicinity had held out for six weeks and were relieved by us. Prisoners are rarely taken; death dominates the battlefield. The Russian corpses often lie in great numbers in front of the villages. They become snowed over and disappear from sight. Now and again when we have to stay for a while near a field of corpses they are piled up, dowsed with petrol and set alight. We cannot bury them because the earth is frozen solid down to a depth of 1.5 metres. A wounded man who can be brought in perhaps survives, but others lying out there freeze to death. The struggle goes back and forth like that. It is no longer StuGs and infantry who fight but also the rearward services of all kinds who are called upon, Army artillery units, construction battalions, supply units, etc. in order to hold the strongpoints along the endlessly long fronts. The infantry companies have long since shrunk in size to a count of heads, but it is best not to dwell on that.

So that is how it looks in rearward areas. In the gaps between villages, through the widely spread woodlands, huge numbers of Russian troops make substantial breakthroughs behind the German front. They join up with airborne troops and partisans to make the hinterland insecure. It is impossible to estimate their numbers. They have huge quantities of weapons, much of them delivered by aircraft. These units interrupt rearward communications severely. We do not have enough troops to fight these large organizations of partisans. We staff the villages along the major routes of communication using Trosses, rearward services and any other groups at hand which we can throw together and then we watch how they get on converting the villages and houses into strongpoints to protect their own skins.

Now and again partisans blockade the roads, blow up bridges and carry out surprise raids on vehicles. This costs lives. If it gets really bad somewhere and the rearward people simply can't hold out any longer and save themselves, then small battleworthy units or squads are deployed with the StuGs. Often in those cases the surrounding villages into which the partisans have settled or are to be found in the area are shot into flame or torched. As noted earlier, StuGs with these operational squads are much feared by partisans.

That was how the winter war looked in Russia. Meanwhile our Abteilung CO, Oberleutnant Haarberg, was promoted to Hauptmann. His personality consolidated the fighting spirit and *ésprit de corps* of the Buffalo Abteilung. It was precisely this harsh winter in Russia that made it clear how much understanding and consideration was required of senior officers in order to protect the men against the vagaries of the climate. As a volunteer in the First World War he had already known two Russian winters. Therefore he despatched teams of lorries to Germany to obtain winter clothing, mail, Army stores and lorry spare parts. On account of its important successes, the Abteilung was known to the offices of Army High Command, which in turn were well disposed to supply the help and support requested.

The bitterly cold months of winter had passed their worst stage. Storms spreading from the south over the snow-covered plain heralded the thaw. On 19 March when the yearned-for orders arrived, our disappointment was great that we would not be going to Germany for a general overhaul. Instead our destination was Mogilev for refresher training.

The Abteilung ordered that preparations be made to leave. All field sentries, security and command posts were withdrawn and the last seven battleworthy StuGs transferred to another StuG Abteilung operational in our area. On 21 March 1942 our entire Abteilung made the journey (350 kilometres) to Mogilev from Spass-Demenskoye by car or lorry. We were hopeful that this transfer might signify a period of leave at last.

Rest in Mogilev, 21 March–1 June 1942

Initially the Abteilung was accommodated in a former artillery barracks on the outskirts of Mogilev. The rooms were intolerably cold and so we moved into blocks of flats previously used by employees of a large automobile factory. Furniture was acquired from nearby. Hauptmann Haarberg was confirmed officially as CO of StuG Abteilung 191.

Mogilev was a town which had had a population of 80,000 before the war. About 30,000 of the people had remained and at most half the houses were still available. A soldiers' hostel, cinema, guest houses and a front theatre were on offer. There was a local brewery and at this time a 'Buffalo band' was formed, six musicians under Hauptwachtmeister Genz. The instruments were obtained from Berlin. The band performed on 'Abteilung comradeship evenings' and also at the soldiers' hostel. The best news of all was the approval for a great wave of leave-taking but this was suddenly cut back to 50 per cent.

Our former CO Major Hoffmann-Schoenborn arrived at Mogilev on 20 May to take his leave of us. The great occasion was celebrated in the hostel and next day he was driven to the railway station in an StuG accompanied by his old loyal followers. After a long wait the Abteilung had finally received a supply of new vehicles, among them StuGs with the L/42 long barrel and reinforcements.

Over the course of time replacements arrived for all vacancies in rank so that the authorized establishment in personnel was met in full. Refresher training brought the preparedness for action to the highest level. The battery commanders at this time were:

Staff Battery: Oberleutnant Tenner
1 Battery: Oberleutnant Kollböck
2 Battery: Oberleutnant Heinzle
3 Battery: Oberleutnant Götz

On 1 June 1942 the Abteilung received orders to make for Kursk, a journey of some 700 kilometres. This took place between 2 and 10 July 1942 via Smolensk, Merkulyev, Karachev, Orel, Chirkusky and Kuritza. The weather was cold and wet and many roads were impassable so that the planned bivouac often occurred very late. No vehicles were lost during transit.

The Abteilung obtained quarters in Kursk, the vehicles were checked over and made ready. The pause enabled the men to get to know the town. It was almost completely undamaged, lively and industrious. A cinema, soldiers' hostel and a front theatre were all at hand. The front lay 60 kilometres to the east of town.

An unexpected change of leadership occurred when our recently appointed CO, Hauptmann Haarberg, was transferred to the artillery school at Jüterbog. His successor, Hauptmann Führ, brought his transfer papers and presented himself as the new CO of the Buffalo Abteilung. It was a sad moment for all when the departure of 'Papa' Haarberg became known. He relinquished his command to his successor Hauptmann Führ on 15 June 1942 and flew back to Germany the same day.

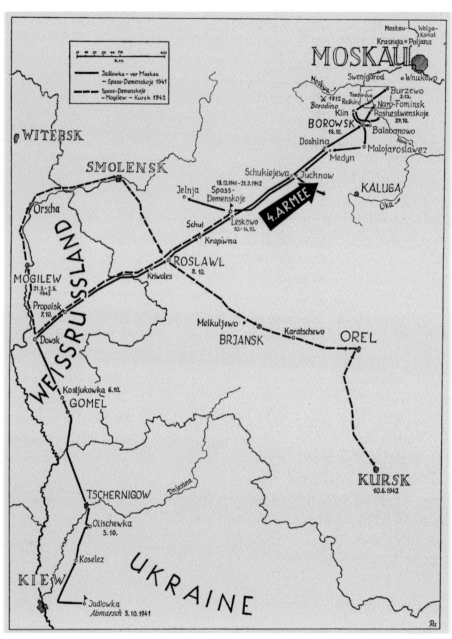

The progress of StuG Abteilung 191: Kiev to Moscow, 5 October to 3 December 1941; winter quarters at Spass-Demenskoye, 18 December 1941 to 21 March 1942; refit at Mogilev, 21 March to 2 June 1942; Kursk 10–27 June 1942.

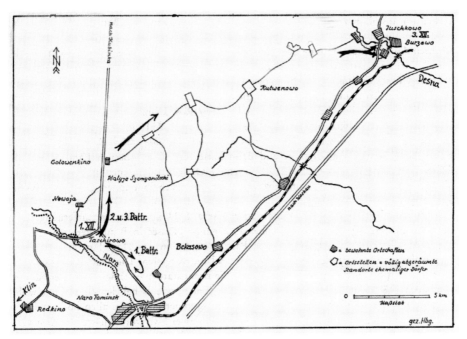

Map of the most easterly point in the Moscow campaign reached by the Abteilung,
3 December 1941. (Key: 'inhabited villages' and 'fully abandoned sites of previous
villages'.

Group photo of officer corps, StuG Abteilung 191. Seated from left to right: Oblt.
Göring, Oblt. Kapp, Oblt. Haarberg, Major Hoffmann-Schoenborn, Oblt. Möller
(fell, 22 September 1941), Hauptmann von Schönau, Stabsarzt Dr Gräve, Oblt. von
Bockum-Dolffs (fell, 7 April 1941). First row standing: Lt. Fuchs, Lt. Lützow, Lt. Barths,
Lt. Nordhoff (fell, 13 September 1941), Oblt. Anacker (fell, 3 December 1941), Lt. Heine,
Oberzahlmeister Barth, Lt. Bingler (fell, 24 August 1941), Lt. Schneermann, Lt. Kollböck,
Lt.Stoll. Rear row: Lt. Heinzle, Lt. Heinrich, Lt. Götz, Lt. Berendes, Tech. Oberinspektor Heder.

Winter 1941: A horse-drawn sled at Spass-Demenskoye, the winter quarters of the Abteilung.

Christmas festivities 1941 with Oberleutnant Haarberg as acting Abteilung CO at Leskovo/ Spass-Demenskoye.

Graves of 2 Battery men who fell near Moscow on 1 and 2 December 1941: Battery leader Oberleutnant Anacker, Leutnant Hälbig, Gefreiter Kumpitsch.

Propaganda photo from a magazine showing a StuG with partial white-paint camouflage and carrying infantry.

April 1942. The 'Buffalo band' at practice at Mogilev. The snow lay on the ground until springtime.

May 1942: resting at Mogilev. From left: Unteroffizier Huhn, Feuerwerker Unteroffizier Kula, Unteroffizier Kühn, senior sergeant radio operator Oberfunkmeister Gutowski, Unteroffizier Weber, armourer Unteroffizier Sücker. At the rear: Unteroffizier Banzhaf, all from Staff Battery.

Hauptwachtmeister Karsten, known as the 'Captain', 2 Battery, StuG Abteilung 191, Mogilev, May 1942.

Oberleutnant Kollböck, commander 1 Battery and later Abteilung CO, fell as Hauptmann, 12 November 1944 at Esseg.

Oberleutnant Helmut Göring, platoon leader, 3 Battery, seen wearing the German Cross in Gold awarded on 19 December 1941.

Oblerleutnant Rudolf Haarberg, commander 3 Battery, Abteilung CO at Christmas 1941, was awarded the German Cross in Gold on 6 January 1942.

Russian prisoners brought in after the fighting at Toropetz, May 1942.

A serenade before a Russian cottage. Visiting is a Gebirgstruppe Leutnant, third from left.

An StuG crossing a ford in the Tim sector between Kursk and Voronezh, June 1942. Oberleutnant Tenner observes the performance of the new long-barrelled StuG delivered to the Abteilung at Kursk.

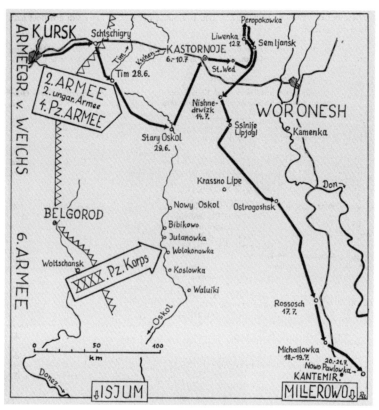

This map shows the route taken by the StuG Abteilung during the offensive towards
Voronezh, 28 June–14 July 1942, and the turn-off to the south, 15 July–3 August 1942.

The StuG was now effective against the T-34 with the newly arrived long-barrel gun.

The circular protective shield fitted around the roof hatch of this observation car would have been made at the Abteilung workshop.

Celebrating the capture of Elista, August 1942. At the right in this photo is Hauptwachtmeister Bruno Bork, author of this book.

The original text with names from the reverse of the photograph: Oberwachtmeister (Owm) Lambacher, Wachmeister (Wm) Ramm, (Owm) Cibrowius, Unteroffizier Küppers, (Wm) Geblhaar, (Wm) Hühn, Hauptwachtmeister Bork. [there are seven names, but only six faces visible – *Trans.*]

"Siegesfeier in der Kalmückensteppe"
"Nach der Einnahme von Elista im August 1942
von l. n. r. Obw. Lambacher, Wm. Ramm Obw. Cibrowius
Wm. Küppers, Wm. Geblhaar, Wm. Hühn
Hptw. Bork

Route taken by StuG Abteilung 191 from Kursk to Mosdok/Caucasus, 28 June to 31 August 1942.

An StuG driven out of cover.

September 1942 at Russkiy ('Büffelskaya') at the foot of the Caucasus. In the photo Unteroffizier Krüger, Leutnant Fischer, Hauptwachtmeister Bork, Oberwachtmeister Cibrowius, Wachtmeister Ebert and Unteroffizier Heinz (3 Battery).

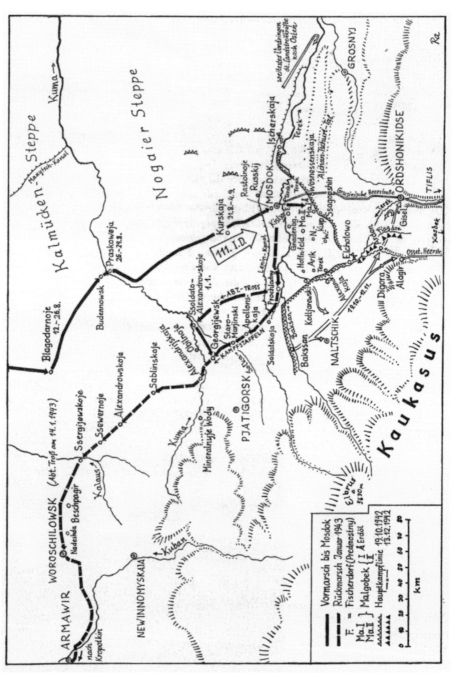

Operational area of the Abteilung in the bridgehead at Mosdok on the Terek, the fighting in the bend of the Terek from 2 September to 31 December 1942 and the return of the Abteilung to the Kuban bridgehead, January 1943.

Hermann Röhm (centre), member of the 'Mühlenbatterie', in front of the quarters, January 1943.

You can hold out longer in the sun. Hermann Röhm extreme right in photo.

Orders being distributed by Hauptmann Müller, January 1943.

Hauptmann Müller reading out the daily orders.

Hermann Röhm drove this Kfz 15 Staff car of the Mühlenbatterie as Hauptmann Müller's driver.

The Mühlenbatterie was wiped out and disbanded in the fighting between January and March 1943. In the photo is a StuG with sparse camouflage, winter 1942.

Ceremony for award of the Knight's Cross to Oberst Georg Scholze, CO, Inf.Regt, on 17 February 1943.

Men of Mühlenbatterie fallen in for the ceremony of awarding the Knight's Cross. Hermann Röhm was transferred to StuG Abteilung 191 on 21 February 1943. Hauptmann Müller was its new CO.

Hauptmann Müller was at Jüterbog on 20 February 1943 when he received his Knight's Cross from the hand of Oberst Hoffmann-Schoenborn. Here in the award ceremony, the decoration is being placed around his neck by Oberst Georg Scholze.

Change of quarters on the return from Terek to Kuban in January 1943. In the foreground is an observation vehicle.

StuGs of the 'Buffalo' Abteilung on the return.

StuGs of Abteilung 191 heading for Kuban, January 1943.

A StuG fitted with the 7.5-cm L/48 long barrel cannon. On the side of the vehicle is a section of reserve track which also served as supplementary armour.

The StuG of the 3 Battery commander in the Kuban area, February 1943. Left to right: Ladekanonier Valentin Klein, Oberleutnant Tenner, driver Griesheimer and gunlayer-NCO Konietzko.

Graves of members of StuG Abteilung 191 in the Kuban bridgehead.

Chapter Four

From Kursk to the Caucasus, 1942–1943

The Summer Offensive, 1942: Attach on Woronesch

After the stormy summer campaign and a winter with many losses and crises, in the spring of 1942 the German Army of the East with its allies stood along a front 2,800 kilometres in length stretching from Murmansk on the Arctic coast to Taganrog on the Sea of Azov. Up to this point both the Soviets and the Germans had suffered severe losses in men and materials.

Hand in hand with their great ally 'winter', the Soviet armies had not succeeded in decisively breaking up the German front, had not delivered Hitler's armies a catastrophic defeat before Moscow, nor obliged them to retreat over the endless snow-covered expanses westwards as the Russians had forced Napoleon's Grande Armée to do in 1812/13.

The German Army had lost much valuable material which could only be replaced slowly by a war industry working flat-out. The great crisis had been survived, however, and the German Army of the East stood equipped for new offensives. Meanwhile the German General Staff had worked on new plans which, if fulfilled, would force the Soviet Union 'to its knees'.

The focus of effort would be in the southern part of the Eastern Front. The Russian armies between the Don and the Caucasus mountains were to be eliminated. The occupation of the Kuban and Caucasian oilfields would provide Germany with valuable economic resources decisive for the outcome of the war. Caucasian oil was at the centre of Hitler's thinking and planning. In his Directive No. 41 of 5 April 1942, the German war aims were set down for the summer of 1942. The plan envisaged:

(1) A thrust by 2 Armee and 4 Panzerarmee from Kursk to Voronezh. In a further thrust, 4 Panzerarmee joined with 6 Armee would advance south along the upper Don to the Kalatch area.

(2) A thrust by 17 Armee and elements of 1 Panzerarmee from Rostov and northwards along the lower Don in an easterly direction towards Kalatch.

(3) The making of small encirclements west of Oskol and on the Donetz.

The long northern flank along the upper Don resulting from this strategy would be secured by the allied Axis armies and in the gigantic encirclements the Soviet divisions on the southern front would be annihilated. In the second operational phase the combined push to the south and the Caucasus would follow.

The basic principle of the first phase of the German summer offensive 1942 was the capture of Voronezh. This city on two rivers was an important armaments and economic centre. It dominated the river Voronezh and also the Don with its numerous bridges. It was moreover the switching centre of the central north–south communications by means of roads, railway and river shipping from the traffic network of Moscow to the Black Sea and Caspian Sea.

On 28 June 1942, Armeegruppe von Weichs began the attack on Voronezh with 2 Armee, 4 Panzerarmee and 2 Hungarian Army. 4 Panzerarmee was the spearhead. At its centre was XXXXVIII Panzerkorps with 24 Panzer Division flanked left and right by 16 Inf.Div. (mot.) and the Division 'Grossdeutschland'. The task of capturing the city of Voronezh fell to 24 Panzer Division, formerly the East Prussian and only cavalry division of the Wehrmacht, converted in the winter of 1941 into a panzer division.

With cover from above by VIII Fliegerkorps, the Soviet defensive positions were overrun, the river Tim was reached and the bridge over the Tim captured intact. With the spirit and élan of cavalrymen, the panzers got to the Kshen river, where they destroyed the Soviet 160 and 6 Infantry Divisions. Here also the bridge was captured intact. The wild charge went on without regard for their unprotected open flanks. When it was necessary to refuel, they grouped up, quickly formed battle groups and carried on. Thus in the hot summer days of 1942, 24 Panzer-Div. emulated those classic powerful thrusts of the opening weeks of the war and showed what well-equipped and rested panzer troops with spirited leadership were capable of against the Russians.

On 30 June 1942, 24 Panzer Division had covered half its route objective to Voronezh when it encountered a Soviet strongpoint. The situation was critical. Three Russian armoured corps attempted to protect Voronezh by encircling the German units which had broken through. The great armoured response against

Hoth's 4 Panzerarmee was a failure. The better German tactics, the extensive reconnaissance and more mobile leadership were victorious against the Russian armour despite their more powerful T-34 and KW tanks.

StuG Abteilung 191 between Kursk and Voronezh, 28 June–14 July 1942

The Abteilung was assigned to VII Armeekorps/2 Hungarian Army. Prior to the day of the attack the batteries and Tross occupied woodlands in the Tim sector. The rearward services remained on call at Kursk.

The first goal to be attained was the Tim river. In the early hours of 28 June 1942, the Armeekorps with effective air support set off and in a surprise attack broke through the foremost Russian position. Our StuGs, together with pioneers and infantry, took on the enemy defences. After breaking through the first staggered defence lines the Abteilung was transferred to XXXXVIII Panzerkorps. 1 Battery placed a platoon with the spearhead unit of 16 Inf.Div. (mot.). On the advance, the Luftwaffe bombed the spearhead, causing substantial casualties among the infantry. While crossing a field of sunflowers the platoon leader Leutnant Klosner fell after being shot in the neck.

Following a brief pause for rest during the night, in the early hours elements of the division occupied the town of Stary Oskol against spirited Russian resistance by a skeleton rearguard.

On 30 June 1942 when 24 Panzer-Div. fought its first major battle, 150 kilometres to the south 6 Armee embarked on its push to the north-east aiming for Voronezh. The Armee Order of 2 July 1942 stated: '6 Armee is completing the encirclement and destruction of the enemy forces still holding out west and south-west of Stary Oskol, and is leading the merging of its fast mobile units into 4 Panzerarmee at Ssiniye Lipyagi (45 kilometres east of Stary Oskol)' (AOK 6 No. 2381/42 g. Kdos v. 23 June 1942).

XL Panzerkorps (3 Panzer Division, 23 Panzer Division, 29 Inf.Div (mot.), 336 Inf.Div., 100 Jäger-Div. among others) were under 6 Armee command between XVII and VII Armeekorps in the area north-east of Voltschansk; they had the following orders: 'XL Panzerkorps will advance with tightly concentrated forces to the north-east as far as the river Oskol and will then build a bridgehead on the east bank of the river south-west of Novyi Oskol. As soon as possible the Korps will then advance to Stary Oskol and link up with the inner wing of 4 Panzerarmee' (AOK 6 1a No. 2505/42 q.v. 2.7).

The operation of the Korps was then upset by a calamity on 19 June when the Fieseler Storch in which the 1 General Staff Officer of 23 Panzer Division was a passenger was shot down. As a result the attack plans fell into Russian hands. Three days before the attack the Commanding General, the Korps CO and the commander of 23 Panzer Division were replaced, which led to great difficulties in carrying out the operation.

On 30 June at 0245 hrs the Korps set out with effective Stuka support and surprised the foremost Russian positions. As the attack went on the enemy offered more stubborn resistance, using many tanks. Aerial reconnaissance surprised us with a report that some of the enemy force had headed off east and north-east on the far side of the Oskol. Korps therefore obtained approval from Armee to advance over the Oskol with 3 Panzer Division, followed by 29 Inf.Div. (mot.) in the neighbouring sector. After crossing the Oskol they were to head north at once in order to create an encirclement with XXXXVIII Panzerkorps in the Stary Oskol area.

Something remarkable was now observed in that, instead of preparing for a major confrontation, the Russians were withdrawing from the threatened encirclement at the Oskol, protected by a strong rearguard, after which they bombed the bridgeheads created on the far bank of the Oskol at Yutanovka, Bibikov and Koslovka.

The first objective of the operation had been achieved, the broad front against the river had paid off. The only disquieting feature was the high casualty rate among panzers and pioneers of 23 Panzer Division. Furthermore, the number of prisoners taken and materials captured was insignificant and no artillery piece was among it. Therefore there could be no talk of 'encirclement and destruction'. The new situation made it essential to advance to the Don without delay to cut off the enemy's retreat. Unfortunately for us, 6 Armee stuck to its encirclement plan and the Korps was not very happy at having to continue the operation to the north as previously ordered. The shortened objectives and changing directions of attack by the divisions to the north, east and south required a high degree of mobility from the Korps. If the numerous changing objectives were nevertheless all achieved, this would be all credit to the Korps, which did not allow itself to be vexed by the inconstancy of the leadership.

On 2 July the first connection with 4 Panzerarmee was made, but not until 5 July in the Krasno–Lipe area between XXXX Panzerkorps (23 Panzer Division) and 4 Panzerarmee (XXXXVIII Panzerkorps), about 60 kilometres south-east of Stary Oskol. The pocket here was sealed but there was nobody inside it. Even here the Russians had moved out with their heavy weapons and hurried towards the Don. From aerial reconnaissance photos it was seen that even there units were being loaded up and so everything pointed to a planned, large-scale retreat.

It was clear that the Russian tactic had pre-empted the German one. They had finally recognized that remaining after the front was breached brought with it the danger of encirclement. They had come to the conclusion that it was only possible to keep up with the Germans on operations if they had at least equal mobility.

StuG Abteilung 191 had meanwhile been assigned to XXXXVIII Panzerkorps to protect its southern flank west of Voronezh. The German spearheads, led by our StuGs, received a message dropped by Fieseler Storch with a smoke bomb that about 200 enemy tanks were on the way from Don to Voronezh.

In order to divert the approaching danger to the flank, XXXXVIII Panzerkorps and the StuG Abteilung engaged the Russian spearheads at once. The tank battle which now broke out raged for several hours and was fought in hilly terrain mostly covered in mist. Russian air attacks supported their armour and also caused casualties in our ranks. Our StuGs 'mixed in' industriously and destroyed thirty-five enemy tanks. Since other panzers were on their way, the Russians refused battle and turned away, screened by a wall of fog in hills to the east. They left behind them the smouldering wrecks of their tanks, among them some Shermans and General Grants. We too lost StuGs with their crews and had many wounded, but these bore no relationship to the losses in the panzer regiments. Our fighting units of the Buffalo Abteilung were withdrawn to somewhere quiet to repair.

Operationally in combat, there were clear differences between the way the StuGs and a panzer group fought and were led. If the panzer spearhead came upon enemy resistance during an advance, irrespective of whether this was artillery or anti-tank fire, the panzers stopped and sought cover if possible. The StuGs then had to take over leadership and engage the enemy, after which the panzers followed. This process led to some tension, and therefore we did not look favourably upon having to cooperate with our panzers.

Meanwhile the rearward services of the Abteilung had left Kursk for Stary Oskol 200 kilometres away on 5 July. We met up with them in the area north of it and settled in quarters at Kastornoye from 6 to 10 July. Vehicles and StuGs were attended to for repairs but for the first time we were short of qualified guncrews, for the many casualties had not been replaced. Therefore the Abteilung had to resort to the men of the rearward services, Tross and workshops who were given a brief spell of training and then drafted into the fighting batteries.

As the daytime temperature on 5 July of 40 degrees Celsius gave way to night, the fast units of XXXXVIII Panzerkorps and 24 Panzer-Div. waited in distant bridgeheads west of the Don opposite Voronezh. On 6 July elements of 23 Panzer Division and the Grossdeutschland Division entered the city. The Russians seemed to pull back. This misled Hitler into believing that the moment was favourable and he gave anew his authority for the conquest of Voronezh.

XXXX Panzerkorps continued the thrust it had already started to the south. 4 Panzerarmee was ordered to free up panzer units as quickly as possible and attach them to XXXX Panzerkorps. Thus began the second phase of Operation *Blue*.

General Timoshenko had drawn up the masses of 40 Soviet Army around Voronezh in order to hold the north wing of the main German forces before Voronezh. His idea was to gain time to enable him to disengage and draw off the mass of his army group from Oskol and the Donetz and cross back over the Don. The city had to be held for as long as possible to delay the German thrust to the south-east. Every day gained was a boon for the Russians.

On 7 July, after heavy fighting, 3 Inf.Div. (mot.) and 16 Inf.Div. (mot.) had occupied the western part of Voronezh but the battalions had not crossed the river, which flowed north to south through the city. Nor in the next few days were they to occupy the eastern part of the city or the bridge at it northern end, nor did they sever the north–south railway tracks along the east bank of the river which were decisively important for Russian supply. The great connecting line from Moscow to the south remained in Russian hands.

Instead of advancing along the Don as planned, and lying in wait for the wavering division of Timoshenko to the east between Donetz and Don, the valuable panzer and motorized divisions of the two Panzerkorps were stuck fast to the city of Voronezh.

In its swift advance to the east, 3 Panzer Division/XXXX Panzerkorps captured first the town of Kamenka, then carried on along the Don further south to take Rossosch on 7 July.

After turning south from Rossosch, the Panzerkorps with all three divisions leading caught up with the Russian retreat. Hordes of Soviet soldiers were following the railway lines and Rollbahn south of Millorov to the south-east. The German pursuers were not strong enough to stop these enemy columns, and because of the resistance around Millerov could not go ahead to form an intended outer eastern pincer on the lower Don.

In this very confusing situation for the Commands, Phase 3 of Operation *Blue* began, which, according to the plan in Directive No. 41, should have been decisive in initiating the great summer offensive of 1942. The advance by the southern pincer with 17 Armee and 1 Panzerarmee began on 9 July. Its aim was to link up in the Stalingrad area in order to encircle and wipe out the Russians caught between the Donetz and Don. As in the north, however, the Russian units in the south only gave battle at particular strongpoints while most of their armies avoided it in the south and east.

The attack by the southern pincer forced the evasive enemy ahead of it and into the great loop of the Don. The Germans had not set up an interception front here because their armies in the north had spent too much time in Phase 1, the conquest of Voronezh, and so the entire operational plan collapsed.

From 15 to 18 July XXXX Panzerkorps continued to defend the Millerov area in order to prevent all enemy breakthrough attempts by day, and this resulted in the capture of about 14,000 prisoners. To the left of this Panzerkorps, XXXXVIII Panzerkorps advanced south via Bokovskaya on 16 July.

On 18 July elements of 1 Panzerarmee arrived from the west at the Korps cordon but lack of fuel prevented an immediate start on the pursuit to the south in the Kalitva Valley. On 20 July, XXXX Panzerkorps reached the lower Don and after heavy fighting set up bridgeheads at Konstantinovskaya and Nikolayevskaya.

Meanwhile 1 Panzerarmee had fought through to the south, crossed the Donetz and was now heading with 17 Armee to Rostov, which was defended with particular stubbornness.

Hitler had decided to split up Army Group South and he dismissed Generalfeldmarschall von Bock for having opposed his divergent operational intentions. Army Group A received Generalfeldmarschall List, and Army Group B Generaloberst von Weichs, and now the ground was prepared for the later disastrous event.

After a week's pause for rest at Kastornoye, StuG Abteilung 191 was sent off to Livenka (60 kilometres), the columns throwing up great clouds of dust on account of the dry weather. Upon their arrival at the new bivouac area, 2 Battery received orders to advance at once to Peropokovka in company with Panzer Regiment 15 to confront enemy tank assemblies (12 July). On the way the StuGs encountered strong anti-tank defences outside the town. Since night was falling, the battery formed a hedgehog and secured at the south-west edge of town facing north. On the morning of 13 July, numerous Russian tanks were seen approaching and these were engaged by the battery's flak. Russian aircraft appeared, enveloped their tanks in smoke and made off. When the smoke cleared, the enemy tanks were nowhere to be seen. The battle group proceeded to Polgoye without incident in order to cover the rear of 9 Panzer Division at the Don. Our StuGs then returned to the Abteilung, which had been reassigned to XXXXVIII Panzerkorps, and on the afternoon of 14 July the entire unit set off to Nishnedevitsk (80 kilometres).

The Advance South to Millerov, 15 July–3 August

Our long advance south began on 15 July. Stassovka was the first goal (80 kilometres). Heavy rainstorms turned the sandy tracks into mud. A day's stop was ordered. There was also a fuel shortage. On 17 July we continued to Rossosh via Ostrogoshsk. For the next stretch to Michailovka (50 kilometres) the Abteilung was attached to 3 Inf.Div. (mot.). The route of advance was totally impassable and another rest day was ordered.

It was not possible to resume the advance to Novo Pavlovka east of Kantemirovka until 20 July. On the way we were stopped by Division and assigned to Artillery Commander 326. Heat, dust and thirst were the unpleasant side-effects of our progress. We made bivouac and were granted another rest day.

On 22 July we set off for Millerov (160 kilometres). About 20 kilometres north of the town we set up our tents in an orchard by the river Kalitva. Now we were transferred to XXIV Panzerkorps. After two days' rest we continued to Tazinskaya (100 kilometres). The terrain appeared to be steppe with thistles and wild grasses. We saw neither trees nor bushes for hundreds of kilometres. The few people who lived here looked like Tartars. The Abteilung set up camp on the outskirts of the village of Tazinskaya and had completed the first stage of its endless journey. We were hopeful of finally having a useful operation to accomplish. We stood 100 kilometres north of the Don. The Abteilung was reassigned to XL Panzerkorps again. The constant change between formations

– 4 Panzerarmee, 6 Armee, 1 Panzerarmee – had now ceased. 6 Armee and 4 Panzerarmee had been sent to Stalingrad, 1 Panzerarmee and 17 Armee to the Caucasus with the next objective being the oil area at Maikop. XXXX Panzerkorps now formed part of 1 Panzerarmee.

When Hitler realized that an encircling operation at the central Don had been frustrated by the quick retreat of the Russians and the delay at Voronezh, he decided that he would encircle and wipe out the enemy forces suspected to be at the lower Don. In order to achieve this, he dropped the nucleus of his great plan, which had envisaged operating against Stalingrad with his whole force and blockading the lower Volga. The encirclement plan could have been successful because he had two panzer armies at his disposal. Hitler was labouring under a false assumption, however: he believed that the Soviets were exhausted. He interpreted the Russian retreat as flight, disintegration and moral collapse, whereas in reality the retreat was strategic. Therefore he ordered 4 Panzerarmee, following the Don towards Stalingrad, to turn about and make for the lower Don at Rostov where, so he predicted, there would be a major battle of encirclement with Rostov at it centre, the greatest encircling battle of the war. Meanwhile 6 Armee continued to Stalingrad without its spearhead, XXXX Panzerkorps, which was en route for Rostov.

On 23 July, the Chief of the Army General Staff, Generaloberst Halder, tried to convince Hitler not to split his forces and only then to move against the Caucasus once Stalingrad had been overwhelmed and the flanks and rear at the Don and Volga had been adequately protected. Hitler brushed aside all the doubts of the General Staff. His belief that the Soviets were largely defeated dominated his thinking. He even transferred most of 11 Armee with five divisions, which had been waiting in the Crimea ready to head for the Caucasus, to finish off Leningrad, and sent the well-equipped SS-Division Leibstandarte to France for rest and reorganization into a panzer division. A little later he withdrew another elite formation on the southern front, Inf.Div. (mot.) Grossdeutschland, and sent it to France. In making these changes, Hitler was relying on information that the Allied major invasion in the West was imminent. Yet these seven divisions withdrawn from the southern front would certainly have been enough to prevent the catastrophe at Stalingrad.

A victim of his own faulty assessment of the situation, Hitler expounded his thinking in the text of Führer-Directive No. 45:

(1) The next task of Army Group A (List) is to encircle and destroy the enemy forces escaping over the Don in the areas south and south-east of Rostov.

(2) After destroying these enemy forces, the entire east coast of the Black Sea is to be occupied, thus taking out the Black Sea ports and the enemy Black Sea Fleet.

(3) At the same time a group of forces composed of fast units is to occupy the area around Grozny, some of which forces are to block off the Ossetich and Grusinish military road if possible up to the heights of the passes. The area around Baku is to be occupied by an advance along the Caspian Sea. These operations by Army Group A will have the cover name *Edelweiss*.

In Paragraph 4 of the instruction, Army Group B had the task of capturing the city of Stalingrad, destroying the enemy defences and blocking the land bridge between the Don and the Volga. Fast units were also to push as far as Astrakhan and there blockade the main arm of the Volga. These operations of Army Group B (von Weichs) had the cover name *Fischreiher* (common heron).

General List (Army Group A) made the best out of what Directive No. 45 prescribed and cobbled together an acceptable plan for the forces he had: the strengthened 17 Armee was to attack Krasnodar from the Rostov area. 1 Panzerarmee (von Kleist) on the left wing of Hoth's 4 Panzerarmee had the job eastwards of it, to leave the Don bridgeheads and advance to Maikop as the outer pincer arm. In this way, in cooperation between the slower-advancing infantry divisions (1 Armee) and Kleist's panzers, the enemy forces presumed to be south of Rostov could be surrounded and wiped out. 4 Panzerarmee on the eastern wing had the security of the flank for this operation. Its first goal was Voroshilovsk. This plan therefore set in motion the advance southwards.

Our Abteilung made camp north of Tazinskaya from 24 to 30 July waiting for fuel. For this reason an order from the Armee to move out could not be obeyed. Even XL Panzerkorps had problems with supply, which made the pursuit of the enemy problematic.

These well-deserved rest days were spent by the men largely doing as they wished. The weather was hot and sunny; the air and water were inviting and the rations good. We received no mail from home because of the perpetual changes in assignment and location.

Oberwachtmeister Stange was appointed Hauptwachtmeister at Staff Battery, replacing myself, Hauptwachtmeister Bork, who moved from Staff Battery to 3 Battery. Hauptwachtmeister Preine transferred to 2 Battery. Oberleutnant Bauer replaced Oberleutnant Göring, who was on the sick list.

On 30 July our new but familiar CO Hauptmann Kapp arrived and addressed his old comrades of the Buffalo Abteilung at roll call. Fuel had come too and the last preparations were made to depart. Most of XL Panzerkorps was already heading southwards.

On 31 July the Abteilung had reached Lissitshanski close to the Don. We were hoping to get a move on from there but were disappointed. We had to rest for several days because of another fuel shortage. Heavy rain interrupted our leisure, but that wouldn't worry an infantryman.

Another reassignment saw the Abteilung transferred from XL Panzerkorps to 1 Panzerarmee.

After the successes of 3 Panzer Division at the Manych, an evil situation had arisen for 6 Armee in the great bend of the Don. The Russian bridgehead at Kalatch was not only defended but being used as the springboard for a counter-offensive. Four Russian armies and two in the process of formation had drawn up to confront 6 Armee: Paulus's XIV Panzerkorps and LI Armeekorps were already under serious pressure while a shortage of fuel and ammunition cut the strength of the entire Armee. This was the result of Hitler having mounted offensives against the Caucasus and Stalingrad at the same time, thus dividing the supply. Because far greater distances in the south had to be travelled first, the concentration of effort to supply the Caucasian front was to some extent set aside.

Hitler realized that 6 Armee was not sufficiently strong to conquer Stalingrad and on 31 July he changed his plan once more. 4 Panzerarmee less XL Panzerkorps was brought out from the Caucasian front, placed with Army Group B south of the Don facing north-east in order to bring pressure on the Soviet Kalatsh front before advancing on Stalingrad from the flank. The addition of 4 Panzerarmee came too late and made no difference to the split of the forces. The burning problem of supply could not be resolved because the entire operation lacked central oversight.

Hitler had manoeuvred himself into a situation from which he could not extricate himself and much depended on what the enemy commanders decided next. In the Stalingrad area the enemy had already set the place and time of the battle. At Army Group A all had initially gone according to plan. III and LVII Panzerkorps had made great strides towards the Caucasus. The oil town and railhead of Maikop had been captured, but all oil compounds had been destroyed and the installation dismantled to some extent. IL Gebirgskorps and V Armeekorps, which had captured a bridge over the Don east of Rostov, had reached Krasnodar and held a crossing over the river Kuban.

At the beginning of August along the entire Steppe front, the motorized unit of Army Group A had crossed the Kuban and Kalmyk steppe in order to halt the Russian divisions there.

Crossing the Don and Manych, 4–8 August 1942

On 4 August, StuG Abteilung was finally under way again, and crossed the Don at Nikolayevskaya. Russian air attacks on the great temporary bridge interrupted the crossing but all vehicles reached the target of Titoff without damage and made camp at the southern end of town. On 5 August we continued through monotonous terrain towards Proletarskaya. Heat shimmered above the landscape. Long banners of dust surrounded and followed our column, the vehicles soon being covered in a thick layer of dust. The men dozed on the vehicles. Ten kilometres north of Proletarskaya we made camp at Mokraya Yelmuta and received another two rest days on account of the shortage of fuel.

The supply of fuel was now a serious problem for us. The distances over which it had to be transported had become so long that the columns of trucks bringing it used a large proportion for themselves. This chronic lack of fuel forced the motorized units to make continual involuntary stops so that the advance and any pursuits suffered constant interruptions.

On our rest days, the steppe climate – to which we were not accustomed – began to affect us. Many men complained of diarrhoea, the first symptom of jaundice. Drinking water could only be obtained from deep wells. Camels worked the machinery bringing the water to the surface. We were approaching Asia. The rations left us hungry. There were no potatoes and we had to get used to the absence of our other usual foods. The intolerable heat exceeded 50 degrees Celsius and the lack of vitamins caused many illnesses.

On 6 August, the Abteilung was assigned to III Panzerkorps, which had the task of protecting the long eastern flank. Two days later the Abteilung continued over the dam to Bereosovka into the Kalmyk steppe (90 kilometres), then we had six days off for lack of fuel.

Upon crossing the Manych dam we left Europe and entered Asia. Hitler's struggle was extending into a strange world. The long river Manych, the demarcation line between the two great continents, is formed by a chain of mighty dams erected to control the area of lakes for the electricity works at Manytchstroy. The crossings over the Manych had been captured in brave attacks by 3 and 23 Panzer Divisions and opened the gateway to the Caucasus. While the assaults by the panzer divisions continued to the south, General Ott's LII Armeekorps proceeded as protection on the eastern flank of Army Group A via Proletarskaya south along the Manych via Kalaus and Kuma eastwards. Regiments of 111 and 370 Inf.Divs covered very demanding distances in the broiling heat. The banners of dust in the steppe at Manych were endless. Each well on the way was besieged by thirsty soldiers and horses.

At Elista, the capital of the Kalmyk Republic, a small motorized fighting group of 370 Inf.Div. had been deployed to capture the town but failed. They had been reinforced by a reconnaissance unit, the Aufklärungs-Abteilung of 111 Inf.Div. led by Rittmeister Goll and our 3 Battery (fighting Staff and supply services) commanded by Oberleutnant Götz. Almost all our 7.5-cm shells and also the reserve of fuel had had to be loaded up. It was 180 kilometres to the objective and naturally this made substantial inroads into the consumption of fuel.

During the 'rest period', the remainder of the Abteilung made an attempt to be of use to the people of Bereosovka. A meeting of farmers was called to get them to restart work in the fields. Officers took on the job of local farmers' leaders, among them Leutnant Harberg, who had good knowledge and experience of agriculture. Four collective farms had to be monitored. The farmers were happy to do the work and soon its success was noted during inspection tours of the fields. It was a goodwill attempt to get the populace out of their lethargy.

In the Kalmyk Steppe, 10–18 August

On 10 August Battle Group Goll set off for Elista, followed by an endless banner of dust whipped up by the column. The terrain was bare of any tree or vegetation except steppe grass. Now and again we passed a jackal or a couple of camels. The steppe horizon shimmered in temperatures of 50 degrees at midday. Tents were put up for the night. The battle group set out at sunrise and on the way the 3 Battery field kitchen somehow caught fire and burned out. The fire spread into the steppe.

On the afternoon of 11 August the battle group met up with the motorized groups from 370 Inf.Div. in their field positions near the town of Elista. After the situation conference and instructions the attack on Elista was set for early next morning at first light. Resistance was soon broken. Our StuGs bore the brunt of the fighting, 3 Battery platoon leader Schlagbaum and a crewman were killed, Wachtmeister Gelhaar and some men of his crew wounded.

The enemy then decamped at speed aboard their vehicles towards Utan Erge. With infantry protection our StuGs drove to the centre of town. The inhabitants welcomed us and appeared friendly and open. The enemy force was pursued into the heights beyond the town, where their rearguard put up a spirited resistance. The StuGs fought here successfully. In the expectation of a counter-attack, strongpoints were set up on the edge of town ahead of our defensive line and later occupied by 370 Inf.Div. After the division was called to the Terek, 16 Inf.Div. (mot.) took over the security aspect of the town and a large part of the Kalmyk steppe.

The region is occupied by Kalmyks, an Asiatic people who speak Mongolian. They originated from north-west China and crossed the Volga with the Mongol hordes. As nomads they wandered with their herds of cattle in a constant search for new pastures. In earlier times they lived in leather tents and lived on a diet of meat. On their migrations westwards the Kalmyks reached the lower Volga in the years between 1630 and 1662, when the tsars allowed them to settle in the steppe between the Volga and Manych. The great Volga floods prevented their mass return to Asia and of those who remained west of the Volga only a few had been prepared to settle in the towns of Elista, Ulan Erge and Yashkul which had been founded by the Russians and administered by their northern lords.

In 1927 the Russians began the enforced settlement of the Kalmyks and made them live in flat-roofed earth cottages. The walls were thick to keep the rooms cool in summer and warm in winter, the roofs covered with dried loam pantiles. The cultivation of foodstuffs, principally for pigs and camels, was scanty in 1942. Dried heating material for the winter is kept in the roof frames. Outdoor hearths are set up for the summer, deep wells provide the fresh water requirement. Small villages are built close to water sources and look like oases. Many of these villages are surrounded by a small stone wall to intercept the drifting sands blown by the often strong steppe winds. Dry steppe grasses are collected with great wooden rakes, trodden down and then stored as additional heating material for the winter. Maize, sunflowers, potatoes and vegetables are cultivated in irrigated fields. Near water sources one often sees small plantations of tropical trees. Fish are very abundant in small lakes and pools along the edges of the Kalmyk steppe. Even though the water has a very high salt content our men found it pleasant for bathing.

In 1940 the township of Elista had 13,600 inhabitants and over sixty industrial concerns. Raw materials and economic possibilities included petroleum, natural gas, chemical salts from the salt lakes, alabaster and Glauber's salt, quartz sand for glass-making and the like. When we took over the town we found a gigantic stock of leather and a factory for the manufacture of fur boots.

On 15 August the Abteilung less 3 Battery StuGs moved out and after 170 kilometres of steppe arrived at the village of Kniginskoye, about 12 kilometres south of Ipatov. The people were emphatically friendly. It was extraordinarily hot and windless over the last few days, only in the evenings did we have something of a breeze. 3 Battery StuGs were recalled to the Abteilung at Blagodarnoye (90 kilometres) on 18 August. We had six rest days. This brought a physically extraordinary operation despite all expectations to a happy end and the men afterwards were not a little proud to have smelled the dust of the Kalmyk steppe. At first the population had been very reserved but once we had their trust they proved hospitable, cooperative and loyal. [Writing his memoir in 1977, the author glosses over the murders and deportations of many thousands of Kalmyks by the Soviet government, particularly from 1926 onwards. Kalmykia today is the only Buddhist province in Russia or even Europe. The practice of any religion then was forbidden under Communism, and in Kalmykia temples were burned down and known believers executed. This would explain why the Germans were welcomed when they arrived in 1942 as liberators, since the swastika is also a Buddhist symbol and the people soon realized that they had nothing to fear from these particular Westerners. However, the author also omits to mention the fearful price the Kalmyks had to pay from 1943 for 'collaborating with the enemy'. – *Trans.*]

An StuG left at Elista was towed back across the steppe. The great heat brought some very welcome rainstorms. For the first time since Kursk we received mail from home. The number of men sick in the Abteilung had increased; jaundice, diarrhoea, steppe fever and malaria were more frequent now so that the batteries had concerns about operational readiness. Drinking water was not always readily available. Coffee made with salty water was a poor substitute for the real thing, and our catering staff had to travel far afield to find good wells. Our surgeon Dr Brankel had many problems with his patients. The anti-malarial drug Antebrin was constantly his last recourse. For the same reason the workshops gave us concerns. During this lay-up reserves were trained for the StuGs and sporting events arranged.

After being refuelled on 25 August, the Abteilung set off for Budennovsk (90 kilometres to the south) and Praskoveya and rested again from 26 to 29 August. It had been realized by the higher-ups that the expanses of the steppe were the wrong place for a normal infantry division, and so 111 and 370 Inf.Divs moved off south from Budennovsk, 16 Inf.Div. (mot.) taking over from them. Assigned to Army Group B, it provided mobile security between Army Groups A and B in the Kalmyk steppe.

On 27 August advanced elements of LII Armeekorps reached the area north of the Terek where 111 Inf.Div. (Generalmajor Recknagel) was to erect a bridgehead at Mosdok, and 370 Inf.Div. (Generalmajor Becker) another one west of it. Since StuG Abteilung 191 also formed part of LII Armeekorps, on 30 August it was sent on a two-day run to Russkiy on the Lenin Canal near Mosdok. This locality we called 'Büffelskaya' and made camp in a small wood. Provisional Armeekorps orders enabled us to conclude that we would soon be in action.

The Bridgehead at Mosdok on the Terek, 2–15 September

After meeting up with 111 Inf.Div. near Mosdok, Grenadier-Regt 50 arrived to relieve the weak 3 Panzer Division defence at Mosdok and handle all preparations for making the bridgehead. Mosdok stood on the north bank of the Terek. The crossing was to be erected on the west side of town facing south-east just west of the Grusinish military road leading south to Ordzhonikidze.

The operation was delayed for twenty-four hours on account of insufficient pioneer equipment being available but the work was completed towards 1800 hrs on the afternoon of 1 September. The time for the crossing was set for 0200 hrs on 2 September in order to surprise the enemy and use the moonlight. For protection against Russian air attacks, in the evening the companies held themselves in readiness in the cellars of the houses near the river.

The river Terek was to play a very important role here. Its source is the Kasbek, the great mountain far to the south, and it flows northwards at first. At Prochladny it bends sharply east and flows through the Nogai steppe into the Caspian Sea. The river is the natural barrier before the oilfields of Grozny to the south. The high, mountainous south and east banks provide outstanding defensive possibilities which the Soviets used to the best advantage. The river hurries eastwards through Mosdok with a wild, tumultuous force. Its bed is lumps of rock and sandbanks. The current is very strong in some places.

At 0200 hrs 11 Company/Inf.Regt 50 crossed the Terek by means of inflatable rafts. The fishing village of Predmostny offered fierce house-to-house resistance before being overcome, and by 0300 hrs the company had passed through the village to reach the anti-tank ditch immediately before the first slope of the many hills. The other companies of II and III Battalions/Grenadier-Regt 50 followed in assault boats; the artillery worked with the entire Regiment 117 (Oberst Barth) to get across.

The Russians made every effort to destroy the bridgehead. Intending to cover the right flank, III/Grenadier-Regt 50 and I/Grenadier-Regt 117 crossed the river but were forced to dig in at the edge of the fishing village by the defensive fire. To reinforce the bridgehead, at first light on 2 September 3 Battery StuGs were sent to Mosdok, the other two batteries following during the course of the day. 2 Battery had a very long wait in the town because the ferry had not been completed. The Russians mounted an unbroken string of air attacks accompanied by enduring artillery fire against the crossing points on the Terek but all of it was ineffective and towards 1700 hrs the StuGs got across. The supply head for the Abteilung remained at Mosdok.

The StuGs were sent to support 11 Company and took up position between the company and the ditch. The weather was cold with rain; overnight the Russians bombarded all positions and Oberleutnant Bauer and two men were wounded. After receiving first aid they were sent to the main dressing station at Mosdok and replaced by reserves to keep all StuGs operational. Three battalions of 111 Inf.Div. formed a half-circle around the fishing village so that the enemy could not see how the bridgehead was being expanded to take larger units. More bridge supports were being brought in for a second bridge. The enemy understood our purpose and maintained incessant air attacks against these bridge positions. Although our flak was too weak to deter them, the pioneers kept at the work to complete the extension and that night 5 Company/II Battalion/Panzer-Regt 201 (23 Panzer Division) crossed the river.

At first light on 3 September I/Grenadier-Regt 50 attacked the line of bunkers in the hills and after a hard fight the important height was taken which gave a view into the village of Terskaya. All counter-attacks were warded off, while III/Grenadier-Regt 50 with StuG support attacked the line of bunkers again and captured some in the left sector to set up a loose contact with I/Grenadier-Regt 50. The infantry had surprisingly few casualties, Abteilung 191 a few wounded. Leutnant Hoppenstedt's StuG had two men wounded by two anti-tank shells which penetrated into the interior. In the right-wing sector our attack on three heavily armed bunkers failed, towards 0930 hrs StuGs, panzers of 5 Company/Panzer-Regt 201 and grenadiers of 1/Grenadier-Regt 117 and III/Grenadier-Regt 50 flushed out the three dominating bunkers to the south.

Good cooperation between all units and weapons branches enabled the bridgehead on the south bank of the Terek to be widened so that the enemy now lost sight of, and immediate influence on, the crossing points. The subsequent completion of the bridge was a glorious page in the Grenadier-Regt 50 history.

On 4 September, twenty-three panzers of Panzer-Regt 201 and III/Grenadier-Regt 117 occupied the Mosdok–Vosnessenskaya highway to create space for our expansion. When the Russians finally grasped what we intended – to advance south from Mosdok by the Grusinish military road to Ordzhonikidze – they feverishly set up one defensive line after another. The advance of our panzers and grenadiers therefore came across a series of anti-tank barriers and anti-tank units. We suffered no losses, and Panzer-Regt 201 destroyed seven T-34s. On the same day II/Grenadier-Regt 50 supported by our StuGs attacked the fishing village of Terskaya. The last houses were taken on the morning of 5 September and a defence set up at the eastern end. The removal of Terskaya provided the eastern flank of the bridgehead with welcome depth.

Meanwhile work had gone ahead at a rapid pace on the Mosdok bridge, which came under repeated air attacks. During one of the night air raids against the Abteilung supplies head at Mosdok, six men of 2 Battery were killed. Our comrades Fischer, Stark, Riegel, Lichtenfels, Klemke and Kästner were given a military funeral at Mosdok cemetery.

On 5 September, our StuGs were attached to Inf.Regt 117 (Oberst Herforth) to reconnoitre and engage the heights in company with panzers. At 0400 hrs next morning the group sortied out on the Vosnessenskaya road. Our StuGs were with III Battalion. Despite good artillery support, progress was slow. Some ground was won but curtain fire from enemy artillery, Stalin organs and anti-tank gun batteries, plus enemy fighter-bombers circling above incessantly, prevented much progress. Halfway between the fishing village and Vosnessenskaya the front had consolidated and heavy counter-attacks by the Russians were beaten off. Upon receiving a report that twenty-five enemy tanks had appeared behind our front, our StuGs had had to turn about but they had not stayed long and so we took over security duties instead. On the night of 7 September our StuGs withdrew to the departure point on the Vosnessenskaya road to form the rearguard and then occupied the readiness area in the fishing village.

Towards 1300 hrs on 8 September Russian tanks attacked a gap in Grenadier-Regt 50's line. The StuGs were alerted, gave battle and destroyed forty tanks, causing the collapse of the enemy attack. At the same time the Russians launched another attack, this time on the Grusinish military road, but II Abteilung/Panzer-Regt 4 and 1 Company/Panzerjäger Abteilung 13 destroyed or damaged a large number of tanks, causing the enemy to abandon their assault. In these defensive battles the StuG of Leutnant Schommer received a direct hit, some of the crew receiving burns; the StuG of Leutnant Hoppenstedt was again hit twice by anti-tank rounds which penetrated the armour, one man, Horstmann, was wounded. Our StuGs then retired to the readiness position at the fishing village.

The operational readiness of the battle group was increased by reinforcements and new StuGs; those of the previous inventory requiring attention were towed to the workshop. Our towing crews were constantly on call, and the workshop team had no let-up.

The Mosdok bridgehead and the smaller bridgehead at Kislyar used by 370 Inf.Div. joined up without delay. The Luftwaffe had aerial superiority again. At midday, when work was started on expanding the bridgehead, the Russians withdrew so the objective was easily attained. A shooting match with a Russian battery at a range of 2,200 metres was very entertaining and successful.

In order to expand the combined Mosdok–Kislyar bridgehead, Army Group von Liebenstein (elements of 13 Panzer Division) was withdrawn from the Isherskaya area to strengthen the Mosdok bridgehead. They crossed the Terek bridge from west to east in the south, demolished various anti-tank batteries and artillery positions and reached the town of Terek at 1800 hrs. This expanded the bridgehead in the west to 10 kilometres.

On 10 September at 1600 hrs, our StuGs sortied in order to improve the front line to the south-west, got behind the Russian lines and surprised the enemy from the rear. The amount of material captured was enormous. The infantry had no losses but on the return journey the StuG of Leutnant Hoppenstedt overturned in the darkness and he was killed. The burial ceremony took place alongside other fallen members of the battery at the Pushkin Memorial in Mosdok. The divisional chaplain and our Abteilung CO, Hauptmann Kapp, delivered the graveside homilies.

On 12 September at 1500 hrs our StuGs, accompanied by infantry, advanced 1 kilometre into the enemy front line. We took many prisoners and weapons. The barrel of Oberleutnant Heinzle's StuG was hit by a round from an anti-tank rifle and needed replacement.

The supplies section of the Abteilung at Russkiy had excavated their accommodation 2 metres deep in the ground against bad weather. The men made their own bunkbeds, tables and so on to make each such shelter homely. The roof was of wood with a covering of planks and roofing felt. For camouflage against observation from the air, bushes and the fir branches were laid over the roof. NCOs and officers generally built their own retreats to their own taste. Much was improvised, such as windows, chimneys and hearths. The talent for invention of the German infantryman was displayed at its best here. Car batteries or workshop generators provided electric light. 'Lights out' was timed for when night fell so that the Russian air patrols at night, carried out by ground-attack aircraft known as 'sewing machines' from their engine noise, or 'the duty NCO' would not spot our campsite in the dark.

In clear visibility by day looking south we could see the Caucasus mountain range ahead of us, from Mount Elbrus far to the west to the Grusinish mountains. The eerie massif of the Kasbek, 5,047 metres high, lay directly before us. It was not often that we could see its snow-capped peak, for it was mostly shrouded in cloud, or mists would conceal it entirely.

The logistical difficulties had now been overcome. The field post was regular; rations, ammunition and fuel were available in sufficient quantities so that we had no worries about the coming winter. A kind of commuter traffic between the 'campsite' and the supplies head at Abteilung brought the men all their needs within reason. Medical care was provided by our Medical Officer Dr Brankel, known as the 'Atebrin Donkey'. Everything had been thought of to make the lives of the men at this remote outpost, far to the south-east of Russia, as pleasant as possible. Army Group A was now entrenched, so to speak, at the Caucasus and Terek. The valleys leading to the Black Sea coast, particularly Tuapse, were blocked by the Soviets and the Terek proved itself to be an almost insuperable obstruction, but it was the last before the old military roads to Tiflis and Baku.

'We cannot go further,' the divisions reported, but Hitler would not accept that, because of a lack of forces, the advance could no longer proceed beyond the Terek and the mountains. He considered that the fault lay with the commanders.

On 7 September Hitler sent General Jodl, Chief of Operations of the Wehrmacht High Command, to Stalino to ascertain from Feldmarschall List why it was not possible to go forwards. Jodl returned, justifying the opinion of List and suggesting, as had List, decisive regroupings at the front. Hitler turned down this idea. Jodl protested, quoting Hitler's own orders and instructions over previous weeks which List had followed precisely and which had resulted in the difficulties in which Army Group A now found itself. Hitler reacted by sacking the Chief of the Army General Staff, Generaloberst Halder and Feldmarschall List. Moreover, he remained determined that the attack on the Caucasus front must go ahead: its oil, the towns of Grozny, Tiflis and Baku, and the ports of the Black Sea, must be captured at all costs. He ordered that the offensive over the Terek must be continued.

The Fighting in the Bend of the Terek, 16–25 September 1942

After the extension of the front to the south-west by combining the Mosdok and Kislyar bridgeheads, by 13 September we had taken Malgobek II and Nishniy Kurp and the fighting had abated. The StuGs of Abteilung 191 were pulled away from the fighting front on 15 September and transferred to Rasolnoye, where the quiet spell was used for overhauls and repairs by an improvised workshop platoon. Constant nuisance air raids were the only problem.

On 16 September when the 16-tonne bridge at Gnadenburg was completed, a newly formed battle group led by Oberst Raczek advanced westwards along the river and captured the village of Terek. Next day I/Panzer-Grenadier-Regt 66 recaptured Height 404. Eighty armoured troop-carriers proceeding in a broad front broke through the morning mist to overrun the enemy positions. Eight heavy enemy guns were immediately included in the German defences, 400 workshop-new and never-fired anti-tank guns of a newly formed 'bazooka battalion' were also captured. The enemy air superiority was making itself noticeable again since many Luftwaffe units had been reduced in size and others withdrawn to the Stalingrad theatre.

On 19 September 13 Panzer-Div. embarked on an attack to break the Russian defences in the mountains at Elchotovo in the glacial valley of the Terek. By evening the Raczek battle group had overcome the enemy in the Kotlyarevski–Uroshainoye–Hoffnungsfeld area and dispersed it to the south and west.

On 20 September, 13 Panzer-Div. destroyed the last of the enemy resistance, advanced to the south on either side of the Arik, won the general line of the Terek bend 4 kilometres south and captured the road, which it then defended using the heights west of point 489. StuG Abteilung 191 rested at Rastolnoye until 26 September and took no part in the advances to the south during that period. The advance on the Elchotov Narrows by III Panzerkorps begun on 24 September resulted in the capture of two villages after heavy fighting. These skirmishes clearly showed the limits of possibility for a panzer division. The high country, rich in woodland, almost lacking paths and tracks but infested with a strong defence in well-camouflaged and developed positions, required a purely infantry attack. Panzers and vehicles could seldom be brought up. Therefore a frontal attack on Elchotov was not possible on account of the strong defence. The panzer grenadiers made their way through the primaeval woods of the mountains east of Elchotov in order to attempt to encircle the locality or capture it from the rear. Panzer grenadiers had become Gebirgsjäger. After almost five days, on 28 September the grenadiers broke into Elchotov and captured it after heavy fighting. The road and railway line at its south were blocked off. The Elchotov Pass was open but insufficient forces were available to take advantage of the breakthrough. Once the fighting ceased, the line reached became the main front.

At the same time LII Armeekorps had advanced as far as the Alchan–Churt Valley, from where it should have been possible to turn east and attack Grozny, then advance south of 13 Panzer-Div. to assist in forcing the Elchotov Narrows and block the Grusinish military road at Ordzhonikidze. Our available forces were too weak for this. Everywhere the 'shirt was too short', as we used to say. The divisions of Army Group A had been whittled down into smaller units at too many places.

StuG Abteilung 191, 26 September–31 December 1942

The Buffalo Abteilung returned to active duty on 26 September when an attack was made on Height 402 in company with I/Inf.Regt 70. Good progress was made through the morning mist, and heavy anti-tank gun batteries in the foothills were overcome. The neighbouring infantry regiment did not come up, allowing the enemy to occupy the gap and fire on our StuGs with heavy flak. The StuGs withdrew into cover but the enemy artillery knew where they were hiding. Three air attacks followed, during one of which Unteroffizier Kowazek was killed. The StuGs now acted as security for Inf.Regt 70. The nights were quiet except for nuisance raids by aircraft.

On 30 September all StuGs of the Abteilung were recalled and returned to the Büffelskaya campsite. On 1 October the Abteilung celebrated its second anniversary, mostly in the earth bunkers. A fourteen-day rest was granted to all but the workshop personnel who had to get the StuGs battleworthy using scrapped parts if necessary. A considerable number of the assault guns were non-operational through battle or technical damage, much of the latter due to the excessive strain and overloading of the materials in mountainous environments.

On 15 October, 1 Battery joined Grenadier-Regt 70 and a Waffen-SS unit, 9/Germania, supported by four rocket batteries and a company of pioneers, to attack Heights 694 and 701. Whoever held these heights could see down the Grusinish military road. After a small gain of territory under enemy defensive fire, the attack halted for a Finnish Waffen-SS battalion to return fire at a collective farm that was shooting at our flank. Our StuGs engaged field positions, tanks and anti-tank guns. The attacking battalions suffered many casualties.

On 16 October five panzers of 1 Panzer Abteilung/SS-Division Wiking came up in support of the new attack by III/SS-Division Nordland against Height 701. The hour for this attack was unusual – afternoon – and the SS Battalion broke through so swiftly that the enemy, who did not have an effective defence in place, panicked. Within thirty minutes the Finns had captured Height 701. A counter-attack by enemy tanks was repelled by our own on the height.

Several of our StuGs received hits and crew were wounded. The damaged vehicles were towed away at once by our recovery unit and brought to the workshop for repair. In due course StuGs that were operational again were driven to the Abteilung supply head at Rastolnoye for readiness when required by LII Armeekorps. It was shown again that it was dangerous to operate StuGs in tall fields of maize and in thickly wooded uplands with few negotiable tracks without cover. Our Abteilung CO Hauptmann Kapp requested LII Armeekorps not to use StuGs for such operations in future. The cannon could only fire ahead and up to 11 degrees either side, and all other weapons were hand-held and fired from outside the panzer.

Increasing our difficulties was the unreliable weather with rain, mist and low cloud. The Abteilung expressed concern at the high number of men on sick leave, which was affecting the operational readiness of the fighting units. It was a type of dysentery rampant in this Armee group. Many men had had to be hospitalized for total exhaustion as a result of the endless diarrhoea.

It had become clear that the attacks by LII Armeekorps in the Terek bend would provide no further operational advantages and accordingly 1 Panzerarmee (Generaloberst von Kleist) ordered III Panzerkorps to prepare a plan to capture the town of Ordzhonikidze, the gateway to the Grusinish military road, by a thrust via Naltchik and then on the northern slopes of the central Caucasus.

The Grusinish military road had been of great significance for centuries. It was an important highway in the Turkish Empire which had once covered the entire Caucasus. Many mountain peoples were Muslim. When the Turkish Empire collapsed, the Russians moved in from the north, subdued the mountain folk and converted them to Christianity. The annexation to Russia followed in 1801. Upon completion of the Christianization process a great cross was erected on the heights above the pass which was then called the 'Pass of the Cross' (renamed Cross Pass by the Soviet government). This pass road is the only usable crossing in the eastern part of the long mountain chain. The following extract is taken from W. Tiecke's book *Der Kaukasus und das Oel* (1970, pp. 296ff):

The plan submitted was approved. After the corresponding reorganization on the morning of 25 October 1942, the assault of Attack Group West from the Bakssam area was unleashed, and that of Attack Group East from Kotlyarevski the following day. On 26 October Attack Group West forced its way into the northern part of the town of Naltchik and secured it after several days of street fighting. The village to its east, Argudan, was occupied by Attack Group East. Then the panzers battled their way unexpectedly quickly south-east via Digora to Alagir, where the Ossetic military road began. The road here is poor and unsuitable for operational purposes. Despite stubborn resistance and difficult terrain – numerous streams flowing down from the Caucasus Massif had to be crossed – Ardon was taken and on 4 November the panzer spearhead reached Ordzhonikidze and captured the radio station, a large factory complex and the airfield – but at what a price!

The territory won that day was 600 metres. Division informed Korps that no further progress would be possible unless the threat to the flanks at Gisel were removed and reinforcements sent. By the third day of the fighting on the fringe of the city, the Russians had got over their first shock and with every passing hour the Germans felt the growth of the enemy resistance. On 5 November, 13 Panzer-Div. advanced only a few hundred metres, then they bogged down at the western and north-western edges of the city. It was clear that LII Armeekorps would have to launch a relieving attack.

In these atttacks by LII Korps, SS-Division Wiking improved the positions at Malgobek I in a surprise push. Our StuGs – repaired vehicles sent to the supply head at Rastolnoye meanwhile – were assigned to the Waffen-SS Division on 5 November and supported their units very successfully. After reaching the objective, they remained there as security against enemy counter-attacks but none came. The StuGs returned to the supply head at Rastolnoye on 8 November. After rain, mist and low-level cloud announced winter, the first snow fell. It became very cold, then came more rain and then a thaw turning the ground into mud. The weather made things difficult.

On 6 November the Russians had begun their counter-offensive against Ordzhonikidze, but none of their attempts to penetrate the German Caucasus front between 18 and 30 November met with success.

On 20 November, Oberleutnant Tenner took over 3 Battery from Oberleutnant Götz, and Oberleutnant Korsen assumed command of the Staff Battery. A new surgeon, Dr Schröder, replaced Unterarzt Dr Brankel. Winter preparations were in hand at the bivouac site, where snow was falling. Thaw, rain and frosts at night kept us busy. Leutnant Harberg held an NCO course. Any vehicle journeys that were not absolutely necessary were banned; travel had to be by panje and cart instead. On moonlit nights the Russian Air Force was very lively and sought the Abteilung campsite but without success.

50 Inf.Div. had meanwhile taken over from SS-Division Wiking at Malgobek I and Verch-Kurp. On the morning of 7 December, sentries of III/Grenadier-Regt 121 discovered that in the course of the night the enemy had dug in on the 'Kusselhöhe', a height which offered an excellent view of the activities of German troops deep into the hinterland. The Russians were ejected with losses on 12 December in Operation *Fuchsjagd*, but on the night of 15 December they were back in occupation. The enemy pressure was increasing.

On 16 December at 0700 a softening up by Russian artillery heralded the expected offensive, whihc soon developed along the entire front held by Grenadier-Regt 121 in the Verch-Kurp sector. By 1000 hrs the breadth of the front in dispute extended 6 kilometres. While the centre held, the enemy made inroads on the left and right flanks of the regimental sector. An important height, 'Stangenhöhe', on the right flank was recaptured by I/Grenadier-Regt 121 in a counter-attack. The ground towards the small Lake Amsee was waterlogged, and here the front was torn open for 2 kilometres. In counter-attacks our infantry brought the Russians to a halt but could not restore the former front line. Both sides dug in; during the night reserves sent up by Armeekorps sealed the gaps and reinforced the positions.

Our 1 Battery led by Oberleutnant Strathmann received orders on the night of 16 December to hasten to 'Stangenhöhe' to support Grenadier-Regt 121. As they drove through the night, one StuG crashed through some bridge railings and came to rest upside down. The enemy pressure against the main front line, especially 'Stangenhöhe', could be reduced but efforts to clear the penetration at Amsee were not successful, the reserves having soon extended themselves to the last. Our StuGs fought doggedly in this confused situation in the bare, undulating terrain and in misty weather with variable visibility against an almost invisible enemy. The StuG of Oberleutnant Strathmann was hit by an anti-tank round: he was killed, the gunlayer NCO and radio operator were wounded. The driver, unharmed, brought the StuG back to the departure area where our new surgeon Dr Schröder gave first aid. Spindig took over temporary command of 1 Battery until relieved by Leutnant Lenz, just back from leave. The same night the battery returned to Nish Kurp.

On 18 December a Russian regiment attacked again from the breakthrough point at 'Stangenwald'. In heavy fighting I/Grenadier-Regt 121 held its positions, supported by 1 Battery StuGs and our artillery, which now concentrated fire on the breakthrough point south of Lake Amsee. The subsequent counter-attack with StuG support drove the Russians back. By evening the main front line was for the most part back in our hands.

On 21 December several enemy attacks either side of 'Stangenhöhe' were beaten off: our StuGs bore the brunt of this defensive fighting and provided the infantry with a firm foothold.

On Christmas Eve, the Divisional CO of 50 Inf.Div. decided that this would be a good time to attempt to regain the lost territory in the watery region near Amsee. After the addition of pioneers, the Alarm Battalion at Pyatigosk, sections of Bicycle Abteilung 150 and 2 Battery, StuG Abteilung 191, the battle groups of Grenadier-Regt 123 stood ready to embark on Operation *Fritjof*.

The exemplary cooperation between StuGs and infantry won ground, and after two hours of hard struggle the enemy was ejected. The former main front line in the watery region was back in German hands. The battle groups rejoiced in having few casualties – 2 Battery had none. The StuGs drove everybody back to the supply head. Now we could celebrate Christmas. The 2 Battery Spiess had set up a tree in a Russian cottage. A Christmas address and snack followed, after which we returned to the bivouac to find the bunkers of the community full of trees, lit candles and tinsel, and paintings done by our men and the Hiwis (Russian volunteers) decorating the walls. The evening of Christmas Day was celebrated with a hot dinner, tea and rum, and smokers' requisites. Between the singing of Christmas carols the battery commanders delivered their Christmas address and then our Abteilung CO, clearly moved, thanked everybody for their 'exemplary conduct as soldier and comrade' and honoured the fallen. His closing wish was: 'I hope we can enjoy next Christmas in peace in the Homeland.' The front was silent over the Christmas period. On 26 December it was so cold that the mud froze into glazed lumps.

On 28 December it was decided that the enemy had held part of the 'Stangenhöhe' for twelve days, which was quite long enough, and our StuGs received orders to prepare to attack in company with units of Grenadier-Regt 121. After an artillery and Nebelwerfer rocket barrage the last enemy resistance collapsed before our advance and the important hill was ours once more.

Verch-Kurp and 'Stangenhöhe' were the target of Russian counter-attacks on 29 December, but these were brushed aside long before they reached our lines. That same day the commanders of 50, 111 and 370 Inf.Divs were summoned to the Commanding General of LII Armeekorps at Gnadenburg, west of Mosdok. General Ott outlined the situation. For the first time they heard the word 'retreat'. Among those present there was no doubt that the most difficult part compared to all previous operations was now before us. Many had seen it coming, but had not wanted to put it into words. Now it was the reality. On the evening of 31 December 1942, the order was given to pull out and withdraw.

After the defeat of 6 Armee at Stalingrad, the next aim of the Red Army was Rostov on the lower Don. This forced Hitler to bring back 1 Panzerarmee, which he had long been reluctant to do.

The Great Retreat began at the Terek. The Staff HQ of Panzerarmee High Command 1 at Pyatigorsk hummed with activity. Besides bringing back the troops, the materials and equipment had to be planned for too. The Korps

Staff drew up the plan for the divisions, and they passed it to their respective regiments.

The preparations could not be concealed from the Russians. The weight of their attack forced us back to the Atchikulak–Stoderovskaya line at the edge of the mountains. XL Panzerkorps also had an imminent attack to look forward to. On 1 January 1943, Soviet tanks and infantry tore open the front between 3 Panzer-Div. and Battle Group Jungschulz north of it, and thrust westwards between them. As a result, the Divisional CO ordered the northern wing to retreat one day earlier than planned.

Chapter Five

The Retreat from the Caucasus, January–April 1943

In the LII Armeekorps sector the front remained quiet. Here the battle-hardened regiments of 111, 50 and 370 Inf.Divs were arming up for the retreat. All supply staff and artillery units superfluous to requirements had already moved out. The Russians came down the flank of the mountains to attack III Panzerkorps on the right wing of 1 Panzerarmee with the idea of encircling it, something they had tried previously, but here again they failed.

The difficult terrain made the retreat by 1 Panzerarmee problematic. While XL Panzerkorps and 111 Inf.Div. crossed the flat steppe, 50 and 370 Inf.Divs and III Panzerkorps had to struggle through swampy land in the bed of the Terek and the foothills of the Caucasus.

On 1 January 1943 the whole of 1 Panzerarmee set off for precisely indicated points on the map. The timetable had been carefully calculated; the Solka–Kuma sector had to be reached quickly. That was where the retreat would stop and be held over the winter. Anyway, that was what Hitler believed but the troop commanders were sure it would keep on going.

On 31 December 1942, StuG Abteilung 191 received the order to retreat. This came as a great surprise to us for our StuGs had travelled with infantry on limited sorties in order to improve the winter quarters. All positions at the Terek and in the foothills of the Caucasus were well prepared for the coming winter. Even our bivouac site Büffelskaya, about 6 kilometres north-east of Mosdok, was well equipped. Now we had to take our leave of this familiar spot. In the early hours of New Year's Day 1943 the general break-up of the bivouac site began. StuG crews remained on call, it being their responsibility to protect the rearguards of the infantry divisions. The Abteilung Tross would join 1 Panzerarmee columns. I was in charge of that personally. In light snowfall, slippery ice and misty weather we set off towards Prochladny, keeping to the timetable. We took our leave of

Büffelskaya depressed and nostalgic. The journey was uneventful. At Prochladny we found the place overflowing with Trosses and troop units. In the afternoon our Abteilung Tross arrived at Ssaldato-Alexandrovskoye and arranged quarters. On the way two of our towing vehicles broke down. Our CO came across them as he approached with the rearguard. Repairs to the ammunition-carrier was not possible; its payload was transferred to the second carrier which was taken in tow by the CO's Kfz 15 Staff car and the first carrier destroyed.

During the rest period all vehicles were topped up to make space in the fuel lorries from the compound stocks. After a hot meal from the field kitchen we retired to a warm bed. The night was cold, the skies starry. The columns set off again on 2 January and arrived twenty-four hours later at the village of Sablinskoye after many interruptions and made bivouac.

On the road again on 5 January the pace was much slower on account of bad weather. The column wormed its way through the snowy landscape lucky to have had cloudy skies during the retreat so far and therefore being spared the attentions of Russian aircraft. From the next bivouac halt at Alexandrovskoye early on 7 January, trucks beyond repair despite every effort were taken in tow by our recovery vehicles. On the final days of this part of the trek in open country the road was our bivouac site. The drivers slept in their cabs, we ate and slept on the vehicles. Five more days and nights passed until on 14 January we arrived at the town of Voroshilovsk and made bivouac near the marketplace.

Earlier elsewhere, units of 50 Inf.Div. had left their positions in the great bend of the Terek on the night of 2 January 1943 and moved to intermediate positions at Mosdok and Gnadenburg. III Panzerkorps gave up Naltshik and headed north-west in stages. The advance of enemy forces from the Elchotov Narrows had to be contained until the main body of the Korps was clear of the difficult mountainous region. Because the Korps had to use the Naltshik–Pyatigorsk highway the greatest discipline was required.

On 2 January the southern wing of 3 Panzer-Div. (XL Panzerkorps) detached, as had been agreed with 111 Inf.Div. At Mosdok, important war installations were demolished and the rearguard left the town early on 3 January. The same day the Russians crossed the Terek and reoccupied the town.

At the beginning of the retreat the three StuG batteries were combined into two strong fighting units led by Oberleutnant Heinzle (2 Battery) and Leutnant Schoel (3 Battery). On 2 January they linked up with the rearguard covering the withdrawal of 50 and 111 Inf.Divs. Meanwhile Oberleutnant Pantel had arrived from Germany with StuGs, other vehicles, spare parts, mail and Army stores. Pantel remained with the StuGs at 2 Battery, the remainder went to the Abteilung Tross. Our surgeon Dr Schröder accompanied the two batteries in an armoured towing vehicle.

On the second day of the retreat our Abteilung CO, Hauptmann Kapp, and his adjutant Leutnant Schommer in a Kfz 15 were involved in an accident on the way to the two batteries while overtaking an StuG. Kapp received head injuries and Schommer was crippled in the right foot. At the scene of the accident their driver was sentenced to three days' close arrest. Dr Schröder got them to a field dressing station. Our CO was diagnosed as walking wounded and returned to the Abteilung after a few days but Leutnant Schommer had to be sent to a military hospital in Germany.

During the day our StuGs skirmished with the Russians and returned with the rearguard when darkness fell. Red Army tanks breaking through the German lines usually provoked panic but our StuG crews were always watchful and would clear up such a situation with counter-attacks.

Provisions compounds during a major retreat were fair game and we would remove all we could until the lorries threatened to collapse under the weight. This sometimes led to nasty incidents with excessively 'duty-bound' paymasters, particularly when they refused to release foodstuffs to the last of the rearguards. Our surgeon and Oberleutnant Pantel were the great 'organizers' for the procurement of provisions for the StuG crews, who were in general left to their own resources.

7 January 1943 was a black day in the history of 50 Inf.Div. and also the Buffalo Abteilung, which lost the crews of 3 Battery under Leutnant School. In the defensive action alongside 50 Inf.Div. they were surrounded and wiped out. Only Oberwachtmeister Lambacher and one man returned to the Abteilung after many days. Totally exhausted and still in shock, they told their story and after a brief period to recover with the Tross, they were transferred to the reserve to regain their health and strength.

Despite all setbacks, elements of 50 Inf.Div. occupied the Solka–Kuma line on the morning of 8 January. The retreat was supposed to end here but the Russians thought otherwise.

The StuGs of Oberleutnant Heinzle, led temporarily by Leutnant Harberg, secured the Rollbahn and later reconnoitred with the infantry to the village of Apollonskaya. At dusk the enemy made contact but the infantry held their positions while the StuGs remained at readiness in the village.

On 8 January the StuGs were assigned to Inf.Regt 121 (Oberst Ringleb). Enemy tanks had penetrated the main front line and occupied a strongpoint. The regiment and StuGs counter-attacked and remedied the situation, destroying five tanks and capturing three anti-tank guns in the process.

On 9 January a strong force of Russian armour and vehicles approached the main front and broke through at several places. After stubborn resistance the Russians were ejected by StuGs and infantry. Three T-34s were destroyed.

News was received that the village of Obilnoye had been occupied by the enemy. The StuGs protected the regiment that night. There was a generally uneasy feeling among the infantry, the tank horror earlier had come as a shock for them. Towards evening the platoon of Leutnant Meining went into action. StuGs transported infantry to retake Obilnoye and recovered four 2-cm flaks with vehicles. The StuGs then continued to Sablinskoye, where they were pocketed by General Westhoven and thrust back into action despite the crews being dog-tired.

Here again the situation was one of mad confusion: in the ensuing counter-attack in company with Michaelis's battle group against Russian tanks which had broken through, our StuGs destroyed three. Mattes's StuG received a direct hit. Oberleutnant Heinzle returned to Battle Staff and brought back with him two sorely needed new StuGs.

On 13 January Inf.Regt 117 ran across a well-defended Russian strongpoint, which they overcame after a fierce fight. Heinzle's StuG was hit and later blew up. Three other StuGs received battle damage and made the return to Alexandrovskoye with difficulty. Here the Abteilung CO reported on our situation to the Commanding General and then occupied quarters in the village behind Alexandrovskoye. The StuGs of reduced fighting status were sent to the bivouac at Voroshilovsk. Heinzle now had only four battleworthy StuGs. Comrade Gerrisch succumbed to his wounds and was buried there.

On 14 January the Abteilung CO received orders to move out to Ssergiyevskoye. It was bitterly cold with snowstorms, no accommodation was available at the destination and so the guns remained at Ssevernoye to support the departure of the infantry from there. When the StuGs eventually arrived at Ssergiyevskoye they found the territory mountainous and not compatible with StuGs. Leutnant Harberg's StuG broke down; it could not be moved and had to be destroyed by explosive charge. The other guns were transferred to Muskulus's battle group. Inf.Regt 50 wanted to deploy them but the terrain proved impossible, instead they were sent to the supply head at Beshpagir, where the remnants of Heinzle's Battery was given quarters. On 18 January the last StuGs of the 191 fighting force arrived at the Voroshilovsk bivouac.

Our surgeon Dr Schröder, who had been responsible for the medical care of the Heinzle Battery since the retreat began, wrote of it so far:

I have not had much of a medical nature to do. Thanks to the discipline of everybody and full usage of the rearguard, the Russians are not attempting anything large scale. My work consists of general organization. It is definitely not bad for us, we are just depressed by the retreat.

At a crossroads we stopped with our StuGs on security duty. What a strange contrast, on the road the endless streams of excited Tross units hurrying back in wild haste. Near the railway rows of dynamited telegraph poles have collapsed, taking down the telephone lines with them. Behind us on the horizon the burning villages bear witness to the recent skirmishes with the pursuing Russians. Yet in this world of destruction, haste and flight we see along the roadside a Tartar heading westwards on his sledge with Stoic calm, followed by an immense herd of sheep. So much tranquillity and imperturbability, as if there were no war and no retreat, he and his sheep all alone in the world.

At Beshpagir we had a warm room for a whole night at last. Tired and resigned, we lay below a miserable lamp and could not sleep because Harberg wants to know if his comrade Stiefel is interested in Egyptology. Yes! Then he can recommend to him Karl May's *Im Reich des silbernen Löwen*. Harberg had it with him, naturally, but to even know the name of an Egyptologist earned him our admiration. The glimmer of a smile at the edges of sad events.

Next morning Unteroffizier Weimer of the repairs team informed us that all StuGs had moved out. The village has been evacuated. I have been left behind with a lorry. We loaded it with flour, then as the Russians stormed the far end of the village the engine failed to start. We could see nothing through the heavy snowstorm. Nobody was recognizable. We all had a really uneasy feeling. At the last minute Weimer saved the day. Sitting on a mudguard, he continued to pour petrol on the carburettor during the whole journey in the most bitter cold. It is an ugly sensation to keep stealing glances back to ensure that 'the comrades of the other side' are not catching up. With much luck we reached our StuGs; our joy was great. A few days more and with the other StuGs we reached the city of Voroshilovsk. It is large and modern for the times. Here we met up again with the entire Abteilung. There was great whirl of activity. The mood of the retreat had mobilized the whole city.

It was very clear that an emergency had befallen the German units. The various Tross and supply units did whatever was necessary of them and then went off quickly. Fleeing inhabitants accompanied them. All roads to the north-west were overburdened. The retreat of 1 Panzerarmee continued, the Staffs watching the course of the retreat with concern. They urged their units to make haste, and the infantry marched and marched despite exhaustion and the greatest bodily demands. Only because they knew that the Russians were behind them was the incredible achieved.

The German divisions of 1 Panzerarmee followed hot on the heels of one another to the north-west. On the southern wing were the regiments of 2 Romanian Mountain Division, 13 Panzer-Div., 350 Inf.Div. and 50 Inf.Div. Their objective was Armavir on the Kuban. At Nevinnomyskaya, German mountain troops coming from the High Caucasus joined them. On the northern wing were 3 Panzer-Div. and 111 Inf.Div., their initial objective being Voroshilovsk. The Cavalry Group 'Jungschulz' operated on the open wing.

The Caucasus line was held by the Germans until 19 January when the retreat continued. The blizzards had stopped, the temperature had fallen to −30 degrees. Russian units made contact again. The road to the north-west became a wandering front. For many horses and vehicles it turned out to be their last night.

The military centres at Voroshilovsk were already in the process of reorganization. Heinzle's StuG 'battle Staffel' had been disbanded to become Tenner Battery and Kollböck Battery. All vehicles had to be unloaded, superfluous items and goods were destroyed. This measure took a lot of pressure off the vehicles and created a great deal of space. It was still a mystery where the retreat was ultimately headed or the condition of the roads we would have to traverse to get there. What we had to be was fast troops, easily manoeuvrable and always ready to fight.

A large section of the Abteilung was entertained by a film show for a few hours of relaxation before the order suddenly came to move out. No sooner said than done and most of the Abteilung Tross was ready. Unfortunately some of the Hiwis were missing from the two batteries. The Abteilung set off westwards for Armavir in the darkness and bitter cold. StuGs from 1 and 3 Batteries made up the rearguard. The Tross arrived at Armavir at 0600 hrs and were allocated quarters on the edge of town. Trainload after trainload stood on the railway viaduct piled high with supplies, materials, seeds, vehicles and much more. We counted forty-two trains, all loaded with valuable goods but unable to leave the marshalling yards because the stretch of track between Bataisk and Rostov was blocked by trains because the Russians had removed the railway tracks at various places. It was a sickening sight. Even German radio was reporting on the critical situation of the Armee.

On 21 January the Abteilung continued in constantly variable weather conditions of frost and thaw, in the late afternoon reaching the railway junction at Kropotkin. Here too the yards were full of trains. The surrounding streets were crammed with convoys coming from all directions. After a brief rest the Abteilung continued with many interruptions to reach Tifliskaya around midnight and occupied quarters. Here we received an order from Armee: anything not absolutely necessary for survival was to be destroyed because of a shortage of loading space. All vehicles were unburdened again, even clothing wagons. The infantry received a new issue of clothing, footwear and underwear, what this replaced had to be taken off and burned. In this way the batteries gained some empty vehicles for use later. In future vehicles were not to be taken in tow but blown up.

On 14 January an Abteilung Infantry Company was formed. All non-essential NCOs and men were transferred into it. Leutnant Harberg was its commander, and within a few hours it saw its first action.

Hitler, who at first had wanted to steer all of 1 Panzerarmee into the Kuban bridgehead, ordered on 22 January that part of (and then on 24 January that all) 1 Panzerarmee was to join the hard-pressed 'Army Group Don' via Rostov. This order was modified by detaching 50 Inf.Div. and 370 Inf.Div. to the Kuban bridgehead. The Armeekorps wheeled via the great Kuban knee to the south-west to form the north wing of the Kuban bridgehead with access to the Sea of Azov.

3 Panzer-Div,, 111 Inf.Div. and the Jungschulz Division joined XL Panzerkorps via Rostov and then attached to Army Group Don under von Manstein.

On 26 January our Tross left Tifliskaya towards Usty-Labinskaya. The journey was tiring and difficult. After many stops the Tross reached the only military bridge over the Kuban river. We spent the night on the road, carried on to Krasnodar, skirted the town and headed next for Sslavyanskaya. With the arrival of the thaw the traffic jam was kilometres long. Any overtaking was not possible on account of the swamps and mud of the terrain. There was no bridge over the river Protaka, only a narrow ford at Sslavyanskaya. The notorious rice road began here, through which the supply and Trosses of II Gebirgskorps, large sections of LII Armeekorps and parts of 1 Panzerarmee had to flow.

The nature of the retreat was now governed by the countless convoys. In six days our Tross covered 20 kilometres. The hoped-for return of the winter cold was delayed, leaving us with a road resembling a large mudbath. Both sides of the thoroughfare were lined with wrecked vehicles. Whenever the clouds parted temporarily, the Russians used every minute for flying and were always given a welcome by our powerful flak. The line of vehicles needed more than a fortnight to get clear of the Protaka and west of it was even worse.

Meanwhile the Abteilung infantry unit had been driven to several hotspots by lorry but not been involved in any fighting. On 29 January they went to Ladoshkaya and found quarters in the town. Early next day orders came to relieve a Romanian squadron on the steep bank of the Kuban. This passed without interruption. Afterwards when they had to secure the road the Russians approached, apparently fortified by alcohol; they were given a warm reception by the StuGs and withdrew.

The security duty was lifted on 31 January and the infantry company drove through Korenovskaya to Kasachye where 3 Platoon secured the Rostov road and the remainder of the company continued 5 kilometres east to a bridge. During an otherwise quiet night Group Bogartz warded off an enemy scouting party. Skirmishes followed during the day; towards evening when all fell quiet once more, the company was brought back to Korenovskaya and assigned to secure the road east of the railway line,

At first light on 2 February a Russian demolition party blew up the bridge and so the river Beissushek now formed the northern border of the main battle line.

On the night of 3 February the alarm was raised and the order given to secure the main road and the wrecked bridge. A semi-circular position was adopted on the road but at first light an enemy battalion penetrated Kasachye village. Our counter-attack at 1100 hrs was successful, the enemy was ejected and then wiped out. The StuG men of the infantry company fought bravely but suffered their first casualties: one dead and seven wounded. The operation received praise.

On 5 February the infantry company was taken to Sergeyevskaya temporarily to man the strongpoints of the new front. During the relief at daybreak Unteroffizier Falk was wounded when he stumbled in the darkness and received a round in the back from his own machine pistol. He was treated at the nearest dressing station; the company went next to Olyovski as divisional reserve.

On 10 February the company travelled to Derbentski to secure the village and bridge until nightfall. On the early morning of 12 February they occupied a new, well-built position at Starovelitchkovskaya and then took over a new sector in the front line. This was at the seam with 50 Inf.Div., 3.5 kilometres distant, with seventy men. The front ran behind a large swamp, currently frozen, with high reeds.

The prevailing quiet allowed the position to be expanded. The weather continued to be changeable, frost at night and a thaw by day with a lot of mud. Enemy units decided to concentrate on 50 Inf.Div. to our left, both sides exchanging ceaseless artillery and machine-gun fire.

On 17 February a major thaw set in. The company's vehicles were made ready and the men decamped towards 2000 hrs without detection by the enemy, reaching the vehicles at midnight. After a short drive it was not long before the vehicles began to sink into the mud, and the desperate battle against the mire failed once torrential rain began. Four lorries, one Kfz 15 Staff car and a towing vehicle had to be immobilized by explosives. Only the field kitchen and provisions lorry could be saved. Next day the company rested at Stavo-Nishe-Stebliyevskaya. The two surviving vehicles were driven along the railway embankment, the only way through the mud. On 20 February the company marched 20 kilometres on foot along the embankment following the empty vehicles and halted without losses at Krasnov-Armeiskaya. It was said to be the coldest day of the retreat. Each man had only his firearm and the clothing he wore. The infantry company then acted as security on the northern side of the village as regimental reserve of Inf.Regt 666. Later 2 and 3 Platoon were in action beside Battalion Maier. The weather was rainy and cold.

On the night of 25 February the company was recalled to the StuG Abteilung 191 Tross, having fulfilled their assignment. The Commanding General praised their assistance. Their losses were two dead and six wounded.

From Voroshilovk the StuG Batteries Tenner and Kollböck (later Pantel) acted mainly as the rearguard for 111, 370 and 50 Inf.Divs. Our surgeon Dr Schröder wrote a report as an appendage to the War Diary as follows:

1 and 3 Batteries had taken over the rearguard. When I decided in favour of Oberleutnant Pantel and 1 Battery, Oberleutnant Tenner was slightly put out. However I had to choose because the operational area of the two batteries lay too far apart. A delightful journey with the StuGs and Tross brought us further west again. Interest seemed to have been lost in where the retreat was heading and when we would get there. Poultry was our staple diet. We had crossed this land twice in a short while and it was still rich.

On 26 January Oberwachtmeister Labusch reappeared. He had long since been given up for lost. Following incorrect directions for the fuel wagon he had driven directly into the arms of the Russians. At the last moment he and his co-driver saved themselves, and then spent two days wading through fields of deep snow. We were overjoyed at his return.

On 4 February we arrived at Kropotkin. Above the town, which had been burning for three days, hung a giant mushroom-shaped cloud of smoke. The railway was blocked by a line of trains 1 kilometre long. I saved all the petrol and oil that I could. On the way we came across the wreck of a 15-tonne lorry, the blower revolving slowly in the wind, the hopeless gesture of a dying giant. I came under attack twice on the open road from Russian fighters. Nothing happened to me. Amazingly, I never saw a real success by their air force.

At Tifliskaya an order came from Armee that everything not absolutely essential was to be destroyed. They needed the space. One thousand litres of our good sunflower oil, the fine tents for the bivouac, all had to be sacrificed. Thousands of the small panje horses were shot dead, the Armee could not bring up the fodder any longer. The last train from Rostov came in, then we were cut off. Behind us the Russians, ahead of us the sea. Tugboats continued to bring troops and the wounded out of the pocket. In fear, they thronged around the evacuation lorries. I freighted out the ill Oberleutnant Kollböck in a Ju 52. Traffic over the ice was no longer possible, and the retreat went slowly onwards. Russians, horses and cattle, dead from the cold and exhaustion, lined the route. Hordes of Russian prisoners were driven back without mercy. Gigantic herds of cattle wandered along with us. We all had ghastly influenza. Our mood resulted from depression at the endless retreating and illnesses. For weeks no ray of sunshine. It was an accursed region. In counter-attacks we inflicted heavy losses on the Russian units harrying us.

On 12 February we made an attack. Formed up in a broad line, our StuGs struck into the flank of arriving Russians and pursued them across the wide plains. Then we rounded them up in a pincer movement, bunched them together and wiped them out.

Fighting was continuing at Novo Dshereliyevskaya railway station. We soon captured it in an assault, closed up, darkness was falling. One StuG was told to go to a stretch of track where fighting was still in progress. A mad exchange of fire ensued and then silence. The driver of the StuG returned distraught, staggering. In the twilight the StuG had skirmished with German panzers. There were dead and wounded. Thus a great operation reached its bitter end. Our Abteilung CO Hauptmann Kapp summoned Oberleutnant Tenner, commander of 3 Battery, to clarify the incident. First he fired a flare into the sky and – see there – it was repeated at once from the other side. They were panzers of 13 Panzer-Div. with which we had almost duelled.

Gone was any joy. Now we felt the wet and cold, and suddenly so tired. I got a fire going in the railway yard, the last time I had done that was at Easter 1942. Twenty-five weary warriors in their damp, steaming clothing crowded around the warming glow. Tongues of flame and dancing shadows gave some life to the large space and lent the men's faces a strange animation. What heavy tired thoughts fluttered through their minds?

On 14 February at Malaya a handful of Russians gave our infantry a hard fight. The medical team was called for. After our attack it looked terrible. Leutnant Treche received a round through the upper arm which broke the bone. They had driven directly in front of the Russian guns on the motorcycle. The driver was killed. Treche ran for his life, chased by the whole pack of hounds. After 400 metres his arm was hit again. He threw off his greatcoat, tunic and shoes and ran in his bare socks, and saved his 'naked life'.

The uncertain twilight of an overcast winter's day hung over the land. A stationary StuG on sentry duty observed passing Russians. We received the radio call. Four StuGs attacked their convoy. Leutnant Förster hit and set aflame a horse-drawn ammunition wagon. The frightened animals broke into a wild gallop, towing the giant torch behind them into the dusk.

On 15 February at Staro-Nishe-Steblievskaya a large catch of fish had been landed. We fetched soap and chocolate from the provisions compound to barter. On 20 February renewed heavy fighting in the swamps. Successes but also casualties, Snow still lay on the ground.

At Vassilishenko the Russians suffered heavy losses. Egon's StuG driver Tenkisch was wounded. I have a lot of work to do. There are very serious fractures from gunfire but we have no dead. The company suffered a heavy bloodletting again. On 24 February we made a crazy run through deep mud to the HQ at Krasno-Armeiskaya. Here we met up with the Abteilung infantry and Leutenants Heinzle, Harberg and Lenz. The Tross arrived later delayed by mud on the road.

On 28 February the batteries moved position to Petrovskaya. At 0500 hrs we arrived at Slavyanskaya. I went with one StuG into the provisions compound. After the paymasters had their photos taken on and in front of the StuG we could take what we wanted. It was my best ever haul. At 1100 hrs we occupied positions and quarters at Petrovskaya. Then followed glorious days of rest and quiet. Every day we bartered soap for our breakfast eggs. We played a lot of skat and held competitions.

On 4 March an attack was begun against the Russians who were pestering us. At Belikov 1 and 3 Batteries together with 1 Romanian Cavalry Division led by General Theodorin (holder of Oak Leaves) launched a counter-attack. This time I had to go along with the infantry because the CO had refused permission for the StuGs to start. Belikov was taken by storm. Great amounts of Tross and materials captured. Later the Romanians struck a medal for it.

On 21 March our Abteilung CO took his leave to join the General Staff. Nero Kapp sang the epic 'Prinz Eugen der edle Ritter'. We were heavy-hearted to see him go.

So, we have reached the Kuban. We loaded up today at Warenikovskaya, a crazy job in the provisions compound. Chocolate, asparagus, chanterelles, fruit and much more. Being active brings blessings! Anything for the poor StuG men! I signed for everything and anything. In the Abteilung I received crazy smiles and handshakes.

At Swistelikov a few kilometres east of the Koka Canal which links the Sea of Azov to the Kuban we had a short summer break. The Abteilung was attached to 50 Inf.Div, being oppressed by strong formations of armour. Three kilometres behind the front we had a football match against the men of the fighting staff. Ivan replaced the terraces with gigantic fountains of earth from his artillery. Then we had a pleasant coffee hour, unfortunately rudely interrupted by an alarm. Immediate scramble into action. In the evening I arrived at the front line. Our StuGs crept up by night and lurked in the bushes.

As our Stukas flew over in the early morning of 27 March, sixteen Russian tanks took refuge close to our lines to escape being bombed. The hotspot was the sector of Inf.Regt 123, the batteries of Art.Regt 150 were firing with all they had.

Concealed, the StuGs waited at fever pitch for the order 'Fire at will'. The enemy tanks came ever closer, showed their flanks at 500 metres. Our StuGs opened fire all at once. Direct hit after direct hit, a shooting festival. Twelve torches over there blazed up as the result of the good shooting discipline of 3 Battery, and no casualties of our own. The survivors were cracked by 1 Battery, only two escaped. Great rejoicing among our infantry.

What sets the character of the Abteilung and raises it above the average of other units? Behind it all I see the obvious readiness for action and the basic attitude of the battery commanders, who do not see grim soldiering as the ultimate fulfilment. Taking into account the liberality and broad-mindedness in the officer–man relationship, it is the officers themselves who give the Abteilung its stamp.

Covered in filth, we returned from the successful operation to be greeted at the bivouac site by a new commander, Hauptmann Müller.

On 30 March the enemy made various fresh attempts at attacks but their troops always fell back under the concentrated fire of our infantry and artillery as supported by Stukas. 50 Inf.Div. settled the question by occupying on 31 March the last enemy position before the final Kuban bridgehead.

On the Don front, meanwhile, 1 and 4 Panzerarmees had ended their involvement south of the river. The delaying tactics of LVII Panzerkorps had prevented the Soviets from closing the Rostov loophole. This frustrated their intended push by strong forces from Bataisk to Tichores and further to the Taman peninsula at the back of 17 Armee. Enemy forces lacking armour support had infiltrated through our lines to form up in small groups at our rear, the intention being to encircle German troops in a pincer movement from north and south at the Kuban before the Germans reached the Taman. The plan came to grief in the field, as did some copies of it. The stubborn German resistance thus enabled units coming from the High Caucasus and Tuapse to fall back on the Kuban bridgehead.

Therefore, as far as the German leadership was concerned, the purpose of the Kuban bridgehead was to 'create a springboard for a new offensive into the Caucasus' when the time was right.

The destruction of our supply routes via Bataisk and Rostov required the setting up of a new route into the Kuban bridgehead over the Taman peninsula and the Kerch Strait. The supply across the latter had to be enlarged considerably so that 17 Armee could receive all it needed, but the icy conditions brought ferry transports to a standstill.

After the heavy losses during the supply to Stalingrad from the air, the aerial supply to the Kuban bridgehead was now to become another honourable page in the history of the German aerial transport units. 'Good old Aunt Ju 52' was the backbone of air supply. They flew from Saporoshye with supplies including ammunition and brought out the wounded on the way back. The departure points were in the Crimea. The landing places in the bridgehead were initially Krasnodar and Timoshevskaya. In the course of the retreat into the Kuban bridgehead these had to be abandoned and new landing places created at Temryuk, Slavyanskaya and Warenikovskaya. In four great and some small steps, 17 Armee returned to the 'Great Gothic Position'.

The departure of the StuG Abteilung 191 Tross had been delayed in early March by long rains. The disbanded infantry company (2 Battery) had returned to the Abteilung to the great joy of the men. Finally, on 5 March the great Abteilung Tross set off and came to a halt after 2 kilometres, the road being totally blocked. For fourteen days, the Armeekorps had been held with its vehicles at the Protoka. The Command HQ of LII Armeekorps was withdrawn for another purpose. The fighting units and StuG Abteilung 191 were now assigned to XXXXIX Gebirgskorps.

On 10 March the weather turned to frost, the great clogged line of vehicles came to life and flowed onwards, reaching Varenikovskaya (airfield) after a few days and nights and then headed for Temryuk. A swampy area, never forgotten by anybody who saw it, now had to be overcome. Another thaw. The route became ever more catastrophic. Great holes appeared in the mud. It clung to wheels and boots. Vehicles abandoned by the wayside reminded us of the retreat from Moscow in 1941. All ranks had to help. Bricks were procured to fill the holes and then stones brought in rucksacks from nearby villages for loading aboard the vehicles as insurance for what lay ahead. Indescribable endurance and tenacity was shown by the thousands of drivers who got stuck somewhere in the terrain or on the road. Often they were left totally to their own devices. The exemplary achievement and conduct of these men was praised and recognized by the highest authorities by the word 'Ostfahrer' – driver in the East.

Meanwhile our vehicle had got across the swamps and then the weather turned cold. The great convoy moved ahead slowly. In a low-level air attack three men of the Staff Battery were wounded. At this time our Abteilung CO, Hauptmann Kapp, took his leave of the Tross.

We continued towards the Taman peninsula. At Vyshesteblyevskaya we stopped for a few days in quarters waiting to be called forward to the Taman ferry. On 21 March, the first day of spring, vehicle groups moved up to the loading quay at Taman and drove aboard the naval ferry barges (MFP) very swiftly. The ferry took some vehicles and thirty men. Steel helmets and weapons had to be set aside and lifejackets worn. A twin-flak on the command bridge was the only protection. Crossing the Kerch Strait, a number of ferries were attacked by low-flying Russian fighters but no serious damage was caused. From afar we saw Kerch in beaming sunshine, an old settlement from antiquity across the blue sea. The Crimea!

The ferries tied up at Kolonka pier and were quickly unloaded. A Staff car then led the convoy of vehicles through Kerch to Feodosia and over the arid hills of the peninsula to Biyuk-Onlar. Here the Abteilung occupied quarters. It was another cheerless region. 2 Battery looked for lodgings in Tchongrav. Many of the men were granted leave immediately, the others remained behind, stocktaking.

The Abteilung Tross was designated 16c Company of the leave-taking Regiment Hahn. Meanwhile 1 Battery Staff arrived from the Kuban bridgehead, reinforcements came from the Reich. Training proceeded in a higher gear. On 12 April 16c Company was disbanded and Buffalo Abteilung was independent once more, being transferred on 24 April 193 to Matfovka. 3 Battery lodged at Novosselovka.

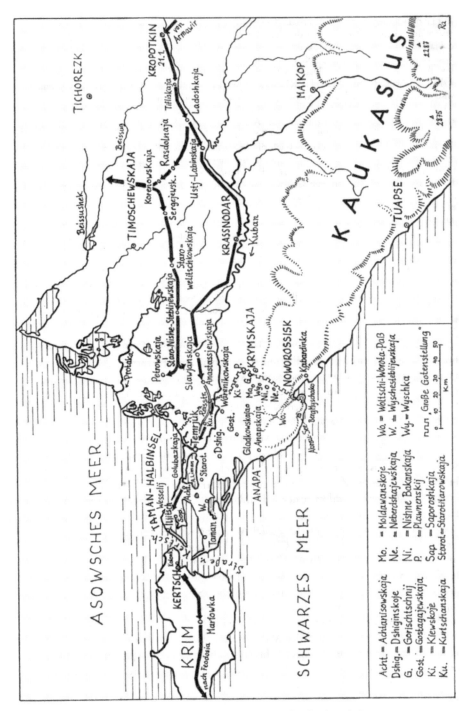

Map of the retreat to the Taman peninsula and Kuban bridgehead, January to
September 1943.

Map of the fighting at Moldavanskaya, 26 May to 2 June, and 16 July to 3 September 1943. The saw-tooth line represents part of the Great Gothic Line and the battlefield at Gorishtshniy, the most fiercely contested area. The arrows at the right indicate the main thrust of the Russian attacks (W. Tieke, *Der Kaukasus und das Oel*, Osnabrück, 1970).

Group photo, Kuban bridgehead, spring 1943.

Hermann Röhm with companions at Odessa, en route to join StuG Abteilung 191, April 1943.

Odessa on the Black Sea played an important role in the October Revolution of 1917.

The Kfz 15 Staff car in which Hermann Röhm drove his CO, Hauptmann Müller. The vehicle has the buffalo insignia on the right mudguard.

Hermann Röhm took over this vehicle on 18 April 1943. His companions are Obergefreiters Beneke and Moddermann, the latter being the CO's radio operator and driver.

The Kfz 15, looking fairly new.

Blaumann of the repairs team changing a wheel at the workshop. Hauptmann Alfred Müller arrived to take command of the Abteilung at Kerch on 17 April 1943.

With colleagues in the workshop at Marfovska on the Kerch peninsula.

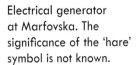

Electrical generator at Marfovska. The significance of the 'hare' symbol is not known.

The Staff car is ready but the Abteilung still awaits the delivery of new StuGs.

Hermann Röhm on leave in his home yard.

Hermann Röhm in tropical uniform.

On technical duties, Kerch peninsula, May 1943.

Farmers delivering wine during a moment for reflection in the commander's Staff car.

A photographic studio also took soldiers' portraits on the promenade at Yalta.

The CO's Staff car on a coastal road near Yalta, May 1943.

Yalta, where the conference of the Allied leaders took place in February 1945.

Hauptmann Müller leading an StuG operation.

A discussion on the exercise of 2 May 1943 with infantry and the first two new StuGs.

Hermann Röhm and companion in tropical uniform.

The new StuG III version G has arrived at the Abteilung at last. Twenty-one of the new guns were delivered on 19 May 1943.

These StuGs are new from the factory and even have the warning on the driver's shield *Achtung! Nicht betreten*: 'Warning, do not step here'.

The StuGs are spray painted dark yellow and in sunlight appear very bright.

In June 1943 the now operational StuG Abteilung 191 being conveyed by ferry from Kerch to the Kuban bridgehead. The ferry *Potsdam* is armed with several quadruple barrel 2-cm flak guns.

A StuG rolls slowly aboard the ferry. Individual StuGs were fitted here with 'aprons' not seen again in later photos.

The StuGs seen here are piled high with ammunition, canisters and the crew's personal baggage. In the foreground is the CO's personal vehicle, a 1939 American Chrysler or Studebaker saloon car.

Hauptmann Alfred Müller giving further instructions. All men are wearing lifejackets, as the Russians kept the ferry under continual attack.

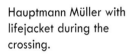

Hauptmann Müller with lifejacket during the crossing.

An inflatable boat on the wheelhouse roof, often hit under fire.

Hauptmann Müller reading orders or field post.

Besides the official Kfz 15 Staff car, the CO had a comfortable personal saloon for 'peaceful' drives.

The CO also had an amphibious car at his disposal. These vehicles were highly thought of by all.

For journeys in the terrain the Kfz 15 was required. Here a rear view with insignia.

Kfz 15 bearing the new tactical insignia of the assault artillery.

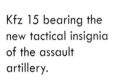

An expanded radio installation, one of the most up-to-date models of the time, made possible communications between StuGs, neighbouring units and the commanding Korps.

Vehicle with 'star' aerial, alongside a despatch rider awaiting orders.

View into the Kfz 15 engine compartment.

In Russia, camouflage became increasingly important as the Russian Air Force grew in strength.

Hauptmann Müller in tropical uniform studying a map, Kuban area, June 1943.

Several men map-reading near a Kfz 17 radio car.

Hauptmann Müller in the Schwimmkübel amphibious car. From 11 June 1943, he commanded Abteilungen 191 and 249.

Hauptmann Müller somehow contrived to obtain a caravan for his mobile quarters, towed from place to place by the Kfz 15 Staff car.

Hauptmann Müller's Staff car and caravan parked at the edge of woodland, Gostagayevskaya, 20 June 1943.

A rest stop with the Kfz 15, in the left of the picture is radio mechanic Radke.

Chapter Six

War in the Crimea, 1943–1944

Operations around Novorossisk, 6–28 April 1943

The new Abteilung CO, Hauptmann Müller, had decided that only one complete battery was to remain operational on the Kuban bridgehead, the others were to rest and replenish in the Crimea. By lot, 3 Battery remained at the front and took three StuGs from 1 Battery. On the night of 31 March 1943, Leutnant Förster's platoon was sent to counter-attack at the right wing of 50 Inf.Div. In this action Förster lost his life. His driver, Unteroffizier Otto, brought his body back for burial at the Kerch military cemetery.

Battery Tenner had been transferred into the Novorossisk area and attached for the purpose of supply to StuG Abteilung 249. Because the Russians had succeeded in building a bridgehead on a peninsula south of Novorossisk, 17 Armee decided that this had to be destroyed. For this purpose Battery Tenner was to operate with 125 Inf.Div. The mountainous character of the region made such an operation dubious from the outset. Mount Myshako, which was occupied by the enemy, was to be taken by 4 Gebirgs-Div. After several day getting there, Battery Tenner arrived in the readiness area, woods in mountains above Novorossisk. The rains had set in and the planned attacks for 6 and 10 April had to be postponed because of fog and rain. A band came to provide music for singing.

On 17 April the operation began. Clouds and mist impeded visibility for the Stuka pilots and in order not to endanger friendly forces they dropped their bombs too far out in the hinterland. The Gebirgsjäger then stormed the crest of Mount Myshako. The defenders, unharmed by the Stukas, offered overwhelming resistance, causing many German casualties and much confusion. The divisional commander called off the attack.

Next day 125 Inf.Div. attacked the western part of the bridgehead, our Stukas and artillery transforming the mountain into a hellhole. 3 Battery operated alongside 125 Inf.Div. but the terrain greatly limited the possibilities for the StuGs. When 'Fat August', a Soviet bastion, was taken, only egg-type hand grenades could be used, hurled from the commander's hatch. To have fired from the forest would have endangered our own forces. Mount Myshako remained unattainable. This was very disadvantageous for us because from there Russian artillery spotters directed the fire of their 17.5-cm and 21-cm heavy guns over Kabardin Bay to fall on our troops on the far side. The attack also resulted in heavy losses for ourselves.

On 25 April the attack on the Myshako bridgehead was abandoned. Both sides had many casualties and our troops had failed to crush the Russian landing head.

After a few days' rest, 3 Battery was withdrawn from 125 Inf.Div. and transferred to Novosselovka in the Crimea, a village about 30 kilometres from Kerch. In difficult negotiations with higher commanders, our Abteilung CO managed to obtain an order that the Abteilung could be transferred to the Crimea for rest and replenishment for both men and machines, the benefit of this being that they would be fully operational for the expected defensive battles to come on the Kuban bridgehead. During the period of R&R, the Abteilung was upgraded to Brigade status and received thirty-one more StuGs together with vehicles and reinforcements. As the result of this expansion and for tactical reasons the Abteilung was referred to alternatively as 'StuG Brigade 191' but this title was not confirmed officially until February 1944.

The refresher periods in the Crimea at Marfovka and Novosselovka were pleasant and diversified. We took over the new StuGs and other deliveries, calibrated the new cannons, staged sporting events, bathed in the sea, attended to the welfare of the troops and had guest evenings. For the first time since its formation in 1940 the Abteilung was equipped with new StuGs and vehicles that were capable of travelling cross-country. Fresh reserves of officers and men arrived from the Reich. Oberleutnant Tenner was promoted to Hauptmann.

In mid-April 1943, when the Russians began their big offensive against the Kuban bridgehead, the Abteilung had to return there immediately, transferring to the area of Gladkovskaya as Armee reserve on 28 April. Good use was made of the fine days at Novorossisk. All vehicles were given a camouflage pattern to suit the taste of the individual crew and the steel aprons protecting the undercarriage sides of the StuGs received a coating of concrete. The CO did not think much of these unauthorized embellishments. He approved some modifications to the StuGs and the camouflage but these had to be standardized over the entire Abteilung. Among personnel changes Leutnant Koch became the adjutant, I was nominated for officer training and Oberwachtmeister Ebert became my successor in charge of the Tross. One week later, 3 Battery moved its bivouac site to a fine oak wood at Gladkovskaya.

Upon its return, 3 Battery, which had remained temporarily in the Crimea in quarters at Marfovka, had to carry out exercise with infantry units (zbV 500, a penal unit) and reconnoitre the front before its readiness for operations could be confirmed. Every monent was now dedicated to training and the full battle readiness of the Abteilung.

Bunkers were dug, fishing nets used to camouflage StuGs, guns and vehicles, the new workshop platoon created a safe place as a repairs yard and the armourer, Wachtmeister Sücker, had his hands full adjusting the new cannon barrels. The Abteilung held an NCO course.

The Kuban Bridgehead, 29 April–end August 1943

At 17 Armee, Generaloberst Ruoff had been replaced by General of Pioneers Jaenecke as Commander-in-Chief. On the Soviet side Marshal Zhukov was transferred to other duties and Colonel-General Petrov had been appointed the new Commander-in-Chief of the 'Northern Caucasus front'.

On 29 April the Russians, having brought up reinforcements and having regrouped, stepped up the strength of their attacks. These now extended along the entire eastern and northern fronts of the bridgehead, its second great battle. In the north of the Taman peninsula they planned to encircle the deep flank of XXXXIX Gebirgskorps from the lagoon region. Up to 2 May, however, all enemy groups arriving in the Kurchanskaya–Temryuk area were either wiped out in several days of individual skirmishes or forced back to the lagoons.

Bitter fighting raged north and east of the town of Krimskaya, in the sectors of 101 and 97 Jäger Divisions. For days Krimskaya was the gloomy symbol for the fighting, endurance and death in the whole Kuban bridgehead. From 29 April to 3 May all positions were held and all breakthrough attempts frustrated by our tenacious resistance. When the energies of the enemy slackened on the night of 4 May, the opportunity was taken to evacuate the protruding and violently overrun bend in the front in favour of the newly prepared, well-built and staggered position west of badly damaged Krimskaya, at Kievskoye and Moldavanskoye.

Between 3 and 5 May, particularly in the region of woods and gorges south of Krimskaya, the Russians filtered through between 9 Inf.Div. and Romanian units into the hinterland, where they barricaded the road to Nishne Bakanskaya all day until being forced back.

On 5 and 6 May the enemy attacked the new positions west of Krimskaya and lost a large number of tanks. On 7 May the attackers suffered heavy losses south of Krimskaya. They had apparently selected this as their breakthrough point.

On 8 and 9 May, using heavy artillery, aerial support and much armour they tried again but paid a heavy price. Powerful superiority in numbers got them a breakthrough at Neberdshayevskaya, but even this could be contained to a certain extent. The Russian storm troops seemed exhausted and we took advantage of it.

On 14 May a battle group under Oberst Göbel including our 1 Battery mounted a counter-attack supported by Stukas on Neberdshayevskaya. Carrying infantry on the hulls, the StuGs drove up near the highpoint held by the Russian where the infantry dismounted for close combat. Scarcely had our grenadiers set up to defend than enemy tanks counter-attacked. The battle group destroyed three in close combat and repelled the following infantry. All in all, in two days of hard fighting the battle group regained a major part of the terrain the enemy had won with such effort and heavy casualties.

Finally the Russians ran out of steam and they lost the second great battle for the bridgehead. Everywhere the German positions had held firm except for the planned evacuation of the bend east of Krimskaya where the front had been pulled further west. The Luftwaffe played a special role in these defensive successes.

We had eight days of grace but a new storm front was building. New enemy preparations had been recognized and the reports solidified into a picture of a concentrated Soviet thrust against XXXXIV Korps at Krimskaya which had had to bear the brunt of past engagements. Supply trains rolled up incessantly with fresh troops, tanks and material from the vast expanses of the Soviet East. The Russian Air Force had also been strengthened. It was soon clear that the new enemy offensive was to be aimed against the area north-west of Krimskaya, and also clear what was the intention: either to roll up the

German front to the east or to attempt to split apart the centre of the front here and force the German units in the north and south to the Sea of Azov and Black Sea respectively.

Finally the Russians embarked upon their expected offensive against the positions of 101 Jäger and 98 Inf.Div. east of Kievskoye. Beforehand Hauptmann Müller had addressed the battery commanders, platoon leaders and StuG commanders of 1 and 2 Batteries and familiarized them with the defensive possibilities of the terrain. The StuGs stood ready for action, 3 Battery was the operational reserve.

The third Soviet offensive on the Kuban began in the early hours of 26 May. Two hours of artillery barrage supported by rolling air attacks from ground-attack aircraft and bombers with thirty to forty fighters as escort. The intention was to cut off the German connections to the rear and subdue our artillery. After two hours of bombardment by guns of all calibres, six infantry divisions and the three tank regiments mounted their attack.

We recognized the tactic of softening up by artillery fire and had previously prepared a strip of land several kilometres wide and deep to absorb the worst of it, occupied only by observers, and we would move forwards to intercept when it all died down.

In the Planvenski sector, the first blow was struck against our front line on both sides of the Varenikovskaya road by their capture of spot height 121.4 at Gorishtshni. This first Russian assault was broken up by StuGs, Pak and machine-gun fire but the pressure was too much and the German lines gave way. The enemy went on to capture a number of villages and achieved a breakthrough of several kilometres. The enemy wave of tanks advanced using the tactic 'stop, fire and advance again'. We were in serious trouble. Calls for help were sent by radio, morse signals, despatch riders and signalling lamps to the command posts and Staffs in the rear.

The reply came back: 'Let the tanks pass – roll through – engage their infantry – hold your positions.' We intercepted the infantry and the breakthrough was thwarted. Now the Luftwaffe came to the aid of the grenadiers and riflemen. Stukas dived on the tanks; Pak guns and flak 88s fired directly at the armoured monsters. A great tank massacre began.

In the afternoon our StuGs counter-attacked. 1 and 2 Batteries with mounted infantry fought with great determination for every dip in the land and every enemy strongpoint. Step by step the Russians pulled back, leaving us in possession of some of the villages they had captured earlier and most of the terrain we had ceded.

On the morning of 27 May, together with penal battalion zbV 500, our StuGs set out to capture Height 121.4. The objective was achieved easily except between Kievskoye and Moddavanskoye where a battle of movement raged.

On 28 May the Russians continued their heavy thrusts against the customary sectors, breached the front again, but the StuGs helped stop the advance and then cleared the area. On 29 and 30 May after Russian assaults on specific points, the raging battle ebbed to a stretch 8 kilometres long. All attacks were fended off except for the loss of Height 121.4.

On the morning of 31 May, German battle groups counter-attacked. Twenty-one guns of StuG Abteilung 191 joined Battle Group Polster. Two batteries of Panzer-Grenadier-Regt 93 with artillery from II Panzer-Art.Regt 13 fought through to the south-west edge of Gorishchniy. A pack of enemy tanks came out to give battle but retired after a T-34 was destroyed. Battle Group von Gaza was unable to force its way to Height 121.4. The forces of 97 Jäger-Div. remained back at Tambulovsky, south of Gorishchniy. At 1500 hrs the German attack was called off and the units pulled back.

On 1 and 2 June the Russians attacked Height 114.1, which gave us a broad field of view over their route of advance. Their attack came to nothing.

On 5 June, starting at 0300 hrs until the evening, the Soviets sent several waves of infantry now and again towards the German positions north-west of Krimskaya in the same area as on 26 May, westwards towards Varenikovskaya, but they had no success.

It was with great determination that the Russians had unleashed these attacks and offensives against the centre of our front. They kept it going for almost a fortnight without really achieving anything. The divisions of XXXXIV Korps had stood firm and so the third battle of the Kuban had not turned out well for the Russians.

After the heavy fighting near Gorishchniy through June until the beginning of July something of a calm set in. Both sides improved their defensive positions. Sport, training – Abteilung exercises with the infantry were held in the woods at Gostagayevskaya–Gladkovskaya – and entertainment were on the agenda during these quiet weeks. With the beginning of warm weather the men wore the newly delivered tropical uniforms, which distinguished them from afar as an elite unit.

The fourth battle of the Kuban began at Krimskaya on 16 July. Our Abteilung was put on alert on 17 July. From 0400 hrs the day before, the German positions received softening-up fire from artillery. This was concentrated on the projection in the front at Height 114.1 and the areas around Heights 95 and 121.4 occupied by the Russians.

Their main thrust was against 114.1 held by 97 Jäger-Div. and to their north Grenadier-Regt 282/98 Inf.Div. The second concentration of effort was in the vicinity of 121.4 held by themselves but surrounded by Grenadier-Regt 290 and one battalion of 98 Inf.Div.

Between 16 and 21 July the fighting for this region of heights was very changeable. Aerial activity by both sides was very intense. Stukas bombed the Russian positions without let-up. The opposing artillery unit duelled all day. Generalmajor Gareis commanding 98 Inf.Div. kept the main front line intact.

On 18 July 3 Battery moved up to the readiness area at Russkoye but orders to advance never came.

On 22 July towards 0530 hrs we were roused from sleep by the heaviest artillery barrage yet. Stalin organ rockets deluged our front line. Enemy ground-attack bombers joined in the attack. Behind the walls of fire two fresh Russian divisions went for the 98 Inf.Div. trenches, concentrating their effort against the sectors held by Grenadier-Regt 282 and the divisional battalion of 98 Inf.Div. They had about fifty tanks supporting their infantry but even so, after three days of trying, no decisive penetration of the German lines had been obtained.

On 23 July the fourth battle of Kuban still raged. At 0530 hrs the enemy attacks commenced as before. This time the effort was directed against I/Regt 282 sector. The StuGs assisted the infantry's defensive efforts until evening. On this day the front more or less held, the only breach was at 97 Inf.Div.

24 July was a black day for the StuGs. At daybreak the enemy artillery unleashed a barrage on the 97 Jäger-Div. sector. Renewed heavy fighting occurred around Height 114.1 but all positions held. 2 Battery was involved in the defence here. For the counter-attack by a battle group of 98 Inf.Div., 1 and 3 Batteries were deployed south-west of Podgorny-Gorishtshny (Death Gorge). Many StuGs ran over landmines in this action, 1 Battery being particularly hard hit. Immobilized, they stood as defenceless targets before the old main battle line, sitting ducks. While outside his vehicle Oberleutnant Pantel was seriously wounded and died at the Russkoye main dressing station. Hauptmann

Tenner, also outside his StuG, received a shrapnel wound in the thigh. An StuG of 3 Battery received a direct hit from artillery, Oberwachtmeister Stühn and Unteroffizier Schäffer had serious burns, crewmen Schnieders and Himmelreich were killed. Their StuG burned out.

Venolet's StuG was hit and came to a standstill ahead of the main front line, three crew got away but the fate of the driver was never discovered. In this fighting the CO's vehicle (driver Röhm) was seriously damaged. Despite everything, the breach at 97 Jäger-Div. was sealed.

After the first tidal wave was spent we expected a follow-up on 25 July but had to wait an extra day, when Grenadier-Regt 282 bore the worst of it again. From 1000 hrs to 1400 hrs the Russians came off worst in close combat, but by 1600 hrs they had recovered and sent in two fresh regiments supported again by fifty tanks. This time they broke through at I/Grenadier-Regt 282 before being ejected and the front line secured, but there was a price to pay for this success.

Leutnant Müller's platoon (3 Battery) was deployed with four StuGs, one of which I commanded. It took three attempts for us to get over the height without coming under fire. Then about thirty enemy tanks appeared from the village ahead and opened fire. Our StuGs attempted to ward them off but without cover we were easy targets. Müller's StuG drove into a shell crater. After a fierce duel my own StuG received three hits. My gunloader Fischer was wounded but we all got out alive. Konietzko's StuG attempted to pull Müller's StuG from the crater but was hit and immobilized; crewman Osterberger was seriously wounded. The artillery now subjected us to a bombardment, the other two StuGs were abandoned and, under artillery fire, the wounded were loaded on the fourth, that of Wachtmeister Harmsen, which took them to the main dressing station.

After leaving my own StuG I joined our infantry in the trenches. At first I was reported missing. I turned up that night at the Abteilung command post with four Russian prisoners whom I had captured as they arrived to inspect my wrecked StuG. I also brought with me the radio code books and a note of the damage. The three StuGs were retrieved next day by the towing team; during this operation Unteroffizier Weiner fell with a round to the heart.

What this proved yet again was that StuG operations in this kind of terrain were untenable, yet despite repeated situation reports by the platoon commanders to Abteilung, it was insisted upon.

On 27 July at 1600 hrs, an unusual hour for an enemy attack to begin, all hell broke loose, violent duels involving tanks against anti-tank guns, fierce infantry skirmishes. Our Abteilung was sent into action. Everywhere that the Buffalo Abteilung surfaced there would be a breathing space and the infantry valued it. 'The Buffalos are coming!' During these Russian offensives, StuG Abteilung was 'a rock in the surf'.

3 Battery received the operational order to defend from Height 95. The StuGs set off, drove through the marked corridors of the minefield and reached the elevation without incident. When the enemy tanks were seen advancing, we received the order 'Fire at will'. By constantly changing our firing positions the attack was beaten off. In the duels, 3 Battery registered hits on fourteen tanks, two of which were put out of action. The 98 Inf.Div. front held but had no answer to a massed attack by thirty tanks.

Casualties among the German infantry were high, although the Abteilung had none. On the return to the readiness area in darkness in the 'Death Gorge', a T-34 lurking near the main front line at 100 metres, illuminated in the light of a starshell, was knocked out.

In an Order of the Day from the High Command, 17 Armee, the Abteilung was mentioned with praise as follows:

StuG Abteilung 191 led by Hauptmann Müller played a decisive role in the defence against a numerically far superior enemy in the last few days. It participated in defensive measures and counter-attacks with great determination, destroying in the Kuban bridgehead ninety-five enemy tanks and several 12-cm assault howitzers. A mention in the Wehrmacht Bulletin has been requested.

Our surgeon Dr Schröder wrote this report on his experiences in the Kuban bridgehead:

I have set up my first-aid post in a bomb crater about 600 metres behind the main front line close to where the StuGs fuel up, reload ammunition and then disappear forward. It is 26 July 1943. Battalion zbV 500, a penal battalion, is advancing. They are good men, mostly good fellows who did the wrong thing at some time or other but are basically decent. Now they have been put into our sector.

I was wounded for the first time today. I was bending over a wounded man when a shell landed nearby. A piece of shrapnel passed through my belt and hit my left buttock. I had a premonition this morning that I would be lightly wounded. Strange, but now I am satisfied, it is behind me, nothing else can happen to me. This was confirmed an hour later. A stray bullet found its way into my bomb crater, hit a man's hand in his trouser pocket, whistled past my head and hit another casualty in the chest as he lay before me.

The battle raged this way and that. I treated seventy wounded today in my pit, nearly all infantrymen. The main front line changes hands often. The casualties on both sides are enormous. The Russians drive almost to the edge of the battlefield with lorries fully loaded with their troops.

It goes like this. After four hours' artillery barrage they attack in hordes on the first day of battle. Once they win a sector they search feverishly for nests. Their tanks roll across our positions. We cannot get at their tanks until they are in open country. Our counter-attack gets under way many hours later. It takes that long until our artillery has picked out their new targets, troops have been reorganized and our StuGs brought up. Artillery barrage again – this time ours – and counter-attack. The previous situation is restored. The numbers of dead and wounded grow. Soon the forefield is strewn with dead and dying. Usually the night brings an enforced lull though this can be deceptive.

In desperate haste under protection of darkness the wounded are transported out, the dead collected, reserves of men and materials brought up. New trenches are dug, old ones reinforced. Rations are distributed. How often the food carriers come with canisters only half full, or empty; every strange sound brings machine-gun fire on them below starshell. Yes, and that means only half-portions or we go without. That is what it is like for the infantry upon whom the main burden of the battle falls all the time, where even the night brings little relief.

27 July 1943. I have been in the bomb crater since dawn. It is now almost calm in the crater. Case after case is treated and transported out. My medical orderly is doing good work. StuGs come and go. There is heavy fighting ahead of the front line. Suddenly panic! The infantry are running back. Russian tanks have broken through. The situation is critical. An Assistenzarzt comes running up, totally flipped. He wants to set up a new dressing station to the rear. It is quite obvious he has lost his head. I hand over my first-aid post to the medical junior lieutenant, gather together all the walking wounded who can carry a rifle and go forward. Infantry streaming back are intercepted. We collect sixteen men and bring them forward. In the late evening two officers and thirty men embark on a last counter-attack, and recapture the front line. Both officers are seriously wounded, one fatally. It seems to us that these thirty-two men decided the outcome of the fourth battle of the Kuban which had been started by ten Russian divisions.

The Soviets have the heavier casualty lists but we also have enough to be going on with. Over the last few days we had fifty-eight StuG men dead and wounded of the 110 men in the fighting batteries.

At the rear a round from the Russian artillery scored a direct hit on 3 Battery kitchen. Achmet lost his head, B. his right leg and another lost the power of speech from shock. For the time being the fighting has stopped. Friend and foe lie together exhausted or bleeding to death, each happy when his neighbour falls silent.

On 30 July the Soviets tried it once more at the nose of the front near Height 114.1. After strong artillery and aerial preparation, twenty of their tanks rolled towards the height, followed by some fresh battalions. StuGs of Abteilung 191 and anti-tank Paks stopped eight tanks of the first wave. The attack continued, then came the Stukas. Bombs fell among the tank formations and on their departure positions. That ended the assault.

Peace descended temporarily over our sector of the front. Both sides improved their defences and rested their troops. The Abteilung ensured that the batteries were fully operational. At Gostagayevskaya the workshop platoon worked flat-out to make every gun battleworthy. New crews were trained up and the existing crewmen drilled in anti-tank and close-combat warfare.

At this time, Oberleutnant Eickhorn took command of 1 Battery. 2 Battery was disbanded, Oberleutnant Heinzle of 2 Battery took the cadre with him to the Reich to found a new unit. Oberleutnant Berg arrived with a new battery but no vehicles to take over 2 Battery, in order that it should be operational at once; 3 Battery had to provide it with two StuGs and crew, no easy decision for the 3 Battery commander.

During the rest period Dr Schröder had made a tour of the Crimea and wrote in his diary:

It is 1 August 1943. Kerch greets me again above a blue sea and beaming sun. Feodosia, Simferopol, Alushka. It is the Alusia of the Ancient Greeks and afterwards a Genoese trading centre. The whole southern coast of the Crimea lies in magnificent colour before my eyes. At Gursov I spent a wonderful evening on the terrace of a convalescent home.

Below us in the park the pines rustled. Black-violet shadows played on the nearby coastal waters. The rocky coast is upstream of Bocklin's 'Island of the Dead' and could easily be it … The early morning finds us high in the mountains, reached by a serpentine road. Above us the great rock Petri, far below the glorious rocky coast and before us the great expanse of the blue Black Sea.

Voronzoff Palace, Yalta, Alupka, the many glorious villas and mansions, the chapel on the needle of rock, everything impresses me deeply. Melons, fresh figs and mulberries for refreshment. I bought a beautiful old gold-silver icon to remind me always of this day.

Balaclava is a real sea-pirates' nest. Only a narrow gap connects the open sea with a natural small harbour basin. High rocks with old fortress towers surround the harbour, the village, and lend it an eerie, forbidding air. The Genoese dominated the coast of Crimea from here.

Not far off is Sevastopol, a magnificent great natural harbour. The town itself is a sad heap of ruins. We passed gigantic military cemeteries, viewed the large defensive fortress 'Maxim Gorki' which played a role in our capturing the town. In the evening we went to Bachshisseray, a bare valley in the rocks. Here we found ourselves suddenly in Oriental surroundings. Mosques with minarets, houses with flat roofs. Bulgars wearing the fez and Tartars people this former capital of the Crimea. It was the residence of the ruler of the Tartars. It became a Tartar province under Genghis Khan and remained independent until the time of the Empress Catherine the Great. Potemkin then prepared a cruel end to its power.

We started back on 3 August. At Simferopol I bought a very fine mocca-mill for Turkish coffee. The Crimea is not Russia; even the people are different, freer. At Kerch we met 2 Battery (cadre) on their way to Germany. On 5 August in the evening we arrived back at Abteilung.

Meanwhile the StuGs had all been restored to working order and the gun barrels newly adjusted by Wachtmeister Sücker. There had been changes at Staff: Leutnant Engelhaaf replaced Leutnant Koch as adjutant, Unteroffizier Treis became the 1st General Staff Officer's secretary and Wachtmeister Schwerdt that of the 2nd General Staff Officer; Wachtmeister Drescher was the new armourer. Benecke, Nordt and Röhm were appointed as crew of the new Command StuG.

For the coming operations, surveys ahead of the main front line had been made and shooting positions set out for the StuGs. Time had been found for patrols to look over the territory. Moldavanskoye, a small town in our sector of the front, was fairly shot to pieces and abandoned by its population. Here we found strange indoor paintings never seen before and works of art. At the

centre of town was a small castle, ruined except for its walls. In the rearward
area we found tobacco plantations and vineyards on slatey soil. The village had
orchards, the apricots were just ripe and our field kitchen prepared refreshing
fruit soups.

In the opening days of August all German observation posts reported
large troop movements. Local reconnaissance activity and incursions had
been repelled. On 8 August the Russians attacked with two divisions in the
98 Inf.Div. sector and on the north wing of 97 Jäger-Div. Our front line held.
The Abteilung drove to the readiness area at Nishne Bakanskaya but was not
required. Over the next few days it moved to the Moldavanskoye area and then
on 11 August to secure the front line around Gorno Vessely where there was an
important height, Vishka.

The fifth battle of the Kuban was announced at 0510 hrs on 12 August with
a barrage on our sector lasting several hours by artillery and Stalin organs.
Russian fighter-bombers dropped their bombs and then attacked our ground
forces. Under heavy artillery fire, 3 Battery StuGs drove to their previously
identified shooting positions and repulsed all waves of attackers. Our own
infantry was unable to prevent the Russians gaining part of the Vishka height
but this was soon sealed off. On driving into the shooting positions the StuG of
Oberwachtmeister Focke was immediately hit by anti-tank fire, and Leutnant
Müller's StuG by an artillery shell, but both crews got out unharmed. The battle
raged until evening. It was a hot and difficult day for everybody in this sector of
the front. The Russian XI Grenadier-Rifle Corps finished in very poor shape.

The StuGs remained in their positions overnight to secure the line; early next
morning the Russians began the usual overture of artillery barrage, Stalin rockets
and air attacks followed by hordes of soldiers, soon halted by the StuGs. Except
for a few strongpoints, our infantry had vacated the line to reduce casualties. Thus
the StuGs stood alone on the height and attempted to hold off the Russians by
their efforts alone. Around midday the Russian attack slackened. Our infantry
counter-attacked and regained that part of the Vishka height lost the day before.
Towards 1600 hrs the Russians signed off by attacking using battalions of women;
once they saw the StuGs the attack petered out.

Tired and drained of energy, the crews returned to the bivouac site with only
a few wounded, including Boos, Kaiser, Klein, Reupke and Scheitzach.

On 15 August, StuGs of 3 Battery – one of which I commanded – secured
the Vishka. In the evening my StuG received a hit from enemy artillery while

in a lookout position. All the crew were wounded: Follmann, Ziesing, Klein, myself. I received injuries to eyes and face. We were driven at once to the main dressing station. 3 Battery StuGs were relieved that same evening by a battery from StuG Abteilung 249.

On 19 August another Russian challenge to the Vishka failed against the steadfastness of 97 Jäger-Div. Subsequent assaults by the Russians to penetrate our lines were far weaker, and degenerated into little more than 'feelers'.

The result of these heavy defensive battles was that despite being outnumbered ten to one, the Kuban bridgehead remained in our hands. We of the Buffalo Abteilung were proud of our contribution to this success in no small measure. Unfortunately in the sector of Army Group von Manstein it was beginning to look probable that even 17 Armee was going to be forced to give up the Kuban bridgehead. The Soviets stopped their offensives against the bridgehead and remained watchful, ready to move in if the Germans withdrew.

On 3 September Army Group A received the order from Army High Command to begin pulling out of the Kuban bridgehead on 7 September. Plans for the retreat, the so-called *Krimhild* and *Brunhild* plans, were drawn up. It had been forced by the situation on the southern wing of the Eastern Front and the defection of Italy. The danger that the Crimea would be cut off from the rest of the Eastern Front was very great. The Armee estimated that *Krimhild* would need ten to twelve weeks if all important materials and large parts of the civilian population were to be brought along with us. Thirty-eight days was suggested for *Brunhild* if it included Wehrmacht property and destroying items of economic use. Both plans involved a retreat in stages to the Kerch Strait with a limited period available for defence at favourable places in the terrain. The 'Kleiner Gotenkopf' – 'Small Gothic Head' – which was connected to the Taman peninsula at only three places, became especially important.

Soviet Landing in Novorossisk, 9–12 September 1943

On 29 August the Abteilung had transferred to Lake Abrau. Dr Schröder described it in his diary:

> That day we undertook a major change of position to Lake Abrau. Once again we gained some benefit. A great mountain lake with endless vineyards and at the

time of the vintage selection. It is already late in the season. Sweet as honey. Never tasted so much and so good.

I have set up my tent at the edge of the beach. We drive around the lake in the Schwimmwagen amphibious car. The workshop has made me some clever hooks for catching pike. Unfortunately the fish have no appetite. On 5 September Oberleutnant Korsen (commander, Staff Battery) took his leave of us. A good-hearted man with a sense of humour, we liked him very much. He left with two Piselinten towing machines.

In the evening I paid a visit to 3 Battery in the mountains. We passed the old position on the Sapunberg. My thoughts went back six months, to the attack on Mount Myshako.

The Teufelsberg towered above, once more we had Novorossisk below us, the Naples of the Black Sea. An unforgettable mood lay over the town and bay, on the other side of which is Kabardinka with its long-range naval batteries which caused us so many problems in April. The sun set like a gleaming sphere. Without speaking we perched on a step in the rock and watched as the world around us disappeared.

The German preparations were naturally no secret to the Russians, who had already brought in troops from elsewhere to extend their successes north of the Sea of Azov. On the night of 30 August, a Russian naval lieutenant was taken prisoner in the port of Novorossisk. Under interrogation he stated that a raid on the inner harbour accompanied by simultaneous landings in the Anapa–Osereia area would also be accompanied by an attempt to encircle at Temryuk. German reinforcements were brought into the harbour and reserves put on standby but nothing ever came of it.

Towards midnight on 9 September a Russian landing force stood off the bay at Novorossisk. Russian artillery, heavy mortars and innumerable rocket batteries then opened fire on the harbour. The long-range batteries at Zemess Bay fired at our troops deep in the hinterland.

Our surgeon Dr Schröder wrote:

It is 10 September. The long-expected Russian offensive has begun. At 0300 hrs a group of Soviet specialists got to the harbour boom and opened it. Shortly after, their landings began on the pierhead. They were seen too late. Their aim was the town of Novorossisk.

Our reinforced pierhead was destroyed by torpedoes. Many landing craft crammed with troops coming from the opposite shore were hit and sunk before they reached our side.

German coastal artillerymen put up a desperate defence but it was not possible to prevent the Russians coming ashore here and there, particularly since the town lay under this box barrage.

At 0800 hrs I received my orders. The StuGs were already heading into town. Just before I got there my small armoured ambulance was spotted by fighter-bombers. Streams of tracer sprayed around me but luck was on my side and I reached the first houses on the outskirts of Novorossisk. A feeling of insecurity crept up on me. There was shooting in the harbour, our StuGs were still at readiness.

Upon my arrival I found Leutnants Winkler and Müller already wounded during a briefing in the terrain. At that moment the order came to attack. Hauptmann Tenner, commander of 3 Battery, was still hospitalized with his wound and so the battery had no officer. I took over the StuG of Leutnant Müller. A Hauptmann of pioneers brought us up to date through a broken window in a tower block. I was to steer to the western part of the harbour. 1 Battery under Leutnant Eickhorn was fighting at the eastern part.

It was 1300 hrs. Our advance was difficult since the town had been shot to ruins. The streets were impassable because of the many shell craters and tram rails bent upwards. Above us infantry fire rattled, interspersed with shell impacts. There is nothing worse than street fighting with no knowledge of the respective positions of friend or foe. At the western end of the harbour the infantry were absent. Had we gone astray?

Finally we made contact. The infantry were very nervous and had casualties. The company commander could not be found. From a neighbouring house a wounded man was calling out pitifully for help, lying in a cellar, shot through the stomach. My conscience as a doctor made itself felt but for the moment the attack was more important. Suddenly no more than 30 metres ahead ten Russians, driven forward at gunpoint by a Commissar, were crossing the road, but too quickly for us to be able to shoot. It was an ugly, uneasy situation. By Very light the infantry indicated the Russian resistance nests. The small wooden structures collapsed like houses of cards when hit by our rounds.

Four hundred metres ahead at a crossroads some of our own infantry had appeared. I was preparing to move up to make contact when suddenly – fire, stars, smoke. I had been hit. I felt like an angel drifting below, could no longer move my legs and noticed how slowly the paralysis and loss of feeling crept up from below. My left shoulder had also been shot through.

The StuG took me to a dressing station where I was unloaded through the commander's hatch. This caused me great pain. In a cellar lit by candles I was laid down on straw. I dictated two letters, one to my mother. The last words melted into one another and then I passed out.

Terrible pain and long-lasting trembling brought me back to reality. I was still alive – for the time being! It was the bitterest disappointment of my life until then. Now I had it all before me. As a surgeon I well understood that I could not know how such wounds would turn out.

The journey to the main dressing station was hellish. Fever and pain made me delirious. I was probably crying. My commanding officer visited me shortly before my operation. I had a slightly guilty conscience: during the heavy fighting expected ahead, the Abteilung would have no surgeon.

Immediately after the operation I was flown out to Taman by Fieseler Storch and from there to Simferopol by Ju 52. In 1944 I was at Freiburg im Breisgau. A two-month leave of convalescence for neurological injuries began at Arlberg in Austria and brought me across Germany to Königsberg. My request to return to what was by then StuG Brigade 191 was not approved and I was sent as medical officer to Artillery Abteilung II/401 at Pilsen. It was unforgivable that I was not sent back to the old mob.

The Abteilung StuGs fought a desperate battle against the Russian landing troops at the harbour basin. Our casualties continued to rise. Communication with our infantry was broken off and we had to identify our own targets under heavy artillery fire. The toll increased: Oberleutnant Eickhorn (1 Battery commander) fell; Leutnant Fischer (3 Battery) was seriously wounded and died three days later in the military hospital at Simferopol. Other officers including Leutnant Strauch and gun crews were wounded so that many StuGs were no longer operational.

Meanwhile German reserves had been brought up: elements of 73 Inf.Div., 101 Jäger-Div. and 1 Romanian Mountain-Div. were deployed in the city at Mefodyevski-Ost; elements of 4 Gebirgs-Div. and 4 Romanian Mountain-Div. at Novorossisk West and Stanichka.

Gebirgsjäger-Regt 91 halted the landings on the western pier and also forced the enemy at the lido and on the submarine jetty into the sea. At 1600 hrs the counter-attack with StuGs in support against the enemy-occupied cold storage depot and cereals quay was unsuccessful. On 11 September the enemy landed fresh troops under the protection of a box barrage. Next day German units attacked the enemy-occupied harbour areas and ejected the Soviets at various places.

Russian attacks to the north from the Myshako bridgehead also failed upon meeting Gebirgsjäger-Regt 91. While the landing operations did not shake the cohesion of 17 Armee, it turned out that the port could not be made usable as planned. The Abteilung withdrew the remaining operational StuGs from the battle area to become the V Armeekorps reserve. StuGs and vehicles were repaired as quickly as possible in readiness for the imminent withdrawal.

Chapter Seven

The Evacuation of the Kuban Bridgehead, 16 September–9 October 1943

On account of the time it would take (twelve weeks), the *Krimhild* plan was discarded and *Brunhild* adopted. The withdrawal was begun by V Armeekorps and XXXXIX Jägerkorps on the night of 15 September. That day the Russians had arrived in the Kievskoye area with seventy tanks and three regiments of infantry, intending to attack the retreating Germans and hoping to get forward quickly on the arterial road to Varenikovskaya. Their progress was blocked by 79 Inf.Div.

On the night of 15 September, German forces abandoned Novorossisk. The enemy pursued them at once along the road to the Volchi–Vorota Pass. At the pass the enemy columns were fought to a standstill but the attempt by the Germans to blow up the railway tunnel was only half successful on account of a technical malfunction. The southern part of the 'Great Gothic Position' was brought back to the southern half of the 'Siegfried Barrier' without much difficulty.

In the course of the withdrawal by V Armee, StuG Abteilung 191 changed position to Anapskaya early in the morning of 16 September, finding progress difficult on account of the muddy paths and tracks.

From 20 September the batteries were deployed as the rearguard for the Tross and other elements of the Abteilung during their move to Gostagayevskaya. 3 Battery was attached to 4 Gebirgs-Div. and occupied the readiness area at Oshernetz, north of Anapa.

On the night of 21 September all three Germans Korps returned to the Hagen Line. The Russians had appeared in large numbers in the V Armeekorps sector and began by making powerful attacks against the southern wing, hoping to intercept German forces leaving the Anapa woods and at the same time making landings in the rear of V Armeekorps from seaward. After they had done that, their plan was to roll up the two northern German Korps before they reached the Small Gothic Head near position 'Bucharest', well up the Black Sea coast. There is no indication that any of this was achieved.

On 22 September, Soviet tanks made inroads into the XXXXIX Jägerkorps sector as far as Pilenko. 2 Battery StuGs and Stukas destroyed all eight tanks which broke through. The supplies compound had to be abandoned due to the destruction of the Pilenko railway yard.

On the evening of 23 September, German troops pulled back to the Rhön–Rüdiger Line. 3 Battery StuGs acted as rearguard at Pyertilebka, taking up a position on the Black Sea coast. The new front ran through Utash. Large Russian troop movements were observed.

As a result of shortening the German front, some troop sections could be released to proceed to Ilyich for the crossing to Kerch. 370 Inf.Div. and elements of 50 Inf.Div. were now attached to Gruppe Becker, which had the task of defending the Temryuk–Golbazkaya area. On 24 September, all three German Korps fought off enemy attacks along the Rhön–Rüdiger Line. At the strongpoint of the defence was 97 Jäger-Div., covering the central land bridge to the Taman peninsula.

V Armeekorps reached the Small Gothic Head position by the evening of 25 September. That night the Russians attempted to make landings in Temryuk Bay to cut off the retreat by Gruppe Becker but after heavy fighting the landing craft failed to make the beach and the carrier vessels were forced back offshore. Originally planned as a simultaneous event, the following morning the Russians developed a heavy attack either side of the Kurtshanskaya–Temryuk road but this was repelled by 50 and 370 Inf.Divs and elements of 101 Jäger-Div. By occupying the Small Gothic Head position the Germans shortened the front substantially and the divisions freed could be transferred out to the Crimea. The defence of the position lay with 49 Gebirgs-Div. and the 19 Romanian Inf.Div. (Sixt).

The Kerch Strait was now a hive of activity. The transfer-out of units followed a strict plan. Voyages between Ilyich and Kerch were made continually by four landing flotillas and Heeres-Pionier-Landungs-Regt 770 using naval or pioneer barges as ferries. The protection of the coasts and escorts was undertaken by small German naval units. For protection of the Kerch Strait itself numerous long-range batteries had been installed on the Kerch coast. This included Generalmajor Pickert's 9 Flak Division with numerous guns of all calibres for anti-aircraft work and other engagements. Luftwaffe transport units also supported the evacuation of the Kuban bridgehead. The abandonment of the Small Gothic Head was carried out in accordance with a plan stipulating the pace, defensive force and crossing capacity.

The Russians were now concentrating their efforts on the land bridge on the road, which had been held by 97 Jäger- and 91 Inf.Divs for over a week. The enemy's preparation areas came under fire from German artillery, with Stukas destroying a large assembly of tanks; these defensive measures being augmented by landmines laid by the pioneers. The same day StuGs of Abteilung 191 carrying infantry on the hulls proceeded to Starotitarovskaya, where the infantry went to prepared positions, the StuGs parking a few kilometres south of the village in readiness.

On 28 September Oberleutnant Hoffmann arrived as the new 3 Battery commander to replace Hauptmann Tenner, now seconded as an instructor with his driver and orderly clerk to the StuG School at Burg. Leutnant Koch was given the Staff Battery to command and Oberleutnant Schumacher 1 Battery.

On the night of 30 September the Russians began heavy shelling. One projectile landed in the readiness area and set some straw alight. During a night attack against the blockade line, a Russian penal battalion waded across the Achtanisovsker–Liman and penetrated 2 kilometres behind the German front. They were spotted and the alarm raised but no definite measures could be taken because it was dark. [This is the only identifiable Russian unit mentioned in this book anywhere on the retreat from the Caucasus to Sevastopol. There must have been prisoners taken from this penal battalion for the author to be able to say that that was what it was. – *Trans.*]

At daylight, from the shore, elements of Grenadier-Regt 666, a platoon of StuGs from 2 Battery and two platoons from light Flak Abteilung 96 engaged the landing craft and destroyed them.

Enemy landings on the Bugasskaya spit of land intended to capture the German positions at Wesselovka. The latter resisted but were unable to prevent an incursion at the seam between the reconnaissance unit Gebirgs-Abteilung 94 and II/Gebirgs-Jäger-Regt 13, although Height 36.4 was held. The German counter-attack failed. Employing all reserves, the Romanian Gruppe Sixt sealed off the incursion at Wesselovka and held it so that the German retreat could go ahead. 1 Armee was able to hold fast to Small Gothic Head for a week.

First the protruding central section of the Small Gothic Head was evacuated. 98 Inf.Div. occupied position 'Vienna' and 97 Jäger-Div. position 'Munich'. 4 Gebirgs-Div. had to fight hard to hold these positions and support the timetable for the jump to Kerch.

On 3 October Romanian Gruppe Sixt disengaged from the enemy unnoticed and by daybreak was already poised to defend in the position 'Bucharest'. Also that day, 98 Inf.Div. in position 'Vienna', defended by artillery and Stukas, held out under attack by tanks and aircraft.

That same night elements of 370 Inf.Div. and 50 Inf.Div. with StuGs of Abteilung 191 as rearguard occupied position 'Berlin'. Most of the remnants of 50 Inf.Div. went on to occupy the 'Pre-Berlin' position. This enabled Gruppe Sixt to abandon the positions 'Bucharest' and 'Vienna', 98 Inf.Div. and 19 Romanian Inf.Div. then headed for the ferries at the Kerch Strait. Regt 13 of 4 Gebirgs-Div. occupied the southern sector of the 'Breslau' position and with Gebirgsjäger-Regt 91 the tongue of land at Kossa Tchushka.

On the morning of 4 October the Soviets attacked the 'Pre-Berlin' position. The men of 50 Inf.Div. supported by our StuGs held firm. The attack south of Ssenaya collapsed, twelve T-34s were destroyed by our StuGs alone, another eighteen tanks by our artillery.

Massed batteries of heavy guns arrayed at Kerch laid a barrage ahead of our sector of the coast. Enemy air attacks against the ferries did little damage because landing stages, barges and other vessels were enveloped in smoke whenever the enemy appeared. Smoke was a dangerous medium in which to operate for their aircraft and caused them losses.

On the night of 4 October the Russians penetrated the German defences and a confused situation developed. First a frontal incursion was repulsed in a counter-attack. Next, elements of Grenadier-Regt 667 occupied the Russian landing point on the Sea of Azov and the enemy group inland south-west of Golubazkaya was wiped out by the StuGs of 2 Battery supported by infantry of III/Grenadier-Regt 666.

After these heavy losses on 4 October the Soviet attacks abated. On the night of 5 October the German companies returned from the 'Pre-Berlin' position to the 'Berlin' position, and Gruppe Becker advanced directly to the loading jetties at Ilyich via position 'Munich' held by 97 Jäger-Div.

370 Inf.Div., and parts of 50 Inf.Div. were shipped across to Kerch on 7 October. In this evacuation phase only 97 Inf.Div. and 4 Gebirgs-Div. were involved, all artillery having been shipped out to emplacements on Kerch.

On 7 October, three Russian divisions with armoured support attacked position 'Munich'. The enemy assault was met by 2 Battery StuGs, Stukas bombed the tanks and our artillery had the range from afar. The Russians retired with heavy losses.

The following morning their artillery bombarded the 'Munich' position again but by then it was uninhabited, Gruppe Müller having transferred to the position 'Breslau' overnight. Believing the occupants of 'Munich' position to have been softened up for what came next, thirty tanks carrying infantry on the hulls now headed to the position but found themselves deluged by fire from our rocket launchers at Saporoshkaya. To the south their assemblies of dive-bombers, rocket launchers and artillery were virtually wiped out.

Towards 1800 hrs on 8 October Gebirgs-Regt 13 evacuated the 'Breslau' position and went to Ilyich for the crossing to Kerch. To provide cover for this last jump, penal battalion zbV 560, reconnaissance Abteilung 97 and our 2 Battery StuGs waited in the 'Ulm' position. When night fell our StuGs drove to the loading bridge at Ilyich and boarded the naval ferries for the voyage to the northern pier at Kerch.

For the voyages of the last units from Ilyich to Kerch, the German artillery set up an impenetrable wall of fire. Soviet night bombers attempted to interfere with the naval ferries without success. Russian artillery scattered the terrain opposite and the loading jetties with indiscriminate blind fire without adversely affecting the sailings. The last Gebirgsjäger went aboard the ferries before midnight, after which the jetties were destroyed by explosives. The last ferry cast off at 0100 hrs on 9 October and the last units arrived at Kerch at 0200 hrs.

During the withdrawal from the Kuban bridgehead the Abteilung CO, Major Müller, was also V Armeekorps roads commander. The evacuation of the bridgehead was therefore carried out as per the timetable to the end. The Armee was brought off to the last company and no weapon of any use fell into enemy hands.

The evacuation was achieved in four weeks, during which time most of the winter reserve of foodstuffs in the bridgehead were brought out, as was the working population and all weapons, ammunition, vehicles and equipment.

The decisive factor was the outstanding *ésprit de corps* of our troops, which was beyond praise.

On 9 October 1943, 17 Armee concluded its Memorandum on the evacuation of the Kuban bridgehead: the Armee had completed its crossing of the Strait of Kerch. With it, a two-year struggle came to its end. It had been unleashed in 1942 in pursuit of crude oil, the raw material so important for the war effort on both sides. When the advance to the Caucasus began, nobody anticipated what a dramatic course the campaign would take. It was a bitter struggle for military positions, for mountain passes, high features, hills and harbours. Despite indescribable efforts and great sacrifices, the goal could not be attained. The German war economy had to renounce its thirst for Caucasian oil.

Chapter Eight

The Struggle for the Crimea, 1943–1944

Those whom the gods would destroy they strike down with blindness. The fighting in the Crimea, the third catastrophe on the German southern wing in the spring of 1944, is an appropriate demonstration of this statement. If anything was unnecessary it was the sacrifice that 17 Armee had to make on the Crimean peninsula on the edge of the Black Sea.

Until then, everything on the southern wing of the Eastern Front had been tolerable. In the course of the Great Retreat, at the beginning of September 1943, 17 Armee had left the Asiatic mainland, evacuated from the Kuban bridgehead in an exemplary manner and had transferred across the water to the Crimea with few losses. The transport of 17 Armee across the Kerch Strait had been a complete success. With the naval units and Luftwaffe it had held in check the Russian presence in the Black Sea.

After the evacuation of the Kuban bridgehead a total of eight divisions were withdrawn from 17 Armee. This weakened the defence of the Crimea substantially. The High Command of 17 Armee – headquarters in Simferopol – was given the defence of the Crimea. Its subordinate units were V Armeekorps on the Kerch peninsula, XXXXIX Gebirgskorps at the Perekop and Ishun Narrows and a Romanian mountain corps. By mid-October 1943 the commanding 49 Gebirgskorps at the Perekop isthmus did not have a single German division at its disposal. A few Romanian divisions, a few units made up of volunteers from the east and some weak artillery forces in the broad sectors of the North was the sum total of all it had to command.

At V Armeekorps it looked no different. 98 Inf.Div., 6 Romanian Cavalry Division, with in addition as Korps reserve 3 Romanian Mountain Division, and the battle-proven StuG Abteilung 191 led by Hauptmann Alfred Müller were available, and 50 Inf.Div. with the task of securing the coastal strips both sides of Feodosia and at the same time extending the Parpatch defensive position towards the east. Two divisions of 1 Romanian Mountain Korps defended the coastal regions and engaged in anti-partisan work inland. There were no true panzers on the Crimea.

Other special fighting units were 9 Flak.Div. under General Pickert and the Army Flak Abteilungen 275 and 279. Generaloberst Jaenecke of 17 Armee therefore had thirteen divisions with which to hold the Crimea. These German and Romanian divisions faced three Russian armies and one tank corps, many independent brigades and thirty infantry divisions, all gathered around the Crimea.

Meanwhile the situation on the mainland front had made a poor start. On 23 October assault troops of 4 Ukrainian Front (Tolbuchin) had broken through the Wotan position and captured the town of Melitopol. General Hollidt's 6 Armee attempted to seal the breach but unsuccessfully. The incursion became a full breakthrough. The Russian steamroller now rolled through the Nogai Steppe to the estuary of the Dnieper. Once they controlled the Perekop Narrows (a strip of land 5 to 7 kilometres wide), 17 Armee on the Crimea would be cut off from all contact on the mainland.

17 Armee Commander-in-Chief Generaloberst Jaenecke, who had led IV Armeekorps at Stalingrad until mid-January 1943 and witnessed the defeat of 6 Armee, saw the danger. In view of this development, a study of the situation, plan *Michel*, was made at Armee HQ which envisioned a retreat by the Armee in stages to the Perekop Narrows where a bridgehead would be established around Voinka. Depending on the situation on the mainland, this could be abandoned as quickly as possible in order not to lose the connection with 6 Armee.

17 Armee prepared and ordered the breakout for 29 October. The day before at 2100 hrs, Hitler forbade the operation. For him the political and strategic arguments for defending the Crimea were the means to stabilize the Eastern Front. It also seemed questionable whether the retreat by the Armee could have been accomplished within eight days. On 19 October when *Michel* was to have got under way, 6 Armee was already split into two parts. On 30 October a Russian tank spearhead arrived at the Tartar Wall at Perekop and one day later sixteen Russian tanks advanced on Armyansk. Thus by 31 October they occupied the narrows at Perekop, yet according to plan *Michel*, most of 17 Armee would not have arrived there until seven days later.

Generaloberst Jaenecke and his Chief of Staff did not give way and now attempted to rescind Hitler's order to defend the Crimea and implement instead a plan for the evacuation of the Armee by sea. There now came into being three more plans: *Ruderboot* in November 1943, later *Gleitboot* and finally at the beginning of April 1944 *Adler*.

The basic thinking here was to empty all front sectors in the Crimea into the fortress area of Sevastopol over six to seven days. Naval forces would then undertake the evacuation by sea. Obstacles and staggered lines of trenches with anti-tank ditches would impede the advancing Russian armour. At Simferopol the two main roads lay in a half-circle around the city and these had to be protected by the 'Gneisenau' position. Sevastopol was to be held for three weeks while the Armee was shipped out from the harbours and quays.

In the course of the evacuation of the Kuban bridgehead, 98 Inf.Div. commanded by General Gareis had taken over the defence of the eastern coast of the Kerch peninsula by 10 October from the 10 Romanian Inf.Div, which had been transported to Kerch by the end of September. 98 Inf.Div. now stood alone defending 100 kilometres of coast either side of Kerch, and this could not be done without leaving gaps.

On the southern wing Grenadier-Regt 282 (Oberst Faulhaber) handled the security, Grenadier-Regt 290 protected the east coast of the Kerch land bridge from Yenika to Vorsovka. I/Grenadier-Regt 290 lay in reserve at Bagerov. Divisional battalions and alarm units took over security duties on the north coast of the Sea of Azov. Three light and one heavy Abteilung of Art.Regt 198 were spread out across the entire divisional sector, strengthened by several batteries of army and naval coastal artillery and Flak.Regt 27. The 6 Romanian Cavalry Division had responsibility for the protection of the south coast to Feodosia.

To defend the 250-kilometre coast of the Kerch peninsula, V Armeekorps had available 98 Inf.Div., 6 Romanian Cavalry and 3 Romanian Mountain Divisions and StuG Abteilung 191. Generalleutnant Deichmann commanded 1 Fliegerkorps with two groups of Jagdgeschwader (JG) 52 and Stuka Geschwader 77. Vizeadmiral Kieseritzky, Admiral Black Sea, commanded the German naval forces.

On the Kerch Peninsula, October 1943

StuG Abteilung 191 after evacuating the Kuban bridgehead assembled at Keneges near Leninskoye. 2 Battery, which had been the last fighting unit with penal battalion zbV 560 holding the last bridgehead, 'Ulm' position, loaded aboard naval ferries at Ilyich at midnight and landed on 9 October without casualties on the Kerch coast. The battalion was brought out at the same time by assault boats. The Abteilung was reunited, but because of lack of space the batteries were scattered among various localities.

1 Battery and the Abteilung workshop were transferred to Novaya-Nikolayevka, 2 Battery lodged at Hirschdorf. The Abteilung was assigned to V Armeekorps Command as from 9 October and was at that time the only armoured unit on the Crimea. The damaged StuGs and vehicles were repaired as quickly as possible, shortages replaced and the personnel brought up to establishment strength. The new surgeon assigned to the Abteilung was Berliner Assistenzarzt, Leutnant (Med.) Dr Henry Gozdz, who soon fitted in.

The period of rest for the Abteilung did not last long. On 21 October 3 Battery had received the order to proceed to the coast of Feodosia where Russian attempts at landings were reported by the Armee. The landing craft had been under fire from artillery and flak and forced to turn back to the open sea. The StuGs of 3 Battery were not involved and returned to the bivouac site. From here the Abteilung Staff, Staff Battery and 3 Battery were transferred to Kongrat in the Feodosia area.

The first alarm at 17 Armee HQ heralded the first crisis. The Crimea was cut off from the mainland, and in the Kerch sector signs of a Russian landing from the Bay of Taman were detected. The increasing adjustment fire from heavy Russian artillery, the grouping up of boats at Kossa Tchushka and at Taman, and the growing activity by Russian aircraft against German artillery and infantry positions indicated this.

On 26 October V Armeekorps was instructed to transfer 50 Inf.Div. to the mainland front. On 27 October Grenadier-Regt 123 took off aboard Ju 52 transport aircraft from Vladislavovka for the lower Dnieper. Bringing up other parts of 50 Inf.Div. from the Feodosia coast took rather longer.

Defence at the Tartar Wall, Perekop and Siwash, 31 October–23 November 1943

While 50 Inf.Div. was in the process of moving out on 31 October, the oral order arrived from 49 Gebirgskorps that 50 Inf.Div. Staff was to proceed immediately, with all troops ready for departure, to 49 Gebirgskorps for action at Perekop. Russian units had wheeled towards the Crimea. The German defences at Perekop consisted only of hastily assembled forces under Generalmajor Weber. These were a Slovak training battalion, the III/Bergmann (Azerbaijani) and companies of construction pioneers. 9 Flak.Div. had two 8.8-cm batteries in emplacements at the Tartar Wall.

On 30 October when the Russian tank spearhead surfaced in the flat terrain it was engaged by the flak batteries and stopped. The flak armoured train *Muhr*, coming from Voinka, joined in the defensive battle and over the next few hours the race for Perekop began.

At once 50 Inf.Div. took over the protection of the Perekop Narrows, Tchongar and Genitshesk with the following units attaching to Gruppe Sixt:

(1) 336 Inf.Div. under Generalmajor Kunze, command post at Karadsha, about 20 kilometres north-west of Dshankoy. This division had been hit hard in the fighting for Melitopol and consisted only of infantry battalions without heavy weapons.

(2) All German forces at the Tartar Wall, and elements of 50 Inf.Div. on their way, came under the Battle Commander of Perekop, General Weber, command post Armyansk. Grenadier-Regt 123 was already operational with 6 Armee.

(3) 10 Romanian Inf.Div. in the right-hand sector of the Sivash front, 19 Romanian Inf.Div. on the Tchigary dam and the Arabat Peninsula, and 9 Romanian Cavalry Division on coastal protection along the west coast, were attached to 49 Gebirgskorps.

On 31 October a strong force of Russian armour attacked the Tartar Wall. Our flak batteries destroyed a number of these tanks but under concentrated tank fire the flak batteries were forced to pull back. Towards evening sixteen enemy tanks with accompanying infantry crossed the Tartar Wall at the northern end of Armyansk, where they were stopped by artillery fire. In the to and fro of the defensive fighting, the emplacements of II/Art.Regt 42 were overrun by the Russians. On the night of 1 November, III/Grenadier-Regt 122 arrived at Armyansk and went on the counter-offensive as soon as its troops disembarked from the train. The battalion recaptured the lost artillery emplacements and erected a new line of resistance north of Armyansk. During the night the Russians added to the force which had broken through and built a kind of bridgehead over the Tartar Wall.

In the evening Generalleutnant Sixt, CO of 50 Inf.Div., arrived at Armyansk. With his Staff officers he gathered up stragglers and units in retreat and placed them into new defensive positions.

On the morning of 31 October, 2 Battery/StuG Abteilung received from its CO the order to proceed north to Bagerov and load aboard a railway transport. On the night of 1 November the battery arrived at Armyansk. Its infantry occupied the defensive position north of Armyansk. Together with flak batteries and the flak armoured train *Muhr* they halted the Russian advance. A number of Russian tanks were destroyed, the survivors drove back under cover, and the infantry dug in.

On the night of 2 November further elements of 50 Inf.Div. arrived at Armyansk. The following morning the Russians left the 3-kilometre-deep bridgehead with reinforcements including twenty-five tanks and accompanying infantry to make the decisive attack on Armyansk, but were unable to overcome StuGs, anti-tank and flak batteries and the armoured train. The main battle line in the eastern section of the Tartar Wall was also held by the battalions of Grenadier-Regt 121.

Simultaneously with the attack in Armyansk on 2 November, Russian units crossed the 3-kilometre-wide Sivash lake and invested Karanki, Ashkadan and Tarchan, against weak resistance from elements of 10 Romanian Inf.Div. The aim of these forces was to block off the road and railway at Ishun and Voinka. This tying-off of the important traffic arteries would threaten the Perekop defences from the rear. Generalleutnant Sixt therefore saw that he was obliged to halt at Voinka those forces which had orders to proceed to Armyansk and from Voinka to counter-attack the narrows at Tarchan and Tomashevka. On 2 November elements of 336 Inf.Div. and a Romanian infantry battalion had advanced via Tomashevka into the narrows. The German battle group in the Tarchan Narrows had gone well forward to take Tarchan and the heights to the north of it. Because he did not have the forces for the expanding battle sector,

2/StuG Abteilung 191 was drawn away from Armyansk and added to the battle group with 1/'Bergmann' commanded by Major Kuhr.

The advance went ahead smoothly and towards evening the battle group dug in. On 3 November Battle Group Oberst Beetz reached the heights of Karanki in a counter-attack and recaptured the town on 5 November. The narrows north of it were closed down while at the same time the left side of the battle group shut down the narrows at Urshin and Tarchan. Thus the Russian landing head on the Tchigary peninsula was firmly in our hands again. It was not possible to destroy the landing head completely, however, because Russian attacks at the Tartar Wall tied down our troops there.

In order to close the breach in the Tartar Wall, the advance to the Tchigary dam set for 6 November was called off and a counter-attack by 2 Battery prepared.

3 Battery was suddenly withdrawn from the Kerch defensive front, loaded up at Bagerov and unloaded at Ishun in the north. It reached Uchvostock overland and occupied quarters.

In the early morning of 6 November our two wing-assault units at the Tartar Wall moved out without artillery preparation. 2 Battery StuGs supported the advance north-east of Armyansk, linking up with Grenadier-Regt 121. Both assault groups were aiming to meet at 'Treffpunkt Zitadelle' with Group Kassner, Pioneer Battalion 73 and II/Grenadier-Regt 121, which had made good progress from the east. Hauptmann Daerr's Pioneer Companie took the Zitadelle by storm but the advance of Oberst Beetz's group (Pioneer Battalion 71, I/Grenadier-Regt 122 and two training battalions) was halted by damage to the railway tracks. Therefore Kassner and Beetz never met up and the plan of attack was ruined. Gruppe Adam left Armyansk too late for the attack to the north against the Russian forces at the Tartar Wall. The attack had to be broken off because of the heavy casualties sustained. Over thirty enemy tanks were destroyed, but the enemy was too strong in the territory. StuGs of 2 StuG Abteilung 191 alone destroyed twenty-seven Russian tanks for the loss of one StuG hit by anti-tank fire and burned out.

Korps ordered, 'Cease attack and expansion of goals reached'. 2 Battery remained as the only armoured unit at Armyansk. Over the next few days the German units were organized into the new Perekop front, and in mid-November 50 Inf.Div. finally took over the defence of the Perekop Narrows. Later 336 Inf.Div. took over all Romanian sectors on the Sivash front.

3 Battery StuG Abteilung 191 was loaded aboard a railway transport at Voinka on 11 November and arrived next day at Bagerov station. The StuGs

and vehicles drove straight from the station into the new operational area of Kerch–Bulganak. 2 Battery took part in the defensive fighting in the north of the Crimea and was not returned to the Kerch front until 23 November. On 27 and 28 November Grenadier-Regt 121 fought off a fresh Russian attack at the Tartar Wall, and enemy thrusts along the Sivash front were also repelled by the German defences. As a precaution the interception positions at Ishun and Tchatyrlyk had been developed, but for lack of numbers the Germans could do nothing to remove the Russian bridgeheads at the Tartar Wall and on the Tchigary peninsula. Over Christmas it remained relatively quiet.

On 8 December 1943 Armee HQ issued an Armee Order of the Day to Army High Command (AOK) 17, Abteilung IIa which read:

(1) In the period from 1 to 23 November 1943 under the leadership of Battery Commander Oberleutnant Berg, with exemplary operational readiness and devotion to duty 2 Battery of StuG Abteilung 191 played an outstanding part in the repelling of all heavy enemy attacks on the Perekop front. In defence and counter-attack it provided the heavily engaged infantry with appreciable relief and effective help.

In particular it had the following successes by destroying:

30 tanks (27 T-34, 2 Kw-1, 1 assault gun)

9 heavy anti-tank guns

6 medium anti-tank guns

2 light anti-tank guns

5 light infantry guns

11 heavy machine guns

8 heavy mortars

37 anti-tank rifles

1 motor car.

I express my special recognition to the valiant battery commander and crews for their achievements in this period of time.

(2) The Commander-in-Chief of Army Group A expresses to all troops of 98 Inf. Div., 6 Romanian Cavalry Division, and to the crews of 1 Fliegerkorps and the naval forces of the Kriegsmarine his special recognition for the outstanding achievements in attack and defence at Fortress Crimea on the Eastern Front.

Signed Jaenecke, General of Pioneers.

The author Hauptwachtmeister Bruno Bork commanded a StuG during various operations in the Kuban and was seriously wounded. Here he is seen posing by a parked StuG in the Kuban region, 1943. The StuG has additional frontal armour attached.

A StuG in the Kuban area, crew not identified. This panzer has no additional armour.

Here it can be seen clearly that the track cover has a 15- to 20-cm overhang beyond the hull. No supports are visible for aprons.

Oberleutnant Egon Pantel (German Cross in Gold, 2 September 1943) meeting his brother Helmut in the Kuban bridgehead.

Hauptmann Wolfgang Tenner, Staff Battery commander and from 1944 3 Battery commander. He was awarded the German Cross in Gold from 16 September 1943.

A StuG of the Abteilung from another perspective.

StuG Abteilung 191 suffered many losses in the heavy fighting between 22 and 24 July 1943. This damaged StuG has a section of 'home-made' additional armour that has been crushed. One metal plate (1) was welded to the outer side of the track cover and the hollow area created filled with concrete (2).

Hauptmann Müller with an unknown Army general inspecting the wreck of a StuG. Parts of the structure and drive shaft were hurled free when the StuG was hit.

Surveying the battlefield after the fighting on 22 and 24 July 1943. StuG wreckage is strewn everywhere.

Shell impact damage to this StuG included the concrete stiffening. It is not know who authorized these innovations or which workshop carried them out.

Hauptmann Müller leaving the Command bus.

The general being driven away in his Kfz 15 Staff car after inspecting the battlefield.

A Propaganda Company man filming the scene. These companies had the task of reporting events at the front in words, photos and films.

A well-camouflaged StuG in a leafy
wood.

The pennant gives no clue as to the
'Buffalo' Abteilung.

The external aerial foot on a Kfz 15.

Hauptmann Paco Herrmann deputized
for Hauptmann Müller during the latter's
leave from the end of October until end
of November 1943.

From left to right: Oberleutnant Korsen, Hauptmann Müller and (probably) adjutant Leutnant Koch. The additional plates on this StuG can be seen to be thinly welded at the seam.

A half-track ammunition transport vehicle 'Maultier' (Mule) after a direct hit. Hermann Röhm stated that although the ammunition was catapulted in all directions by the hit, none of it exploded.

Unteroffizier Hahn, the author Hauptwachtmeister Bork, Oberwachtmeister Gruber and Wachtmeister Heinz.

The fiercely contested town of Novorossisk on the Black Sea. In the background are the Caucasian mountains.

Gutted Black Sea villas at Novorossisk. The town and harbour changed hands frequently between the Russians and Germans. The death toll here was high.

Vineyards by Abrau Lake, Kuban
bridgehead, September 1943.

Lake Abrau, Kuban bridgehead.

Hermann Röhm grape-tasting in a Lake Abrau vineyard.

Hermann Röhm ashore after a drive in the lake to wash the Kfz 15. The radio aerial was unscrewed, the steering paddle can be seen at his right hand.

The Kfz 15 with all radio equipment removed.

View of the extensive vineyards around the lake.

Willi Schwerdt preparing for an amphibious drive.

September 1943: Oberleutnant Korsen in conversation with Hauptmann Müller shortly before the evacuation of the Kuban bridgehead.

Hauptmann Müller at the wheel of a Schwimmkübel amphibious car. The vehicle had good qualities for the purpose. The reserve wheel forward is absent.

Three StuGs parked by the wayside awaiting orders to proceed to the ferry for the Kerch crossing. The raised side armour plating up to the base of the commander's hatch is clearly seen.

First of the loading up, late summer 1943.

Hermann Röhm on a ferry, November 1943.

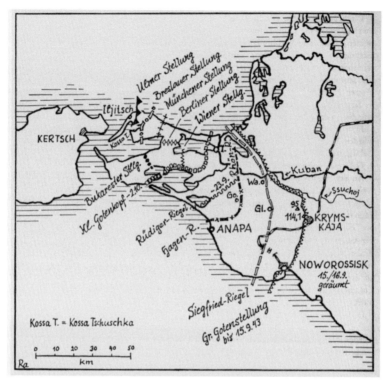

Map of the defensive positions in the Kuban bridgehead between
16 September and 9 October 1943.

A StuG III Ausf. F crossing a pioneer bridge.

Wooden beams and planks for bunker- and bridge-building were shipped to the Crimea, which has little woodland. Notice two MFP naval ferries in the background.

The narrow-gauge railway used for the transport of materials on the Taman peninsula.

The fate that awaited anything that could not be dismounted and transported out.

A Famo 18-tonne tug with an observation car in tow.

1 Battery StuGs aboard a naval ferry, October 1943. The StuG at the left has side aprons to protect the gun from lateral fire.

Pause for a smoke on the Kerch peninsula. The reserve wheel is just visible below the Kfz 15 running board.

Men of the Abteilung map-reading near an old windmill, Kerch.

An Oberwachtmeister posing against a StuG.

Great interest in a captured T-34.

The original Russian identification symbol can be seen in the triangle on the turret side of the captured T-34.

Hauptmann Paco Hoffmann tried out the driving qualities of the T-34. The photo gives an idea of the thickness of the armour and shows the detail of the driver's hatch.

The Russian T-34 arrived in large numbers at the front in 1941/42 and was the principal opponent of the StuG. This 1943 model was captured on the Kuban bridgehead and transported to Kerch. Provisional German 'Balken' crosses indicate the tank as a German trophy.

Defence of the Kerch Peninsula, 1 to 20 November 1943

When the race to Perekop began during the course of 30 October 1943, German reconnaissance reports piled up at 17 Armee HQ. From these it was obvious that the Russian coastal army was preparing to jump across the Kerch Strait.

On 31 October three large ships on a westerly heading were reported coming from the port of Taman with heavy air support. German artillery broke up the formation, the ships made smoke and disappeared.

Feigned enemy landings were made against the north-east coast on 31 October while the Russian 386 Naval Infantry Battalion went aboard landing craft at Taman. Other elements of the Russian 18 Army also prepared to embark. On the night of 1 November the battalion landing craft approached the Kerch coast at Eltigen and for an hour from 0230 hrs the Russian artillery fired across the Kerch Strait on targets at Jenikale, Kerch and Eltigen.

386 Battalion came ashore at Eltigen and overwhelmed the 6 Romanian Cavalry Division defences. Sector-Commander Kerch South, Oberst Faulhaber, at once roused the resting Reserve Battalion I/Grenadier-Regt 282. Their counter-attack threw the Russians back to the cross on the Heights of Eltigen before the enemy resistance hardened and the push faltered. Prisoners stated that the Eltigen landing head was to have been extended by up to 10 to 15 kilometres in the first night as the springboard for their 18 Army. Their 56 Army was to have created a base north of Kerch.

Overnight, advanced Russian forces attempted to expand the landing head while the Germans brought up fresh reserves in the attempt to prevent it. Neither side was decisively successful. Russian air superiority was oppressive.

After a brief situation conference V Armeekorps brought in its Korps reserves. 1 Battery StuG Abteilung 191 (Oberleutnant Schumacher) set out at full speed for the Russian landing area at Eltigen. 3 Battery was loaded aboard a train transport at Feodosia for Kerch where they unloaded in a suburb and set up their readiness area on the north-west side of town. The crews were forced to seek shelter in cellars and the ruins of houses against the enemy artillery fire and persistent air attacks.

With the support of 1 Battery StuGs the landing head was substantially narrowed. Fresh Russian troops now landed with heavy infantry weapons and light anti-tank guns. Pioneer Battalion 46 and 11/Grenadier-Regt 282 came forward as reinforcement.

During the night our StuGs occupied the departure position with infantry protection. The gun crews were ordered to maintain radio silence and await the infantry reinforcements. Our CO made sure that StuG commanders received maps divided into quadrants to enable aimed shooting in darkness or poor visibility.

Oberst Faulhaber commanded the German-Romanian forces. His opposite number was the Russian, Colonel Gladkow. The Russian 18 Army tried to make the decisive thrust at Eltigen. With fresh forces on the morning of 3 November they caused I/Grenadier-Regt 282 to fall back but the planned breakthrough to the north-west came to nothing.

In the morning our StuGs came under fire from Russian naval guns. Visibility was very poor in the misty conditions. After the infantry from Grenadier-Regt 282 arrived, the counter-attack began.

After we had travelled 3 kilometres our StuGs came under fire which strengthened, causing the infantry to dig in. Three StuGs drove to the high point of our infantry in order to obtain a better field of fire. It was not advisable to go any further, for damage to tracks was likely in the ruins and debris. An enemy trench with Russian troops was discovered. The range was too short to fire their cannons and so two StuGs, covered by the third, drove along the trench throwing hand grenades from the commanders' hatches into the trench. This operation was successful. The enemy fire against our StuGs was fortified by mortars and anti-tank rifles, requiring cover to be sought to elude visual detection. The attack was eventually called off because of our infantry losses.

Towards midday visibility improved. The StuGs of Weisgerber and Girschkowski noticed landing craft at about 1,400 metres distance protected by a heavily armed gunboat. Both StuGs opened fire using delay-fuse and armour-piercing shells alternately against the targets. Hits were observed on landing craft and the gunboat. Suddenly our StuGs came under heavy fire. Weisgerber's gun received a hit on the gunlaying equipment, the optic being destroyed; the gunlayer Obergefreiter Horak received wounds to neck and shoulder. Both StuGs were then recalled by radio to the departure area. After negotiating 'Spanish rider' wire obstacles, they returned to the departure area which was now being pounded by naval guns offshore. 1 Battery remained several days in this position in order to provide the infantry with moral support. The landing head at Eltigen was now blockaded by German motor-minesweepers and

Schnellboote (fast torpedo boats – S-boats or MTBs) operating from Kamysh Burun. StuG commander Weisgerber reported on a new operation thus:

> We were just celebrating the birthday of a group leader of the infantry when we received new orders. With four StuGs we drove up to the old position in the height. Our infantry had been holding it and were visibly overjoyed that we would be cruising around in their neighbourhood. Our flak was shooting out to sea without pause. The Soviets were searching for the S-boats of our Kriegsmarine with searchlights, and our side was doing the same, looking for Russians ships, and whenever one was caught in the beam the flak fired at it. It was the devil's handiwork.
>
> We received the order by radio, 'Cleanse plan square X with infantry at first light!' I was also informed by radio that there would be six StuGs in action.
>
> At the time ordered we attacked with infantry and threw the Russians out. There were no enemy anti-tank guns present, only Russian naval infantry and mortars.
>
> In the grey mist of morning I saw the Russian gunboat again: it was listing, but still trying to fire at our StuGs. I informed my neighbouring gun, Wachtmeister Kühn, by radio of the sighting. We broke through a wall together and saw the gunboat about 800 metres ahead of us. We scored one hit after another on the gunboat and the effect of our projectiles was devastating. The boat exploded, fiery cascades lit up the entire surroundings and then through our optics we saw groups of Russian infantry lying on the beach. We opened fire on them with percussion-fuse projectiles and they soon vanished. Suddenly they returned with anti-tank rifles and later anti-tank guns. I spotted a 4.5-cm anti-tank gun as it was changing position and scored a direct hit.
>
> We remained with our infantry for the time being in the patch of ruins until receiving new orders by radio. Some 100 metres from us the Russian naval infantry had broken through. We understood the situation at once and fired with all three guns at anything which moved. Without our support the infantry then sealed off the area and cleared it.
>
> Towards daybreak Russian Boston bombers with many Yak fighters as escort came over in four waves and practised carpet bombing. This caused the StuGs no casualties, but not so the infantry and flak. The bombers were followed by several waves of Ilyushin-2 aircraft which attacked using phosphorous rockets. This forced us to change position to higher ground because the grass was burning all around us. From our new viewpoint over the sea we sighted Russian ships, but these were

too far out for our gunnery. Besides, we were forbidden to shoot because of a shortage of ammunition. Our CO, Hauptmann Müller visited us frequently and said that we would soon have the task of cleansing Russian bridgehead at Eltigen.

Over the next few days we were very active, either on security work or making short attacks. Our StuGs were scattered far and wide across the terrain. In order to get to them one had to risk life and limb because the terrain was open country, and anything which moved on it attracted immediate enemy fire. It was rare that we got out of our StuGs. Meanwhile we heard that the commander's StuG was missing. Oberleutnant Schumacher and his crew failed to return from a reconnaissance mission.

The Russian bridgehead at Eltigen could probably have been narrowed by our existing forces but not cleared out. An attack by the Romanians on the Eltigen landing head on November 1943 was not successful.

On several nights German light naval forces based at Kamysh Burun sailed for the northern part of the Kerch Strait to lay mines but were unable to pass the heavily armed island of Kossa Tusla. Simultaneous with the landings by Russian naval infantry at Eltigen, on 2 November infantry of the Russian 56 Army boarded landing craft of the Russian Fleet. That evening the long-range Russian artillery batteries, aided by their air force, pummelled the Kerch coast to soften it up for attack. The barrage lasted two hours, a hail of shells and aerial bombs falling on Kerch, Yenikale, Mayak and the 5-kilometre wide coastline. When the artillery fire suddenly stopped, Russian infantry units sprang ashore at Yenikale and Mayak.

The German coastal defences were overrun and wiped out. The brunt was borne by II/Grenadier-Regt 290 protecting Yenikale and the adjoining III Battalion at Mayak. As a result of the critical situation to which this gave rise, 98 Inf.Div. Command decided to occupy the heights east of Baksy and Dshankoy during the night and have another look next morning.

The Russians did not make much progress at Yenikale. III/Grenadier-Regt 282 bent its left wing back. The remnants of II/Grenadier-Regt 290, the divisional battalion which had been brought up, and 1/Pioneer Battalion 198 erected a new front from Dshankoy to Height 102 to Kapkany which resisted all attacks made against it.

Not far from Mayak, 8 Battery/Art.Regt 198 set up a circular defence to protect the positions until morning, when they kept firing until out of ammunition and then destroyed the two still intact guns. The survivors headed west with their last rounds of small-arms fire. True to their objective, this battery was the breakwater against which the Soviets battled in vain and were thus denied their success that night. On the morning of 3 November the extent of the landings could be surveyed. At Yenikale and Mayak the incursion proceeded apace. The Russian Air Force was present in waves and wiped out every nest of resistance. In the Kerch area the battle raged along a 5-kilometre-long front. The cohesion of the German defensive front had been shattered.

The Russian main thrust was concentrated against Baksy and Height 175; a second centre of effort was developing against Height 102 at Dshankoye. 3 Battery Abteilung 191 at readiness at Kerch went into action with I/Grenadier-Regt 290 south of Baksy and stalled the Russian advance. All other enemy attacks were beaten off. By the evening of 3 November, the Russian 56 Army had won a bridgehead 8 kilometres broad and 5 kilometres deep at Baksy. It was clear, however, that the Russians were exhausted and the force of their attacks was abating, and they did not resume the offensive until 9 November, by which time reserves had strengthened the German defences.

On 9 November the Russian offensive at Baksy continued, but was parried from the heights. At that they switched the centre of effort of their attack to the north, where they threw back 11 Romanian Inf. Battalion from the high ground. During the night the divisional reserve and one platoon of 1 StuG Abteilung 191 came forward and on 10 November reoccupied the line abandoned by the Romanians. In the late afternoon a breakthrough was reported at the I/Grenadier-Regt 290 sector through which the Russians advanced towards Adshim Ushkay, and on the morning of 11 November three Russian divisions, pouring out of the Baksy region, came across a gap which they widened on all sides. Adshim Ushkay was taken and now they wheeled towards Kerch. At the eastern end of Kerch a new resistance line was set up with the remnants of Grenadier-Regt 290.

Grenadier-Regt 123 (50 Inf.Div.), free at the Dnieper, was now flown to the Kerch front. At the same time the Russian advanced assault troops had reached the territory east of Bulganak and Heights 133.3 and 125.6. The Soviets thought that they had the breakthrough to the Crimea but they had not reckoned with Grenadier-Regt 123, which had just landed at Bagerov airfield. I Battalion was taken at once to Bulganak in a convoy of lorries and recaptured the heights there, and together with III Battalion in the north and II Feldausbildings-Regt 218 under training in the south, a firm line was established. The Russian intent to roll up the German front from both ends was therefore thwarted.

Bulganak now became the centre of effort for the Red Army. New units formed up to face the German front. The backbone of the German defence was initially StuG Abteilung 191 commanded by Major Müller. Later StuG Brigade 279 arrived in the Crimea from the northern theatre. StuG Abteilung 191 was used on the eastern and northern fronts, depending on the development of the situation.

On 12 November the Soviets attempted in vain to break through the German front at Bulganak. Two days later the Russians entered the fray with masses of armour. The hardest fighting yet for Bulganak began. In this sector III/Grenadier-Regt 123, which had just been flown in, was slotted between I/Grenadier-Regt 123 and I Battalion/Grenadier-Battalion 121. III Battalion was the dam against which all enemy attacks came to grief. Battalion CO Major Bärenfänger was the soul of the resistance. Nine enemy tanks were destroyed in his sector.

The weather improved such that on 16 November a greater deployment of Stukas and fighters over the Kerch area was possible. Several Stuka attacks on Baksy and other targets of the Russian bridgehead hampered movements. The new major offensive at Bulganak began on 20 November and the Soviets breached the main German defensive front south-east of Bulganak. The spearhead entered the town but was ejected by II/Grenadier-Regt 123 supported by elements of 3 Battery StuG Abteilung 191 with heavy losses in tanks. The StuG of Oberfähnrich Konietzko destroyed four T-34s. Enemy supporting tanks held back and then fell victim to the Stukas. The point of incursion was sealed by a counter-attack and the area cleared of Russian forces. This was the last serious Russian attack in November, and the Russians limited their efforts to testing the German main front line for weaknesses.

17 Armee never managed to destroy the Bulganak bridgehead and until the evacuation of the Crimea it remained a serious threat. In the long run the Armee could not keep two bridgeheads in check (Bulganak and Eltigen) and also prevent the enemy entering through Perekop or at other feared landing sites. The Armee had no more reserves. At Kerch they took a deep breath and then decided that the Eltigen bridgehead had to go, only this attack seemed to promise success. V Armeekorps was given the job of planning and carrying it out.

3 Battery StuG Abteilung191 was relieved from the Bulganak–Kerch defensive front by one platoon of 1 Battery and sent to Ssaraimin via Bagerov. Here they settled in quarters and recovered their strength for further efforts. From 26 November until 2 December 1943 they held field exercises with 6 Romanian Cavalry Division. The riders received the last polish, their horses remained in the stables. They were a proud outfit and they promised, after the exercises in the field, that they could launch a successful attack. Meanwhile the Abteilung Staff and Staff Battery were transferred on 20 November from Kongrat via Stary Krim-Feodosia to Marfovka. Oberleutnant Laubmeier, recently arrived from Germany, took command of 1 Battery, succeeding Oberleutnant Schumacher, missing in action since the beginning of November during the narrowing of the Eltigen bridgehead.

The Eltigen Bridgehead, 4–11 December 1943

V Armeekorps had ordered 4 December 1943 to be the day for the attack. The responsibility of destroying the Eltigen bridgehead fell upon 6 Romanian Cavalry Division, some units of 98 Inf.Div. and StuG Abteilung 191. The bridgehead was a rectangle 800 x 3,000 metres in extent.

On 3 December readiness area and departure points were occupied by our assault troops. The attack was to be supported by German and Romanian artillery, aerial forces and flak. The plan of attack for the Abteilung set out by Oberleutnant Hoffmann was as follows:

1   Battery would support the advance from the south to the coast, carrying it forward northwards.
2   Battery would thrust from the south to the north-east, supporting 1 Battery.
3   Battery would push frontally to the centre of the bridgehead and separate it into two halves.

At 0630 hrs on 4 December our artillery barrage began and the attack on the Russian lines commenced at 0700 hrs. The Soviets responded at once by laying a barrage from their heavy artillery situated on the Taman peninsula that was intended to halt the German advance. Russian fighter aircraft supported the defence of the bridgehead using phosphorous rockets and their cannons. A large number of enemy aircraft were shot down by our flak and other guns used in anti-aircraft roles.

The German attack with Romanian support made little early progress. The Russian ground defences – anti-tank guns, mortars and anti-tank rifles – sought the StuGs as the primary target from trenches, bunkers and ruined houses. 1 Battery StuGs supported by men of Pioneer Battalion 46 took on the anti-tank guns, mortars and landing craft first. The Romanians were daunted by the heavy defensive fire and the StuGs then attempted to carry out the attack with the pioneers alone. Fire was maintained on all enemy positions sighted until all weapons were silenced. The pioneers disarmed the mines ahead of the Russian positions and laid a corridor to guide the StuGs through. The slackening of enemy resistance now allowed them to proceed through the corridor and trenches and head for the commanding heights of Eltigen, which afforded a good panorama of the coast and the Russian landing beaches. On one path to this height we discovered the burned-out StuG of our former battery commander Oberleutnant Schumacher, who had fallen with his crew during the operation to shorten the breadth of the bridgehead.

From this height our StuGs were able to engage other nests of resistance and sank a large number of landing craft offshore. Then they rolled down to attack the positions from the east – therefore from the rear. Around 200 prisoners were taken and a huge quantity of ammunition seized. The StuGs of Oberleutnant Laubmeier's 1 Battery remained in these positions in order to prevent further Russian landings and also to protect the flank of 2 Battery using Romanian assault troops.

2 Battery led by Oberleutnant Berg, attacking from south to north with elements of 6 Romanian Cavalry Division, made no progress forward after the initial successes, the advance being brought to a standstill by extensive minefields and heavy defensive fire. The Romanians, having suffered many losses, could not continue. In the absence of the infantry escort, the StuGs had to pull back.

3 Battery commanded by Oberleutnant Hoffmann achieved no useful successes on the first day because the attack strip lay under heavy artillery fire and the air attacks were incessant. Here too the Romanian infantry did not remain with the StuGs and so the advance faltered. During the afternoon, while outside his StuG searching for an infantry officer, Oberfähnrich Konietzko

was seriously wounded. A despatch rider carried him across his back from the foremost front line. This much-liked colleague died of his wounds later in a military hospital.

The first day of the offensive against Eltigen had shown us that the bridgehead would not be taken so easily and the second day was equally fruitless due to the absence of Luftwaffe support.

Our CO Major Müller put together new directions of attack for 1 and 2 Batteries for 6 December.

3 Battery was to reach Eltigen and then wheel north. 1 Battery, coming from the west with one platoon, was to wheel south before reaching Eltigen and wipe out the remaining nests of resistance in the ruins. 2 Battery was to lead the attack from south to north, the aim still being to split the landing head into two halves.

The attack on 6 December went off well according to expectations. Stukas bombed ahead of our attack field again. StuGs and men of 6 Romanian Cavalry Division formed spearheads again from west and south. 1 Battery made a successful attack from west to east, knocked out some of the Russian defences behind the heights west of Eltigen and created the pre-conditions for splitting the bridgehead. On the last push, however, it lost two StuGs to anti-tank fire and engine damage. 3 Battery also had bad luck. Some of its StuGs were trapped in a minefield and became non-operational, Oberleutnant Hoffmann and five men, Herich, Roos, Niebergall, Klinger and Trojahn, were wounded. Nevertheless the battery fought through to Eltigen and found that the Romanians had occupied it. 2 Battery carried out its objective without casualties.

Russian Colonel Gladkow, commanding the Eltigen sector, saw what was afoot and with about 800 naval infantry he broke through the cordon in the north on the night of 7 December, overran a Romanian battery, forced his way into the old ruined fortifications as far as Mount Mithridat near Kerch, ejected the weak defences and installed himself in the position on the heights. Oberst Faulhaber gave the alarm readiness order and put together forces for the encirclement.

The last attacks by the StuG batteries were made on 7 December. 2 Battery was assembled and sent to Kerch to become involved in the fighting around Mount Mithridat. 3 Battery followed two days later. The attempts which had been made until then by Aufklärungs-Abteilung 150 and by elements of

I/Grenadier-Regt 282 and Pioneer Battalion 46 had found the Russian battle group stronger than expected. Because the StuGs were unable to engage the resistance nests on account of the rocky terrain, they sought them out systematically. The attack on the positions on the heights proceeded very slowly because the enemy had dug in well and was offering stubborn resistance. He was also being given air support and artillery protection from the Taman peninsula. Furthermore there were galleries through the mountains which led down to the precipitous coast.

The bitter fighting for Mithridat went on until 10 December. Few Russians were prepared to surrender; most fought to the last man. This bridgehead had become especially strong through further Russian landings at Kerch South, and 3 Battery coming from Eltigen was deployed here.

On the night of 10 December, 2 Battery stood north of Mithridat. Because it was no longer possible for the StuGs to do anything about the resistance nests, Battery Commander Oberleutnant Berg ordered StuG machine guns to be dismounted and under his leadership he attacked with his gun crews and accompanying infantry. In close combat the crest of the mount fell into German hands and shortly after midnight the last enemy positions on the mountain were ours. The enemy had had enough and the Eltigen landing head was defeated. Two thousand prisoners were taken. Along the beach at Eltigen the tally of craft captured or sunk was three gunboats, twenty-four landing craft and numerous motor launches and small craft.

For the Armee operationally this was not of great significance, but it was for the whole southern wing of the Eastern Front. If we had not captured this bridgehead it would not have been possible to have held the Crimea for so long. StuG Abteilung 191 under the command of Major Müller played a major part in the overthrow of the bridgehead at Eltigen. It took part in attacks and defence with the greatest commitment and energy. For this achievement by the Abteilung on 15 December, Major Müller was the 354th soldier of the Wehrmacht to be awarded the Oak Leaves to the Knight's Cross. Many decorations and promotions within the Abteilung were the reward for its operational readiness and bravery.

On 11 December with the support of the StuGs of 3 Battery, the remnants of Colonel Gladkow's force at Kerch South was surrendered with many prisoners taken. The colonel escaped in an assault boat.

Other Fighting at Kerch, 10 January–March 1944

After securing the area, the StuGs were withdrawn and the crews returned to quarters. On all Crimean fronts there was now a period of quiet. Snow and thaw interchanged. The Christmas festivities were planned by the batteries as before but not enjoyed as in previous years. The old circle of comrades had been much reduced by wounds, death or transfers. New reinforcements from the Reich were appearing all the time in order to replace the losses, and welcomed into the 'Buffalo community'.

The front remained quiet at New Year. The German defensive front had been extended and reinforced. It now followed this line at Kerch: Kerch harbour–Keteries river–north railway station–brickworks–Heights 30.9, 133.3, 95.1 and 165.5–Tarchan–Azov Sea coast.

After days of fog and rain the weather improved on 9 January 1944. The Soviets were preparing another strike against Kerch. On 10 January they made a surprise attack on the Bulganak bridgehead between Height 125.6 and the Azov coast. III/Grenadier-Regt 290 broke apart on this front. It was only the beginning of a new offensive and soon extended over the entire northern sector. Battle Group Biermann at Bulganak held, but Height 125.6 was lost to the Russians. At the same time Russian forces landed at Cape Tarchan and captured Heights 88.5, 136, 165.5 and 115.5. This meant that all the high ground south-east of Cape Tarchan was in Russian hands for the first time. The German forces here (Grenadier-Regt 290) were ejected and after daybreak an attack by fighter-bombers forced out the others. It could be seen that the second breakthrough would ensue at Kerch for a large-scale pincer movement against the German defences.

After rolling up the German main front line at Height 125.6, a bitter battle raged for Heights 133.3 and 95.1. The intervention of III/Grenadier-Regt 123 under Major Bärenfänger was decisive, for which he received the Swords to his Knight's Cross.

V Armeekorps recognized the Soviet intention and brought up all reserves into the defence. On 10 January at midday the batteries of StuG Abteilung 191 were sent out. The Abteilung command post was transferred initially to Katerles, later to Skasilov-Fontan. Our CO placed the batteries at the centre of effort of the German battalions. Thus 3 Battery fought in the Cape Tarchan region and 1 Battery with Fusilier Battalion 198 at Bulganak around Height 133.3. After a struggle lasting twenty-one hours all high land on the Sea of Azov with the exception of Height 115.5 was in German hands again. The StuGs played a major role in this. Despite blizzards and bitter cold, the artillery, infantry and StuGs fought with great determination against the numerically greatly superior enemy but the casualties were heavy. On 11 January Unteroffizier Henne and Obergefreiter Lederer fell. The StuG of Oberwachtmeister Linke was hit and there were also wounded here.

The Russians resumed on 12 January after a quiet night. Their Garde-Infantry Corps rolled over II and III/Grenadier-Regt 290 and won territory. Only a few men managed to make their way back to the west. Many remained behind in medical bunkers and rooms and were captured, among them four doctors with medical orderlies. Both battalions lost two-thirds of their former establishment. Only on Height 95.1 did elements of I Battalion resist all Russian attacks. The remnants of Grenadier-Regt 290 and Fusilier Battalion 198 set to work putting up a new resistance line.

2 Battery of Abteilung 191 hastened to assist as the Russians with greatly superior numbers of infantry supported by tanks aimed to break through against a Romanian battalion. This threatened that the German forces north of it would be forced to the sea and encircled. Because the situation in this sector was totally confused that night and chaos threatened, it so happened that the StuGs of 2 Battery had joined a Russian column of infantry unrecognized for twenty minutes. Not until the StuG commanders became unhappy and fired up a flare to which the response was not correct did they realize their situation. The guns opened fire and sought their targets at will. As no German reserves were at hand, Hauptmann Berg decided that he should bring the Russian advance to a standstill with his battery. Within a few minutes leading his panzers, Berg had personally destroyed two Russian tanks, the other panzers three more and an enemy self-propelled gun. This stopped the Russian advance and Berg now took the brave decision to use this success.

Taking command of a Romanian reserve company, he led the men on foot towards the Russians. After a hard struggle control was regained over the main front line; Berg saw the opportunity to force home his advantage and without infantry support led his battery against the wavering enemy, inflicting on them serious casualties. His battery destroyed fifty-five enemy tanks that day, of which Berg himself accounted for twelve.

His personal contribution and fast decision-making in threatening situations in the fighting on Kerch was one of the reasons for his award of the Knight's Cross. Notification was given to Berg on 6 April 1944 and he received the decoration from the hands of the Commander-in-Chief, Generaloberst Jaenecke at Sevastopol on 21 April.

On 13 and 14 January 1944, heavy fighting concentrated around the Heights 133.3 and 165.5 and the main battle line was held with difficulty. The order to recapture Height 115.5 was issued under the cover name *Seestern* with the support of 1 and 2 Batteries of Abteilung 191. The operation was a failure, with high casualties. The attacking infantry were unable to overcome the strong Russian defence and the two StuG batteries also suffered losses. Leutnant Mludez and Unteroffizier Asshof were seriously wounded, Obergefreiter Beck was killed inside his StuG by an anti-tank round.

Towards midnight on 22 January the Russian artillery took the eastern side of Kerch and the harbour under fire, which increased to barrage strength. At 0200 hrs III/Grenadier-Regt 282, holding the position, was attacked and overrun while Russian units made landings in the harbour behind the southern wing of the battalion. The entire southern wing of the German front at Kerch then collapsed. The highway to the port was defended and held by elements of Pioneer Battalion 198 with the support of 3 Battery StuGs. General Gareis (98 Inf.Div.) reported to the Commanding General, Allmendinger, that his division was bleeding to death. Since the Korps had no reserves, Allmendinger saw himself compelled to insist that 98 Inf.Div. held its sector of the front. There followed very heated discussions.

Meanwhile 73 Inf.Div. had been relieved from its quiet position at Melevoye on the Dnieper and flown to the Crimea. I/Grenadier-Regt 186 and Pioneer Battalion 173 were the first units to land at Kerch and their timely arrival averted a catastrophe by occupying a new line of resistance and holding it.

A lull now settled over the Kerch front. The units of 98 Inf.Div. were rested alternately. General Gareis was 'given a sick note' and sent back to Germany. On 8 February 1944 Oberst Reinhardt took over the remnants of Gareis's butchered infantry division.

After the fall of Nikopol, the Russians spared their units in the Crimea. It was bound to fall sooner or later. In February and March the Kerch front remained quiet. Our StuG batteries (apart from one alarm platoon) were withdrawn from the defensive front for R&R. This was the lull before the storm!

On 28 February 1944 StuG Abteilung 191 was officially declared to be a Brigade.

On 27 March 3 Battery was loaded up at Bagerov and early next morning the rail transport arrived at Vladislavovka, where the StuGs were unloaded and made for Kahisan, where they occupied quarters.

In Operation *Adler* the Parpatch position was thought of as the first line of defence after the withdrawal from Kerch. 3 Battery was to cooperate with SS units in this defence. For this purpose exercises were to be carried out and began on 3 April 1944.

The battle for Kerch called upon all German units not absolutely essential elsewhere. 17 Armee had construction troops renovate the old fortifications and installations at Sevastopol. Preparations were made for the planned timely removal of divisional supplies so that in the case of an alarm the infantry would have all the transport room it needed to reach Sevastopol in great leaps. The Armee would determine removals from the Crimea. Even Marshal Antonescu insisted on the evacuation in order to have his troops available for the defence of Bessarabia. Hitler brought him round, however, by promising to strengthen the defence of the Crimea by sending fresh units.

On the mainland the front was moving ever more westwards. The town of Cherson on the lower course of the Dnieper had been abandoned by the Germans. Now 4 Ukrainian Front was preparing an assault on the Crimean Narrows and had put together two armoured corps and eighteen divisions for the purpose. At the same time the Russian coastal army in the Kerch bridgehead was ready to attack to the west. On 30 March 1944 Feldmarschall von Manstein, Commander-in-Chief of Army Group South, now renamed Army Group 'Nordukraine' and Feldmarschall von Kleist, Commander-in-Chief of Army Group A, now renamed Army Group 'Südukraine', were relieved and replaced by Generaloberst Model and Generaloberst Schörner. 17 Armee in the Crimea now became part of Army Group Südukraine commanded by Schörner. The evacuation of Nikolayev meant another supplies port lost for the Crimea. Once again Marshal Antonescu asked for the evacuation of the Crimea because it seemed certain that the last port, Odessa, would soon be lost. Hitler refused.

Final Battle of the Crimea, April 1944

The remnants of the XXXXIX Gebirgskorps Divisions still occupied the Tchatyrlyk position. At dusk, Battle Group Hoppe carried out spirited thrusts against the Russian armoured spearheads in order to create time and space for the right wing of the Korps to move off to the south. This it did on the night of 12 April, Hoppe providing the rearguard, and occupied the B-position at Dzurti.

Because of poor signals communication, 50 Inf.Div. and large sections of 111 and 336 Inf.Divs had remained stationary at Tchatyrlyk. The situation there became critical when on the morning of 13 April fighting flared up on their front and the enemy made incursions. The retreat had to be diverted to the 'Gneisenau' position. The three divisions moved out, the retreat being partly managed with columns of lorries, constantly defending against Russian attacks on the flanks. The battered German divisions reached the B-position at Dzurti on the night of 13 April.

A few 3 Battery StuGs protecting the Voinka–Dshankay Rollbahn suddenly realized that they were alone except for Russian armoured and motorized units in the distance heading south, with StuGs keeping a wary distance behind. On their return, the few StuGs became involved in skirmishes. Those guns no longer in working order were abandoned and destroyed with explosives, the crews then acting as infantry protection. At Aibar they met German motorized units including some 3 Battery StuGs. Major Hoppe was now able to increase his battle group to fourteen StuGs and a light flak Abteilung which took over protection of the German column on the flanks.

Although the Soviets frequently surrounded the battle group, their forces must have been very light for the Germans always managed to break free in the night and continue through to dawn at a fast pace. On 13 April Hoppe detoured to Kadir-Bali to break an encirclement and release the German infantry trapped there. Returning in the afternoon to Tishi, Russian units were encountered. The StuG of Wachtmeister Lissmann received a hit, the commander receiving serious wounds; the StuG of Unteroffizier Thomas was hit by anti-tank gun fire and blew up, but not before the crew managed to get free.

In the evening the retreat continued southwards, Battle Group Hoppe bringing up the rear as before. Passing through the village of Avet, they came under fire, light flak Abteilung 86 and the men of the battle group replying as they drove by at high speed. No serious casualties were sustained. At

Kontugan farm they came across enemy forces again in a false flag event that was illegal under all conventions of warfare. Kappe had opened fire at once, but the other side raised the German warflag. Kappe ordered the ceasefire, which the Russians answered with a sudden concentration of surprise fire. The StuGs of Plath and Lissmann were hit and set aflame. This was a skilfully constructed Russian anti-panzer trap. It was destroyed using every StuG cannon and machine gun and every 2-cm flak gun of the Abteilung, and the German force then departed. Its fighting vehicles and lorries veered to the left and rejoined the battle group later.

Upon reaching the 'Gneisenau' position, our troops found it to be partially occupied by Russian forward forces and a struggle ensued, after which the Korps ordered its troops to retreat to Sevastopol via various intermediate positions.

On the night of 14 April the units of XXXXIX Gebirgskorps headed south, passed through the Alma Valley and set up in interception positions on the southern heights where Generalleutnant Sixt, commander of Battle Group Sixt, took command of 50 Inf.Div. once more.

The main thrust of the Russian pursuit lay on the Dshankoy–Simferopol railway line. Hauptmann Berg led the rearguard composed of 2 StuG Brigade 191. The StuGs were also here forced to fight spread out against Russian tank packs. On 13 April Berg reached the Sarabus airfield, the eastern pillar of the 'Gneisenau' position, which had to be held until the last stragglers arrived. In the morning the enemy attacked Sarabus, first in the north, then from west and east. Battle Group Sixt formed a hedgehog manoeuvre. First all the wounded were flown out from the airfield and then on the night of 14 April Battle Group Sixt broke out to the south-west and fought through via Bulganak, west of Simferopol, to the German forces. On this occasion 2 StuG Brigade 191 formed the spearhead.

On the afternoon of 13 April spearheads of Russian armour, which had previously gone around Sarabus, were waiting at Simferopol, from where they were driven out without a shot being fired and surrendered in the evening. Twelve hours previously Generaloberst Jaenecke had had his Staff quarter in the city. Since 12 April the commanders of 17 Armee calculated that from this point the Crimea would be abandoned. The evacuation by naval vessels of the Kriegsmarine began according to plan. Rearward services, Trosse, non-combatants and prisoners of war were already being continuously shipped out. According to Operation *Adler* everything could be accomplished in eighteen days. Unfortunately it did not work out like that. All hopes were dashed. Hitler ordered: 'In the long run Sevastopol must be defended.' With that order the tragedy involving the brave German divisions and units on the Crimea began. In vain the Commander-in-Chief 17 Armee, Generaloberst Jaenecke, but also Schörner, commanding Army Group Südukraine, and Zeitzler, Chief of the General Staff of Army High Command attempted to persuade Hitler to abandon his senseless order. All of Schörner's attempts and efforts to get Hitler to change his mind fell on stony ground. The fiasco of the never-give-an-inch strategy was about to run its course on the Crimea.

The aim of the Russians now was to reach the fortified area of Sevastopol before, or at the same time as, the Germans got there. The focus of effort lay along the Simferopol–Bachtshissaray road.

Oberst Betz had been given the task by Armee to block off the most important roads to Sevastopol. Two infantry battalions, six flak batteries, the remnants of StuG Brigades 191 and 279 and the armoured train *Muhr* lurked in positions on the heights north of Bachtshissaray. Before noon on 14 April the Russian armoured and infantry columns came along very incautiously, received the defensive fire of Battle Group Betz and were almost totally wiped out. Forcing the pace of the retreat, this time advantage enabled the troops of XXXXIX Gebirgskorps and such artillery as had been saved to reach the fortification line at Sevastopol. The regiments arrived worn out and reduced in numbers. On the way many men had not kept up: dead, taken prisoner, missing. Countless wounded had had to be left behind. The rearguards fought all day against the pursuing Russians: StuG crews who had had to abandon their panzers due to damage by enemy fire or material breakdown fell into the hands of the Red Army or partisans. Only a few, such as Wachtmeister Lasch, managed to reach the German defences at Sevastopol.

Battle Group Betz held the high ground until 15 April and were forced back, stage by stage, until giving up the struggle next day. The retreat of the battle group into the fortified area was covered by our own artillery.

At this point in time, the first elements of V Armeekorps coming from Kerch were arriving at the fortified area. When the codeword *Adler* was given, the troops at Kerch were still 250 kilometres from the 'Gneisenau' position. They began moving out on the night of 11 April. The Tross, flak units and the Romanians were already flowing by the afternoon without regard for material losses; bringing out the men was the main aim.

73 and 98 Inf.Divs moved out during the evening and occupied the Marienberg position on the Tartar Wall, 30 kilometres west of Kerch. As far as possible, the units were taken back by columns of lorries. The Russians were aware of these withdrawals. A regrettable nervousness had spread such that ammunition stocks were fired off, compounds and bunkers blown up, and radio traffic was rife. This made it easy for the Russians to recognize the beginning of each new withdrawal movement. When the last rearguards pulled out of the positions at Kerch, the Russians were close behind them. There began a competition, with many casualties between the motorized Russian units and German troops who were unused to being on the move due to the long period of trench warfare they had endured. Besides the infantry, V Arneekorps only had horse-drawn units for its heavy weapons.

Only 1 Battery of StuG Brigade 191 had seen fighting action at the Kerch front, the Trosses of battery, Staff, Staff Battery and workshop were already in the hinterland.

The StuGs of 1 Battery commanded by Oberleutnant Laubmeier stood with the rearguard troops. As soon as the withdrawal had begun they became enmeshed in the defensive battle with the Russian armoured spearheads. One StuG platoon was at I/Grenadier-Regt 213 on the retreat from Katerles to Bagerov when it was noticed that their 3 Company was missing. Two StuGs went in search with infantry seated on the hull, and at the railway line 3 kilometres east of Bagerov they found the lost unit, Oberleutnant Jaeger's 3 Company of 3/Grenadier-Regt 213 strung well apart, four Russian tanks with mounted infantry following close behind the stragglers. The two 1 Battery StuGs headed for the Russian tanks, firing as they rolled, and the Russians retired into a gully. Although other enemy tanks were seen moving up, the two StuGs remained until they picked up the last stragglers and drove back with them.

I/Grenadier-Regt 213 got away from Bagarov with a convoy of lorries: I Battalion 'Mez'/Grenadier-Regt 290 was late in getting away and the ring of Russian tanks closed around them very quickly; few survivors got through to the west. Twelve hours after giving up their positions at Kerch, large sections of 73 and 98 Inf.Divs had been lost.

The 1 Battery StuGs fought it out with Russian tanks out in open country: when the battery wanted to fall back on the Parpatch position, they found their path blocked by enemy tanks. During the evening when they broke through, not recognized at first by the Russians, they destroyed one T-34 and in the resulting hiatus the battery fought its way through and arrived intact in the new defensive position into which it was integrated immediately. Those StuGs no longer operational 'went to the workshop': they never arrived and the smoking wreckage fell into enemy hands.

The V Armeekorps retreat having taken on a catastrophic character, our CO Major Müller was appointed roads commander of V Korps by General Allmendinger. Besides commanding the brigade he had to direct the entire withdrawal of the Korps. Because the Russians coming from the north were already at Simferopol and – if they were bold enough – could turn up at the rear of V Korps within an hour, the Korps headed south in order to continue the withdrawal along the coastal road via Sudak–Yalta and then head west.

On the morning of 13 April the last V Korps rearguards emerged from the northern part of the Parpatch position under Oberst Schmidt, who led his last men to Ssaly in order to keep the mountain road there open to Sudak. Meanwhile the battle group of Oberst Faulhaber on the heights around Zürich Valley held back the pursuing enemy. The Russian sent up fast forces intending to cut off the road back, and soon the first Russian tanks arrived from Stary Krim and shelled the columns at the entrance to the pass. They lost nine tanks to return fire and these now blocked the road.

The central sector of the Parpatch position was held by the remnants of 73 Inf.Div.; the 6 Romanian Cavalry Division had not occupied the southern sector. Enemy forces now pushed unhindered for Feodosia. The Germans pulled out of the town on the night of 12 April. The remnants of Romanian units and V Armeekorps Trosse were transported out from the port aboard naval barges, and the first forces of the Red Black Sea Fleet arrived at Feodosia on the morning of 13 April. Because of the premature loss of the port, 73 Inf.Div. could no longer use it and had to fall back on Ssaly for the pass road to Sudak. Stary Krim to the north had to be avoided since it was already occupied by the enemy. In the west and north elements of the 98 and in the east of the 73 Inf.Div. held up the enemy advance and the stream of vehicles flowed through the pass.

To traverse the pass road through the Jaila mountains was no easy matter. It proved impossible to get the horse-drawn artillery through: the guns were destroyed and the animals shot. The feared involvement by partisans did not occur. On the evening of 13 April the column reached the small town of Sudak:

that night naval barges took out large sections of the units arriving and brought them to Balaclava near Sevastopol. The last barrier groups supported by five StuGs of 1 Battery, Brigade 191 held the area around Sudak until midday on 14 April when the positions were abandoned by the German rearguards. That evening the mass of V Armeekorps reached Alushta. This was the first pause for rest since the withdrawal from Kerch. Rested groups manned the defences. From Alushta too the ferries brought out the last elements of 98 Inf.Div. and stragglers and put them ashore at Balaclava. On the morning of 15 April, the remnants of 73 and 98 Inf.Divs came to Yalta by lorry. The German rearguard left, with enemy tanks held at a safe distance by 1 Battery, StuG Brigade 191.

A stream of vehicles and convoys hastened along the coast road westwards to Yalta, the first vehicles arriving at midday, rations distributed and the vehicles refuelled up. The provisions and supplies compound at Yalta was emptied and the column set off once more. Scarcely was it beyond the town than it received fire from the mountains. Fire was returned from the moving vehicles and from every barrel, including the quadruple flaks. The partisans called it off and a lull prevailed.

On 16 and 17 April the last sections of V Korps reached the fortified area of Sevastopol. It was a great surprise that the retreat had been carried out so successfully under pressure from a more powerful enemy. The Soviets had apparently considered it to be impossible and had therefore not taken stronger measures.

All German divisions had arrived at Sevastopol in tatters. What the men had achieved on the march and in battle was unprecedented. It had been a murderous withdrawal in which nearly all heavy weapons and equipment had been lost. The divisions were little more than regiments, the Romanian units close to dissolution. The fighting strength of the Armee on 16 April 1944 was approximately 19,500 men, all now hoping for a speedy evacuation from the Crimea, but their hopes were not to be fulfilled so soon. V Armee was now sent to hold the southern sector of the great fortification at Sevastopol.

All men of 1 Battery StuG Brigade 191 who had no StuG or vehicle were loaded aboard naval barges and brought from Sudak and Feodosia to Balaclava. From there they went by Siebel ferry to Sevastopol to take over prepared StuGs meant for Brigade 279, and rolled out ready for action under the command of Leutnant Strauch to the barriered area at Bachtschissaray. This was controlled by Oberst Betz whose job it was to keep Russians tanks back from the heights.

The defensive operation with support of the StuGs was a complete success. When the barrier was lifted, our StuGs went first as an interception reserve under General Pickert and then returned later to Brigade. All StuG crews of 2 and 3 Batteries StuG Brigade 191 who had no vehicle upon arriving at the fortification line were taken by mule or lorry to the Sevastopol city centre to find quarters. The city was coming increasingly under attack from the air and by artillery fire and so initially the men sought new quarters on a height outside Sevastopol. However, during an artillery barrage Gefreiter Hofmann was killed and other men were wounded. Their stay here was not a lengthy one, for they were either returned to unit or shipped out to Romania.

Chapter Nine

Sevastopol, 16 April–13 May 1944

After the arrival of the shrunken divisions in the fortified area of Sevastopol, approximately five German regiments had been defending the fortress perimeter since mid-April. Its artillery consisted of what had been saved from the XXXXIX Armeekorps allocation. The main front line was well developed, but only tactically important positions had been provided with strongpoints in depth. There was no second or third line occupied by reserves. The old Soviet bunkers and forts had not been reinstated and could only be used as military dressing stations and readiness areas. The positions south-east of Sevastopol were in poor condition. V Armeekorps had no heavy artillery and few infantry heavy weapons except two batteries of StuG Brigade 191 with full staffs. General Pickert commanded a weak flak division for the whole fortress. The Luftwaffe presence was forty-six machines which operated from the airfield at Chersones.

The Russians had twenty-nine divisions, two armoured corps, three artillery divisions and a dozen independent brigades with a total of 470,000 men poised to storm the fortress of Sevastopol, therefore more than 6,000 guns and 600 tanks, and two air armies with fighter-bombers, bombers and fighters standing by for the great offensive. The Black Sea Fleet, however, remained in its hiding places for the time being. This had the advantage for the Germans that the impressive port of Sevastopol could be used to its fullest extent to ship out the German troops on the mainland.

Armee Order No. 3 dated 16 April 1944 for the fortress of Sevastopol stated: 'In the defence of the fortress there is to be no step back. Behind us there is only the space needed for the life of the fortress and the Black Sea.' Nothing in this order hinted at the evacuation of Sevastopol and the transfer of 17 Armee to Romania. Nevertheless the men trusted in their officers and they had the memory of the successful evacuation of the Kuban bridgehead to fall back on. They knew nothing of the struggles between the Armee and Army leaderships with Hitler, who had strictly forbidden the evacuation of the Crimea. Both

Korps were to defend their sectors to the last. V Armeekorps had to ensure that the Soviets could not use the approaches into Balaclava harbour. XXXXIX Gebirgskorps had to set up the central strongpoint of the defence in the Meckensia High Road area.

Between 16 and 18 April the Russians attacked the northern front and were repulsed. 2 Battery of Brigade 191 (Hauptmann Berg) took part in these actions, first north of Severnaya Bay and later joining the brigade again at the main front. Scarcely had 1 Battery been given its defensive sector than it was sent to carry out a relief attack on the Balaclava–Alupka road where troops fighting their way through the Yaila mountains would be arriving. When groups of infantrymen began to filter down they wept with joy to see the StuGs. Russian tanks made a brief appearance but after a duel they returned to cover, to be replaced from a protected position by a heavy anti-tank gun which concentrated on the StuGs. There was nothing for it but run for cover; during this operation the brakes on one StuG failed. Since it could not be towed away it had to be set on fire and allowed to roll down a slope to burn out, the crew being picked up by other guns. The enemy tank spearhead followed cautiously since it had great respect for StuGs in general. The guns then returned to their departure point.

Leutnant Strauch had supervised the construction of a bunker for StuG crews on a slope of the Sapun mountain. It was meant to protect the men against artillery fire and air attacks, which were becoming stronger day by day. Priority targets were the airfield, the ammunition dump and the harbour area. Our fighters and flak shot down a large number of enemy aircraft daily, but it made no impression on the number of air attacks we received.

Meanwhile Brigade 191's rearward services had been shipped in stages across the Black Sea back to Romania. But by order of the Führer such evacuations were forbidden, therefore the workshop teams had all returned to the Crimea. Major Müller ordered them all back to Romania because the technical personnel were no longer needed at Sevastopol, and once on the other shore again they were to find ways of reactivating the brigade. Happy faces were to be seen as they disembarked once more in Romania since this meant salvation from death in the Crimea or on the sea. Once our CO had recognized the military situation at Sevastopol as hopeless he decided to send the other operationally unused StuG men to Romania by the sea route. An evacuation group was formed. Each battery had to release thirty men into it. 3 Battery was disbanded for tactical reasons and its still-operational StuGs were distributed to 1 and 2 Batteries.

Two gun crews were also transferred to the complements of these two batteries, the remainder went to Staff Battery. The StuGs of Brigade 279 were taken over by the two batteries for use as anti-tank companies armed with Panzerfaust and 'stove pipe' (*Ofenrohr*) anti-tank rockets. When the Russian major offensive against Sevastopol began, these companies stood at the centre of the fighting at the Nikolayevska Height. It was their final sacrifice on the Crimea.

When the evacuation groups were assembled, Major Müller took his leave of them with a short address and wished them good luck for the voyage. It was a long way to Romania and they knew they might need it. On the night of 22 April the groups were driven to the harbour. Loading up was very slow and halting because the quay for transport ships was in range of enemy artillery. During embarkation there had already been some dead and many wounded, and the loaded naval barges cast off as soon as possible in order to get free of the danger zone.

After a certain time the wind was forecast for Force 6 and the barges, unable to cope with rough seas, had to turn back. The barge with Leutnant Jentsch and sixteen men aboard returned. They came ashore and sought refuge in the harbour area. The night of 23 April passed peacefully. In the morning they reboarded and the convoy of nine vessels under Luftwaffe protection set out for Romania. They came under enemy air attack twice, the bombs missing the convoy although several men were wounded by strafing from the aircraft. These wounded were transferred to floatplanes later. The convoy arrived at Konstanza at about 2300 hrs. It had been a hellish and unforgettable voyage for the StuG men. The evacuation group was given temporary quarters in Buzau and transferred later to Colasei, the collection centre for Brigade 191.

The Russians made comprehensive preparations for the attack on Sevastopol. They tested the German front with local thrusts and their artillery zeroed in on the harbour. On the morning of 23 April, their 51 Army commenced its attack on the north front, heralded by massed artillery fire and rolling air attacks which even included the city of Sevastopol. The centre of effort was concentrated either side of the high road at the southern end of the Belbek valley, and that running from the Oelberg to the north-west via Belbek to the Koberberg. When the western sector of the north front threatened to collapse, reserves were brought up and won back the old main front line.

On 24 April they began their attack with Oelberg at the centre of effort. In response the German armoured train *Michael* operated from within the railway tunnel, emerging to fire its salvoes and then steaming back inside. The two air forces fought a bitter battle in the skies. The following day the Russians arrived with new, rested forces while the Germans had to use all reserves in order to retain their positions. Gradually the fighting abated.

On 27 April the enemy attacked the V Armeekorps positions to the east but these withstood the onslaught. In the Sapun Heights–Strassensattel (crossroads) sector the Russian attacks were made with armour support which desisted on meeting the fire of the twenty guns of StuG Brigade 191 under the command of Major Alfred Müller. The brigade was the great prop and backbone of the German defence. Waiting unseen in favourable positions, they would emerge in bold thrusts, destroying numerous enemy tanks and separating the infantry from the armour. Russian attacks on the German position also failed on 28 April, and no trench between Balaclava Bay and the Sapun Heights was lost. Even the weak remnants of 7, 111 and 98 Inf.Divs and the three Romanian mountain infantry regiments between them also held the line.

On 27 April when Generaloberst Jaenecke considered the catastrophe unavoidable, he sent a telex, meant for Hitler, to Army Group Südukraine. Schörner forwarded it at once to Führer HQ. Jaenecke, who on 24 April had requested information about the promised two divisions of reinforcements, asked for one division at once for support. He also wanted 'freedom of action' for his Armee in the Crimea.

On 19 April Generaloberst Jaenecke flew to Berchtesgaden and once more tried to get his way. Hitler remained firm with 'No'. Sevastopol had to be held to the last man. Hitler also assured him that reinforcements and new weapons were being sent to the Crimea and that Sevastopol and the peninsula had to be held another for two months until the start of the imminent invasion in France.

When Generaloberst Jaenecke arrived on 1 May 1944 at the headquarters of Army Group Südukraine at Galatz, the order for his removal was awaiting him. He was forbidden to go back to the Crimea and returned embittered to Germany. The new Commander-in-Chief of 17 Armee was General Allmendinger, and Generalleutnant Müller assumed command of V Armeekorps. The replacement for General Konrad (XXXXIX Gebirgskorps) was the Oak Leaves holder General Hartmann, a very handicapped man for he had only one arm and one leg. For the new major offensive of the Russians, the most important commanders of 1 Armee had been replaced. Despite Hitler's 'No', Armee High Command 17 was preparing the evacuation of the Crimea.

On 5 May at 0900 hrs the great Russian offensive against the north front of the fortified area of Sevastopol began. The thrust of five divisions and the air force fell on the 336 Inf.Div. positions on the heights. The Stellenberg was given up and bitter fighting continued around the Oelberg. After two days the fighting groups in the north sector had been much reduced and it seemed only a question of time before the positions could no longer be held with reserves.

On the morning of 7 May, Jeremenko's coastal army attacked the positions of V Armeekorps in the east. After a long artillery barrage the Russian tanks and infantry attacked in masses towards the weakened German regiments of 73, 111 and 98 Inf.Divs. Enemy fighter-bombers overflew the area shooting at anything that moved. The main effort was concentrated along the Kamary–Nikolayevka road to the crossroads at the southern foot pf the Sapun Heights.

After heavy defensive fighting the fronts held by 73 and 111 Inf.Divs were torn open. The men of V Armeekorps fought on at the old hotspots: in the Pioneer Gorge, at the English Cemetery, on the Sapun Heights, at Weingut and on the Nikolayevka Height. The German front at Kadykivka and south of it crumbled. Towards midday the Russians were immediately before Hohe Batterie, Bunker-und-Buschberg, Adlerhöhe and Herzogstand.

Our StuGs supported the infantry defensive battle in every conceivable spot. Thus 1 Battery with the last reserves of 73 Inf.Div. carried out a counter-attack from Strassensattel Berg to Kadykovka, forcing the Russians back. The incursion was cleared and the front closed up once more. Next the enemy threw in masses of men and materials, and succeeded in breaking through and going round the mentioned island of communication. The German counter-attacks with StuG support demanded more and more strength and spirit of sacrifice from the reserve troops. Accordingly the casualties were heavy and the reducing numbers could be seen visibly. In the evening a strong enemy group succeeded in breaking through at Strassensattel to occupy the Weingut Nikolayevka road. Once again the incursion had to be sealed off by interception reserves. In the XXXXIX Korps (north front) sector the battle continued on 7 May. The positions were held by calling upon the last reserves. Wild aerial activity dominated the day. German fighters and flak claimed 120 enemy aircraft shot down.

The defeat of 17 Armee could be seen coming by the evening of 7 May. It had not a single battalion in reserve. In the evening a foot battalion arrived at Sevastopol by sea, not enough to make any difference. The Armee decided to pull back the north front and recapture the Sapun position in order to gain the two days it needed to evacuate the Crimea. That night the north front was pulled back in two phases codenamed *Wildkatze* – wild cat:

(1) Into the harbour protection position on the north bank of Severnaya Bay and
(2) To the south bank of Severnaya Bay.

The Kriegsmarine and Hitler were displeased with the pulling back of the front. In a telephone call Schörner informed Zeitzler, C-in-C of the Army, that the V Armeekorps front had collapsed and that the C-in-C General Allmendinger himself had given the order to retreat. Therefore the matter was out of Hitler's hands.

On the night of 7 May the units of XXXXIX Korps proceeded without much interruption to the harbour protection position. 336 Inf.Div. slotted into the old front of V Armeekorps at Inkerman. 50 Inf.Div. held the harbour protection position for twenty-four hours and then occupied the southern bank of Severnaya Bay. The Chersones position had been occupied by the remnants of 2 Romanian Mountain Division as a precaution. The Staff of Armee High Command 17 and Sea Command Crimea transferred their command posts into the fortification works 'Maxim Gorki II'.

All units at a loose end were then formed into two battle groups: one of four battalions under Oberst Faulhaber and the other of two battalions commanded by Oberstleutnant Marienfeld. 1 and 2 StuG Batteries were assigned to both battle groups. On the night of 7 May the Russians pushed forward and in the morning captured our fighting islands (Adlerhöhe, Windmühlenberg and Bügelberg). On the Höhenkamm west of the Serpentine the remnants of Grenadier-Regt 50 were expelled but fell back on the anti-tank gorge position.

Meanwhile the Faulhaber and Marienfeld battle groups with 2 Battery in support advanced towards the English Cemetery in order to cut off the Russian spearhead. In the course of the subsequent fighting some StuGs were lost with their crews. The two tank-destroyer companies also suffered heavy losses. Once these companies had reported more than sixty dead and missing they were pulled out, the remnants then receiving the approval of V Armeekorps to transport out to the Romanian mainland under the leadership of Oberleutnant Heise. The worst of it was not yet over, however, for on the naval transport they suffered casualties from Russian air attacks and only about forty-five men joined the reserves. Our CO Major Müller played a major role in saving the remains of Brigade 279.

The first task of 1 Battery was to relieve the Romanians encircled in the north-east at Kamylshly. Our flak cleared the way to the eastern end of Sevastopol where the StuGs, with troops seated on the hull, received enemy anti-aircraft and artillery fire. The StuGs made smoke and returned to the departure point. A fresh advance supported by quadruple flak guns and Me 109 fighters got them through to rescue the Romanians, and then fight their way out. Russian tanks made no attempt to interfere – possibly out of respect for our cannons.

In a night attack against a Russian thrust the StuGs received fire on the flank. Thanks to the circumspection of their drivers they managed to escape this precarious situation and bring about a decisive turn in events. The accompanying infantry had suffered heavy casualties and so from the StuGs the crews used infantry weapons to mow down the tightly packed attacking Russians. During this attack nearly all the infantry ammunition was used up. The operation was successful and the StuGs suffered only minor casualties.

Battle Group Marienfeld supported by StuGs of 1 Battery regained Weingut Nikolayevka from the enemy and the vanguard established contact with Grenadier-Regt 70. The turn towards the English Cemetery was unsuccessful, Grenadier-Regt 50 being forced back along the Serpentine–English Cemetery road. On the night of 8 May the remnants occupied a newly built line on the city outskirts of Sevastopol.

In the southern sector 73 Inf.Div. maintained cohesion in the face of strong enemy attacks but towards midday Hohe Battery and towards evening Karan were lost. At the same time fresh enemy forces came into the breakthrough area near the English Cemetery. Battle Groups Faulhaber and Marienfeld were now in great difficulty.

On 8 May 1944 the cautious and brave officer commander of 1 Battery, Oberleutnant Laubmeier, was awarded the Knight's Cross. When the Sapun Heights were lost, at 2115 hrs, Schörner sent a telex to Führer HQ: 'Request evacuation, as the continuing defence of Sevastopol no longer possible,' and at 0215 hrs next morning AOK 17 received the order 'The Führer has approved the evacuation of the Crimea.'

The basic conditions were to hold the Chersones position and if possible the Nikolayevka position in order to keep the Russians as far away as possible from the loading harbours in the Chersones bays.

On the morning of 9 May 17 Armee had 120 flak and artillery barrels at its disposal. Ammunition was in short supply. In the south the remnants of 73 Inf.Div. had been ejected, the Windmühlen mountain had been captured by Soviet forces and the main German front had been pulled back to a line based on Kloster Georgievsky. This was how the Russians saw the southern part of the Chersones peninsula from the Karan Heights.

A fresh attempt to recapture the Nikolayevka position between the English Cemetery and Weingut Nikolayevka was made with the support of the StuGs. III/Grenadier-Regt 122 won back the Weingut. Battle Group Marienfeld was unable to proceed with its advance to the English Cemetery since it was held by Russian heavy weapons. The same problem confronted Battle Group Faulhaber. A thrust to the south was not contemplated because the casualties would be too great. Even the batteries of Brigade 191 had losses: Leutnant Vieten, Wachtmeister Schmitt and others had fallen, Oberleutnants Berg and Koch, Wachtmeister Weisgerber and many others were wounded during the last engagements of the StuGs.

At midday on 9 May the entire German defensive front moved off but soon crumbled. By 1500 hrs the Russians had occupied the southern and eastern parts of Sevastopol. The last elements of 50, 98 and 336 Inf.Divs fought through to the Chersones position. This chaotic retreat brought with it more heavy losses. The CO of 50 Inf.Div., Oberst Betz, was killed in an enemy air attack, Generalmajor Hagemann, CO of 336 Inf.Div., was seriously wounded.

According to the plan, V Armeekorps was to have command in the Chersones position. After the collapse of the V Armeekorps, XXXXIX Korps took over. By using all available means, at first the Chersones position was held. The last airfield at Chersones lay within the reach of Russian artillery. The last Me 109 fighters left for the Romanian mainland; 17 Armee now had no protective roof. Only the most intrepid and indestructible pilots continued to land their Ju 52s during the following nights to bring out the wounded. Meanwhile the divisions arranged their survivors into units and put together new battle groups under energetic officers. On 10 May the German defence was firmly established in the Chersones position. German and Romanian soldiers fought with the greatest bravery and denied the enemy any gains in territory. The StuGs of Brigade 191 had occupied new positions and had always been the last men facing the enemy during the retreats. Now, despite all their efforts and enormous numerical superiority, the Russians were unable to roll up the front. Widely spaced and cleverly camouflaged, the StuGs were the only heavy weapon in the Chersones position. It had been well planned and well developed. The main battle line was a continuous infantry trench with access trenches and concrete bunkers. This gave the battle groups the opportunity to receive support, even good rations and adequate supplies of ammunition were available. Because the peninsula had no water, soda water was used. Veteran infantrymen led by proven officers set up small battle groups with the remnants of the various troop units. These were designed to be used as assault and interception reserves. In 98 Inf.Div. sector there were still 250 men – a considerable force in this situation.

Brigade 191 had its command post in Fort 'Maxim Gorki II' together with all assault artillerymen for whom there was no operational employment, among them the Staff with Wachtmeister Treis (IIa), Wachtmeister Schwerdet (Ia), the armourer Wachtmeister Sücker and others. According to the evacuation orders all horses were to be shot and thrown into the sea, another of the senseless ideas that were thought useful in the Crimea.

Now all eyes turned to the preparedness and operational abilities of the Kriegsmarine. On the night of 8 May convoys with a carrying capacity of 20,000 put to sea and were expected at Chersones on the night of 10 May. That day other convoys set out for Sevastopol from Constanza and Sulina. The fate of 17 Armee hung upon the success or failure of the seaborne evacuation.

The intention was to embark on the night of 10 May. There were 30,000 men in the Chersones position. The Navy agreed. Anything seaworthy was sent over. More than 190 German and Romanian vessels sailed. Their total carrying capacity was 87,000 men, more than sufficient. The distance by sea from Sevastopol to Constanza in Romania is 273 nautical miles. The plan did not look bad but depended on what the enemy did from the air and with submarines, and was also influenced by wind and weather. As soon as the armada sailed from Romania it was detected by Russian air reconnaissance. And then attacked. There was insufficient fighter cover, for the German machines had only a small radius of action which extended for no more than 100 kilometres from the coast. Here the Russian Air Force had superiority. The sailing was delayed first by the onset of bad weather with Force 8 (fresh gale) winds from the north-east. Smaller units had to turn back, vessels with weak engine power had to reduce speed, which meant that the vessels of the first transport group did not arrived off Chersones until the early hours of 10 May.

At first light the vessels of the first group were attacked from the air 2 nautical miles off the Chersones coast. Undaunted, pioneer landing boats and Siebel ferries carried out the embarkation. At the loading places in the various bays troops crowded together. Everybody was anxious to go. The ships lying in the roadstead were under continual attack by Russian bombers and torpedo-carrying aircraft. There was no German fighter cover and the flak was insufficient.

The *Totila* had already shipped 4,000 men aboard when it was hit by three bombs, leaving her adrift and burning. The ship sank two and a half hours later. Only around 200 men could be saved. The *Teja* was 20 nautical miles out of Chersones heading south-west when torpedoed by Russian aircraft and sank towards 1500 hrs. Only 400 men of the 5,000 embarked survived. Other ships and boats was attacked and sunk, several hundred more men being drowned. A number of Brigade 191 and 279 men were aboard these maritime casualties but their story cannot be told because none of them reported and no passenger list survived the sinkings.

Meanwhile the Chersones positions had been divided into two sector areas commanded by Generalmajors Böhme and Reinhardt. On land the Russians attacked seven times with several waves. Especially in the southern sector the fighting was very bitter. The 73 Inf.Div. battle group with the Naval Battalion Klemm, remnants of 9 Flak Division and Brigade 191 StuGs fought off all attacks successfully. The Buffalo Brigade stood firm like a rock in the surf. One Russian tank attack resulted in a loss to them of twenty tanks. The casualties which we sustained were large but not disheartening. The Artillery CO of XXXXIX Korps, General von Gallwitz, fell in action. Our own brigade also had deaths but the names never became known.

Since it could be predicted that the next naval transports would not be arriving on the evening of 10 May, the battle groups received the order to hold the Chersones position for another twenty-four hours. The disappointment was great but they held out. On the night of 10 May only small numbers were got out because the stormy conditions offshore made embarkations aboard ship very difficult. All Staffs were shipped and a large number of wounded flown out by Ju 52 transport aircraft. Nevertheless many wounded remained in conditions of indescribable suffering and were to be found in the casemates at the fort, in the embarkation bays, concrete bunkers and anti-shrapnel trenches. They were collected up, brought to the waterside for shipping out and put aboard naval barges as quickly as possible. At midday on 12 May they reached Constanza. Saved!

On 11 May the Russians resumed their attacks. The field positions and the fort lay under permanent artillery and salvo-gun fire. Soviet fighter-bombers and bomber aircraft attacked incessantly. Several times the remnants of 1 Armee beat off heavy attacks. The enemy broke through at 'Batteriehügel' held by 98 Inf.Div. but were ejected in a counter-attack also involving the die-hard stalwarts of 1 and 2 Batteries of StuG Brigade 191. Battery commander Oberleutnant Laubmeier and several crewmen were wounded. In order to cover the last withdrawals by the troops from the Chersones peninsula, eight StuGs of our brigade commanded by Leutnants Strauch and Jarratsch were left behind in the area enclosing Fort 'Maxim Gorki II', the precipitous coast and harbour because it was by no means certain that these StuG crews would not fall captive to the Russians. This was a very difficult decision for our CO.

The remaining StuG crews of both batteries went aboard naval ferries on the night of 11 May under mortar fire. A Danube steamer in the roadstead took the men. On the voyage to Constanza the ship came under air attack on several occasions; Hauptwachtmeister Knaak (2 Battery) and others lost their lives.

On 12 May the CO came to the conclusion that time was running out. He sent the last men of the brigade who were unoccupied to the loading jetties to get away with the last boats. He followed later to monitor the evacuation. He reached the steep coast under artillery fire and found there hundreds of German soldiers, wounded, stragglers and men without weapons searching for cover along the beaches, before them nothing but the open sea. A few hours previously naval ferries had taken off soldiers and wounded but a number still had to await the next ships, arriving at an unspecified hour.

The CO thought to himself that there was no getting away from here. He was an StuG man whom the Russians had learned to fear, in the bend of the Don, at the Kuban bridgehead and in the Crimea, a specialist for hopeless situations. Not for nothing was his StuG Brigade 191, the Buffalo Brigade, feared by Russian ground forces. It was understandable that the Russians left the attack on the Chersones peninsula for last.

After some hours a single naval ferry crept up to loading jetty K5. This was probably the last chance for the remaining soldiers. Many infantrymen stepped over the wounded and fought their way aboard. Our CO, Major Müller, hurried over and shouted, 'The wounded aboard first, or I shall shoot!' He had the ferry cleared, the wounded were then brought aboard, the rest followed in good order until the ferry was full. It cast off swiftly and headed for Romania, without the

CO and some of our men. Now he sat among them on the sand and encouraged them not to give up hope of rescue.

After some time a boat appeared from the fog and mist lying over the sea. Signals were given and it approached the loading jetty. Minutes later all men and our CO were aboard. The overloaded naval vessel then turned about and disappeared into the mist. During the night some of the evacuees were taken aboard S-boats. Our seriously wounded 2 Battery commander, the Knight's Cross holder Oberleutnant Laubmeier, was aboard an S-boat. All S-boats arrived early next morning at Constanza.

The last 17 Armee battle groups knew nothing of the tragedies at sea and all thought they were soon going to be shipped out. Fate then ran its course, even for those who had fought to the last shell. During the course of 11 May all battle groups received the order to report to the individual loading jetties at 2300 hrs and to safeguard themselves during the loading operations, They were also told that that should the vessels not arrive at the embarkation points they were to seek other possibilities.

On the evening of 11 May the evacuation fleet lay in the roadstead in sufficient numbers, but could not find the loading jetties. The Naval Commander Crimea, Konteradmiral Schulz, went on board the command boat of 1 S-boot-Flotilla at 2100 hrs. It had been his intention to steer the flotilla to the loading jetties himself because the command radio structure no longer functioned. The admiral's S-boat attempted to get to the ships in the roadstead quickly but was suddenly enveloped in a fog which grew ever thicker. This was no sea fog but artificial smoke. In the course of the last month the Kriegsmarine had a set up a large smoke-making installation around the harbour and inlets to protect military structures, anchorages and landing bridges from the sight of enemy bomber crews and so make aimed bombing raids impossible. Now – by mischance – these containers of smoke-making materials had been hit and activated by enemy artillery fire. Even our own units had released the intact barrels, not suspecting what they were for. Impeded by the wall of smoke, at first the ships had not attempted to find the anchorages. Admiral Schulz had rounded up a couple of ships and guided them to the anchorages but the majority could not be found because they had returned to Constanza at daybreak. Even the lighthouse at the end of the spit of land at Chersones could not be seen. Those ships still present picked up the waiting men without any problem.

Meanwhile the battle groups went to the loading jetties at night and waited for the ferries. Fortunately for us the Russians noticed nothing of the last movements out. From the north front the last 2,800 men of 50 Inf.Div. were loaded aboard ships and ferries. The remnants of Grenadier-Regt 123 with Major Teschner watched in vain for the next ferry. Further south, 111, 336, 98 and 73 Inf.Divs abandoned the Chersones position. Here too the battle groups arrived at the advised loading places without enemy pressure. The men of 98 Inf.Div. waited to be embarked in the inlets at Kruglaya and Kamysheva (east bank). Here the cliffs were nearly all steep with only a narrow froth of sea at the foot. There were no ships. The men felt betrayed. After a long wait the groups divided up independently and sought the ships, by chance finding some Siebel ferries and other small boats. By runners and shouting, the men of 98 Inf.Div. received the news. All units and men of 117 Grenadier-Regt/111 Inf. Div. were also loaded. A few Staff people and the last machine-gun rearguard remained behind, and their fate is unknown. Most of 73 Inf.Div. survivors went aboard ferries, the rest were saved by a submarine hunter (UJ-boot). The last ferry departed at 0300 hrs on 13 May.

The Divisional Commander of 73 Inf.Div., Generalmajor Böhme, was found later at his command post and taken prisoner by the Russians. Similarly, the men of 336 Inf.Div. got away in boats and ferries but the few who remained with the rearguard and had not got away in time stayed behind.

111 Inf.Div. was worst hit, the division to which StuG Abteilung had had the closest ties in actions at the Dnieper, at Elista, on the Terek and in the Crimea. No single vessel of any description found its way to the appointed loading jetty. In despair the men stood on the shore of the steep cliffs and searched the empty sea.

Our StuG crews led by Leutnant Strauch made every attempt to escape from the Crimea but this was not to be. At dawn on 13 May an S-boat neared the steep coast, navigating by the lighthouse. Strauch guided the boat towards the loading jetty by the use of lamp signals, and sent radio messages to the StuG crews to leave the guns and make for the jetty. Leutnant Jarratsch and his platoon on the harbour side of the positions was also notified. As the S-boat came in it received fire from Fort 'Maxim Gorki II', turned away and disappeared into the mist. That was the last boat to be seen from the shore.

On the morning of 13 May Russian tanks arrived at the last veil of defence before the loading jetties. The resistance of the last group soon weakened.

Artillery fire fell on the beaches, the enemy tanks held back. In the blind spot created by the steep coastal wall a couple of thousand men had sought shelter from enemy fire. These were the last remnants of 111 Inf.Div., of the brave Romanian mountain troops and StuG Brigade 191. There was obviously no point in resistance. With open hatches, the panzers rolled up slowly and raised the barrels of their cannons towards Sevastopol. Divisional Commander Generalmajor Gruner marched up to a T-34. A gun fired and he collapsed. He died later in a Russian field hospital.

Then the Russian infantry attacked the unarmed Germans, shouting in rage, shooting and striking out at their defenceless prisoners. Officers were identified and led away. The Russian Hiwis, our loyal helpers, were put against the coastal wall and murdered. More than 1,000 men began the arduous trek into Russian captivity, including the StuG crews, led away with the others. They had all done their duty to the utmost beyond the limits of human tolerance and fought to the bitter end.

A large number of them returned home after years of captivity, among them Leutnants Strauch and Jarratsch, Karl Reuter, Zahnen and many others whose names have not come through to us.

A gallant Armee was sacrificed to achieve nothing. Officers and soldiers of all Wehrmacht branches of two allied peoples, a blood brotherhood, fought bravely and with all they had against the looming defeat.

Sevastopol was a catastrophe on the scale of Stalingrad, brought about by a human weakness and consecrated by soldierly virtues. Here they shone once more.

A telex from AOK 17 of 23 May 1944 to Army Group Südukraine stated:

In the fighting in the Crimea from 10 April to 13 May 1944 under the outstanding leadership of its commanding officer, holder of the Oak Leaves Major Müller, StuG Brigade 191 destroyed 137 tanks, 48 anti-tank and anti-aircraft guns and a large number of other weapons and vehicles. The brigade, already well proven in its defensive struggle in the Kuban bridgehead, destroyed its 445th enemy tank on 12 May 1944 and proved again its outstanding valour and readiness to fight. A mention in the press and by radio has been requested.

At Colasei, near Buzau in Romania, the surviving Crimean warriors of the Buffalo Brigade met again. The subsequent weeks of rest and relaxation

A captured T-34 on the rail transport. This tank was a dangerous opponent: well-armed, fast and mobile across terrain.

were gratefully accepted. As the memory of their dreadful experiences began to fade, each man recognized that the brigade – measured against the losses in infantry – had come through relatively tolerably. Whereas all operational StuGs and most of the equipment had been lost, the personnel level had been maintained to a reasonable extent. We hoped that the brigade would be re-equipped and rearmed, and the men therefore spoke rightly of 'saving the Buffalo Brigade'. They were united in attributing the major service to our commanding officer, Major Müller. After a couple of weeks of rest the brigade received the order for refresher training and transfer to the troop training depot at Schieratz, south of Berlin.

On 30 May 1944 they loaded at Slobozia-Cilesu station and travelled by train via Kronstadt, Arad, Timisoara, Subotika, Stuhlweissenburg, via Vienna, Prague and Breslau to Schieratz, arriving on 30 June 1944.

On 15 June 1944 command of the brigade was given to Hauptmann Kollböck, a former officer of the brigade. Major Müller was at first given command of the Tactical Training Staff of the StuG School at Magdeburg and became the commanding officer of the school in August 1944. He was therefore a successor to the earlier Commanding officers of StuG Brigade 191, Oberst Hoffmann-Schoenborn and Oberstleutnant Haarberg.

The StuG of Hauptmann Paco Hoffmann, Crimea, November/December 1943. This gun also has 'supplementary armour'.

StuG '302' of Abteilung 191 at Kerch on the Black Sea coast, November/December 1943, with supplementary armour fitted.

Most crewmen wore the green and white reversible jacket with the green side outward. The carrying of reserve track segments on the StuG was important for repairs or replacements on the spot due to wear and tear or mine damage.

A StuG version F at the rear of a column in the Crimea.

Hauptmann Paco Hoffmann was seriously wounded on 6 December 1943 during an attack on the Russian bridgehead at Eltigen.

A victory celebration following the fighting around Eltigen.

A Romanian general distributing decorations to StuG Abteilung 191 crewmen.

Marfovska, early December 1943: StuG Abteilung 191 on parade. Hauptmann Müller drove to Simferopol on 20 December 1943, came under partisan fire on the way, and then flew to Führer HQ to receive the Oak Leaves to his Knight's Cross.

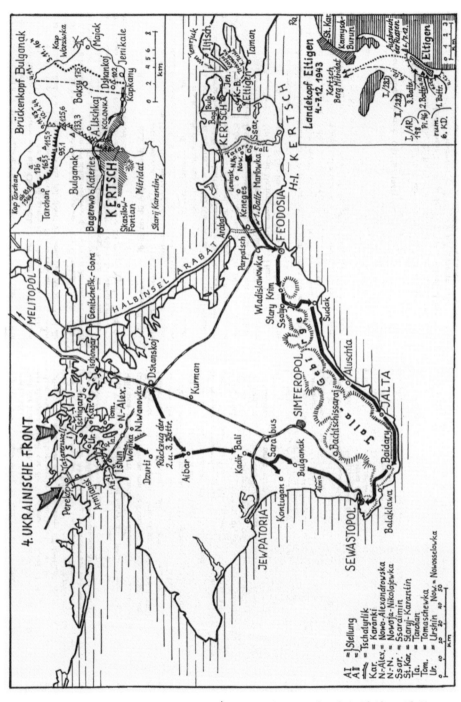

Map of the operations of StuG Abteilung/Brigade, Crimea, October 1943 to 13 May 1944.

Crew of the StuG of Oberfähnrich (cadet senior grade acting sergeant) Koniezko. From left to right: Gefreiter Grasenack, Koniezko, Obergefreiter Lederer (seated on gun barrel), Gefreiter Thomas. The 7.5-cm barrel received a direct hit from a T-34 on 12 November 1943.

A StuG during the fighting around Eltigen, December 1943. The slope of the side armour caused by the supplementary armour can be seen clearly here. It is absent from later photos. Either it made the StuG too heavy or the protection factor was inadequate.

Hauptmann Alfred Müller receiving the Oak Leaves to his Knight's Cross from Adolf Hitler, probably 22 December 1943. The official date of the award was 15 December. On 26 December Müller was promoted to Major effective 1 December 1943.

Major Müller in his StuG, spring 1944. Notice the splinter deflector spearhead ahead of the hatch, the scissor binocular SF 14Z by the commander's left hand, the angled mirrors in the rotating cupola and the gunlayer's SFL telescope which was coupled to the firing instruments.

Major Müller with Knight's Cross and Oak Leaves in the commander's hatch of his StuG.

Major Müller with his crew. StuG Abteilung 191 was redesignated StuG Brigade 191 on 28 February 1944.

Hauptmann Müller(1) as he then was at a situation conference with Romanian officers before the attack on the Russian bridgehead at Eltigen (4 to 7 December 1944). The German officer wearing the Knight's Cross (2) was not a member of the Abteilung.

Two items of radio equipment with long upright rod aerials served for the command of the Abteilung and communications with senior command units at Division or Korps.

Major Müller in his Kfz 15. Note the aerial fixture at the right side of the vehicle.

Driver Hermann Röhm with his commander Alfred Müller.

Hermann Röhm wearing a 'Russian cap' near his Kfz 15.

Hermann Röhm at his 'workplace', the driving seat of the commander's Kfz 15.

Hermann Röhm as Obergefreiter (non-NCO lance-corporal) with colleagues.

Hermann Röhm in a slit trench, February 1944.

The Kfz 15 after one night's snowfall.

The 1944 period of spring mud caused many problems for vehicles, the gearing was particularly prone.

The port of Feodosia, spring 1944.

By April 1944 German and Romanian troops had been forced back to the fortifications at Sevastopol. The photo shows a village spring and washplace somewhere in the Crimea.

A view over Feodosia to the Crimean mountains.

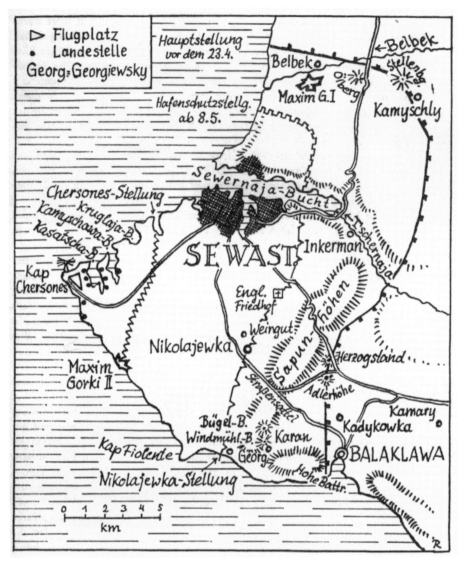

The final battle for Sevastopol between 16 April and 13 May 1944 resulted in a huge number of casualties for the Germans.

After returning from leave, at the end of April 1944 Hermann Röhm reached Constanza in Romania. The photo shows warships in the harbour at Constanza. These had the task of evacuating the Army of the Crimea to Romania.

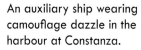

An auxiliary ship wearing camouflage dazzle in the harbour at Constanza.

A fully loaded MFP naval ferry arriving at Constanza after crossing the Black Sea. These ferries could only be used in relatively calm conditions and were not seaworthy as such.

A recently unloaded naval ferry at the quay in Constanza.

To arrive at Constanza harbour meant survival!

A converted trawler with flak armament took part in the evacuation of the Army of the Crimea.

A Ju 52 on the airfield at Constanza.

On 7 May 1944
Hermann Röhm
travelled in the bomb
bay of this Heinkel
111 from Constanza
to Sevastopol for a
four-day Odyssey, and
returned on 11 May.

Engine maintenance on
a Heinkel 111.

A Ju 88 on the Constanza airfield. In the background is an Me 109F.

While waiting for his flight, Hermann Röhm had a chance to look over the aircraft present, here an Me 109F.

A Fieseler Storch reconnaissance aircraft of Aufklaerungsgruppe 14 at Constanza.

Chapter Ten

Defending the South-Eastern Front, 1944–1945

_____

The General Situation in the Balkans

After the Russians had defeated Army Group South Ukraine, their next priority was to effect their political aims in Romania and Bulgaria. This appeared to them so important that they used the greater bulk of their forces for this purpose and for the time being relegated their other military operations to second place. Sections of 2 Ukrainian Front pursued the escaping remnants of 6 and 8 Armee by driving them in front of them without much effort. They gave orders to the now Communist Romanians to create an army to liberate Transylvania.

German Army Group South set about the task of defending Transylvania as far as the eastern Carpathians with a will. About five divisions from 8 Armee and splinter groups from other units had escaped from the great collapse and now occupied the eastern Carpathian passes alongside 1 Hungarian Army. The southern wing of the latter was at the Borgo Pass and the northern wing alongside 1 Panzerarmee. The situation south was less favourable. 6 Armee had only been able to save small numbers of fighting troops from the Dnieper. A substantial part of the Tross and rearward services, together with the Luftwaffe ground organization, having beaten a way through the suddenly hostile hinterland, arrived via Sereth at Buzau and then, joining the defenders of the Ploesti oilfields, made their escape within a long convoy, under extreme conditions. Finally they negotiated the Predeal Pass via Kronstadt to the north, where new battle groups were assembled from these remnants to form the nucleus of a new 6 Armee.

On 5 September 1944 the Russians occupied Kronstadt and then attempted to push northwards. Between the inner wings of the German 6 Armee and 2 Hungarian Army was a yawning gap into which the newly formed Communist

Romanian forces had ventured to thrust, supported by strong Russian units in the Walachai (the 77,000 square kilometres of Romania north and north-east of Bulgaria), from where they could break into all southern Carpathian passes in Transylvania.

The German leadership recognized the danger, and its weak forces succeeded in repelling the Romanians. The Russians counter-attacked, placing the bulk of their forces in the area south of Klausenburg. Although the fighting raged until the end of September, the Russians failed to make the breakthrough. Even the eastern Carpathians held out. Therefore the Russians gave up attempting to wipe out the forces of Army Group South and changed their aims instead into a greater operation.

Now they lay low in Yugoslavia and the Hungarian plain, poised ready to strike at Budapest in the expectation that Hungary, the last East European Axis partner, could be separated from Nazi Germany. In order to stall this hidden Russian agenda, Hitler had to strengthen the south-eastern front with fresh troops.

The Defensive Struggle in Yugoslavia and Hungary, mid-September–early October 1944

In the framework of reinforcing the Balkan front, StuG Brigade 191 was given a new operational area. After a long period of leave, the brigade had been re-equipped at Schieratz and was now up to its authorized establishment in men and materials. It was now clear to all that the coming actions would be defensive. The fighting in Yugoslavia, along the Romanian border and in Hungary from the autumn of 1944 until the spring of 1945 would be a fresh chapter in the history of the 191, and the last.

StuG Brigade 191 posts as at 1 August 1944 were occupied as follows:

Adjutant: Leutnant Erich Müller
Surgeon: Assistenzarzt (Med. Lt.) Dr Gozdz
Technical Inspector: Hauptmann (Ing.) Scheubel
Cdr, Staff Battery: Oberleutnant Egelhaaf
Commander, 1 Battery: Oberleutnant Winkler
Commander, 2 Battery: Hauptmann Berg
Commander 3 Battery: Oberleutnant Koch

At the beginning of August 1944, a large section of the brigade entrained for the south. After a long journey with many stops (including Vienna) they arrived at Lescovac south of Nisch and occupied quarters on the edge of town. The transports with the StuGs and equipment from Altengrabow were brought by Oberleutnant Werner on 24 September via Vienna, Budapest and Belgrade. The last transport arrived at Peterwardein on 10 October. From there the assembly location was reached via Belgrade.

At Lescovac the brigade was reinforced by the addition of an independent StuG battery originating from Abteilung 201 which had fought in the Balkans (Greece and Bulgaria). The battery had only a few StuGs (howitzers and cannons), the remainder consisted of infantry platoons equipped with the most modern infantry weapons and vehicles. The battery commander was Oberleutnant Krech, the two platoons were led by Leutnants Wagner and Neumann. The new Infantry Escort Battery was incorporated into Brigade 191 as 4 Battery on 1 September 1944.

For the brigade this strengthening was of great value, making it more mobile operationally and in defensive manoeuvres. It was also able to perform without outside assistance as a small powerful battle group, especially in anti-partisan work.

In the rest days from 1 to 5 September, the town of Nisch was subjected to bombing. These air attacks were aimed at interrupting the withdrawal movements of Armee von Weichs and also mobilizing the remaining Bulgarian units and General Staff to resist German forces. On 15 September, our brigade was transferred to Niska Banya, east of Nisch, the seat of the Bulgarian General Staff with some troop units which had switched to being our enemy some days previously as the result of the defection of Bulgaria from the Axis.

The brigade acted. The Bulgarian resistance was broken, the General Staff taken prisoner and sent off at once into the hinterland. Sections of the tank school at Nisch (Bulgaria and Yugoslavia) had made a run for it with the tanks and self-propelled assault guns there, returning two days later to Nisch, where they opened fire on our StuGs. This attack was intercepted by our batteries and put down with many casualties. All tanks were destroyed bar one which made off towards Bulgaria. Our brigade had only minor wounds to report. The StuGs then set up security around the town. The most urgent task for the brigade was to secure the retreat of Armee von Weichs from Greece and to stop the pressure from enemy forces coming from Macedonia.

Meanwhile the German training staff under Oberleutnant Sturm, sent with some StuGs for the now-defunct Bulgarian assault gun weapons school at Nisch, came to us. Sturm's mission was over: later, south of Belgrade, commanding his StuG he was seriously wounded and fell into enemy hands.

On 18 September 1944 the Brigade Staff, Staff Battery with workshop, 3 and 4 Batteries and the entire Tross of the brigade was sent north from Nisch to Pancevo, north-east of Belgrade. The convoy reached Belgrade without incident, crossed the Danube by ferry and took quarters in Pancevo. 1 and 2 Batteries left Niska Banja on 19 September to continue to protect the retreat of Armee von Weichs, fighting off enemy attacks or partisan raids. Each battery reached the destination without losses of any size and also took quarters at Pancevo but did not rest there for long.

Army Group von Weichs was now in full retreat from Greece, southern Yugoslavia and Bulgaria. The retreat was under threat from the east. There were two major difficulties: the extraordinarily industrious and ruthless activities of the Tito partisans and the breakthrough of Russian troops at Turnu Severin with the associated crossing of the Danube at the Iron Gate.

Meanwhile 2 Battery at Pancevo was attached to 2 Panzerarmee and Battle Group Oberst Kaulber. On 27 September, 3 Battery received the order from Battle Group to proceed to the north-east. The nine StuGs set off with the support Tross and provisions staff from Pancevo towards Werschetz. After a short rest there they carried on to the Romanian border and crossed it towards Denta on 28 September. Here they had their first contact with Romanian forces as enemies but the latter made themselves scarce at once. Since the enemy remained quiet, 2 Battery was withdrawn to Moravita towards evening.

On the night of 30 September Battle Group Kaulber, including our StuGs, returned to Werschetz for the StuGs to be loaded aboard train transports, destination Gross-Betschkerek (Hungary), where they arrived the next day. The wheeled vehicles of the battery followed on the land road. After the StuGs were unloaded they drove at once to the readiness areas on the Theiss front which had only a few strongpoints manned by German and Hungarian units.

Meanwhile the Soviets had been continually bringing up reinforcements to the west at Arad. These then spread out northwards and arrived in the area east of Gyula and Salonta. Armoured concentrations had also been transferred from the Klausenburg area south of Grosswardein. At first this threatening advance was supposed to be opposed by units of 3 Hungarian Army to prevent them coming down from the mountains into the Theiss plain but that was clearly not within their capabilities.

Hitler had probably recognized the Soviet intention but did not have the forces to oppose it frontally by strengthening the Hungarians. Instead the idea was first to assemble a panzer group and then build a strongpoint in the area around and west of Grosswardein in order to cut off the Russians by a thrust to the flank. 6 Armee was to carry this out. The request by Army Group to haul back the well-advanced front of 8 Armee and 1 Hungarian Army was rejected, however. The only alternative was to take as many troops away from the southern front as possible and add them to the panzer group.

When the first panzer division to arrive skirmished successfully against the Russian advance south-west of Grosswardein, the expected Russian offensive was unleashed against the Theiss front on 5 October. 3 Hungarian Army was overrun immediately. After a few days the Russians were at Szentos, Szegedin and west of Betshkerek on the Theiss river, which they proceeded to cross. At the same time the southern wing of 2 Ukrainian Front went via Pancevo towards Belgrade, and 3 Ukrainian Front crossed the Morava at Svilajnac and turned from the south towards Belgrade.

The Defeat of 2 Battery, Early October 1944

At the end of September 1944, Soviet troops crossed the Danube at Turnu Severin, an area occupied by elements of 1 Gebirgsjäger-Div. under General von Stettner. Seeing himself threated by Russian armour coming from the east, he requested Army Group to send panzers or equivalent defensive weapons. Here follows a report by Hauptmann Berg, commander of 2 Battery, StuG Brigade 191:

> As commander of 2 Battery in the first days of October 1944 I received from Army Group an order to move out to the area west of the Iron Gate. This was to be done from Belgrade through the mountains to the east. The Army Group panzer reconnaissance company which had been sent to look at the roads came back with the opinion that the mountain was impassable because much of it was only mule tracks. My representation to Army Group that an operation by StuGs in the area made no sense tactically got me the old heave-ho and an order to

proceed south from Belgrade to the former royal radium-deposit baths at Nisch and Niska Banja. From there I was to head north, partly following the Bulgarian frontier, then through the Timok Valley via Zajecar to the Negotin region.

We got there, meeting some partisan groups along the way, which were dealt with by the battery which, by the way, had no infantry support. At Negotin I reported to the Staff of von Stettner's battle group which, apart from the Gebirgsjäger and now my battery, consisted of stragglers which included naval men from the Danube Flotilla. The battle group was therefore encircled by mainly Russian troops. As a 'wandering band' we now attempted passage through the mountains to the west towards Belgrade to meet up with German units. The StuGs fought here and there along the way in operations which were perhaps unique. In the valleys and on narrow mountain paths we fought it out with Russian self-propelled assault guns armed with 15-cm calibre cannon and destroyed some. We also had to cope with hand grenades hurled down from the slopes above us so that even at night on these almost footpaths we drove with the hatch shut.

By day we supported the mountain infantry in their defensive battles and counter-attacks in the mountains and hills which would certainly have been deemed totally unsuitable for StuG operations beforehand. The battles of the 'wandering band' involved substantial losses on the way via Majdanpek towards Smederovo.

Since we had no tactical communication with Brigade or Armee, we were soon running short of food and ammunition. Occasionally small quantities were dropped to us by the Luftwaffe, but not enough to keep our force going. The wounded had it worst of all because they were forced to remain in the band with us.

Literally with its last reserves of strength, the battle group fought its way into the area south-east of Belgrade, oppressed on all sides, and kept going in the hope that Belgrade was still occupied by German troops. As we neared the capital we received the very depressing information that not only Belgrade but also wide areas west of it were now in enemy hands. I reported forward that my StuGs would soon roll to a standstill for lack of fuel, and each gun had only a few rounds left with which to fight off a weak enemy attack.

General von Stettner held a conference of commanders at which he let us know that from Führer HQ he had received the order to attack the enemy in Belgrade. He did not intend to implement this order. The battle group was to destroy all materials which could not be carried, then we were to form up into several powerful units and attempt individually to break through the double encircling ring that night.

All vehicles and equipment which could not be carried were made unusable and with the onset of darkness the groups formed up and broke out of the encirclement one by one during the night. Occasionally hand-to-hand fighting occurred with the Russians: at dawn I met another group and learned from General Stettner's Staff officers that the general himself was missing. There followed days and nights of laborious forced marches through mostly overgrown terrain, and bloody encounters generally with Tito's partisans.

In one of these actions in the Avalla mountains south of Belgrade, among others, Leutnant Kuhn – our good Malinki – fell. We used this term, Russian for 'little boy', to mark with respect all those of 2 Battery who did not survive these murderous encounters. And so finally after weeks, the remnants of the 'Royal 2nd' met up again with the remnants of the former battle group von Stettner, then German troops around Semlin, and then the brigade itself.

There was a very bitter balance. 2 Battery had been all but wiped out; besides Leutnant Kuhn, twenty-eight NCOs and forty men had not come back and their fate is unknown. I formally passed the survivors of 2 Battery to Oberleutnant Egelhaaf. They went to Lehrbrigade II at Altengrabow, I was sent on a commanding officer's course at the StuG School, Burg.

Another report by a survivor of 2 Battery sheds light on the plight of his colleagues who were involved in the fiercest fighting and then went into captivity. Wachtmeister Hans Lasch reported:

2 Battery was on the move from Belgrade to the south via Nisch and from there northwards towards Zajecar. On the way the brakes of my StuG failed and had to be repaired on the spot. Once that was done I wanted to catch up but then received an order by radio to fetch a medical convoy from Nisch and escort it north. I set off at once and at Nisch after a conference with the convoy it was decided that my StuG would lead it. We agreed on the speed and took the main road north for Belgrade. Everything was going well at first.

A few kilometres after leaving Nisch an ambulance ran over a landmine laid by partisans. Now we knew that an increased level of caution was required. Near the village of Zitkovac my own StuG ran over a landmine, damaging the drive wheel and track. At once we came under fire from the mountains and the nearby maize fields. We returned fire with hand weapons but were unable to use our machine gun, which had been damaged by the mine explosion. The enemy fire increased and all vehicles of the convoy were shot into flame even though each was clearly marked with a red cross flag. When the partisans saw that we were immobile and not returning fire, they concentrated their fire on my StuG. The personnel of the escort got out, we remained in the StuG and kept quiet. Soon we were surrounded by partisans, had to get out and were taken prisoner. Some of the partisans spoke very good German. We were interrogated for hours until they appeared satisfied with our answers.

After a few days of captivity my crew and I managed to slip away unseen from a night camp. We headed north, met up with partisans again and two members of my crew were killed. Unfortunately we had to leave our dead where they lay.

For days we headed north with the greatest caution, moving only in darkness through the mountains and woods. Overcome with hunger and thirst, exhausted and in rags and tatters, weeks later we found the brigade at Semlin. We were given a hero's welcome since we had been listed as missing. I returned to Germany to Lehrbrigade II at Altengrabow with the others of 2 Battery.

The survivors of the former 2 Battery later fought on the Eastern Front. Lehrbrigade III was formed from Lehrbrigade II at Altengrabow and went to the Eastern Front on 22 January 1945 as part of a battle group to relieve Posen, and reached Meseritz-Schwiebus as ordered.

The prevailing circumstances were so chaotic that the CO, Hauptmann Wagner, felt obliged to reconnoitre with several StuGs. In a short while the brigade itself was encircled by Russian forces. Some of the men attempted to get to Frankfurt an der Oder. An assault spearhead led by the CO broke out, the remainder under Hauptmann Schmid reached the river Oder on foot five days later and crossed at Guben. This group lost Hauptwachtmeister Ebert killed; 2 Battery commander Oberleutnant Egelhaaf was wounded and died later in military hospital.

After the Brigade underwent restructuring it was sent at the beginning of April 1945 to Freienwalde-Fürstenberg. When the Soviets launched their major offensive on 16 April, the new brigade withdrew, fighting north of Berlin to Wittenberg on the Elbe. At the beginning of May, 1 and 2 Batteries crossed the Elbe and surrendered to US forces. From this, the last StuG men of the former 2 Battery of StuG Brigade 191 would return home to Germany.

The Fighting In and Around Belgrade, 5–15 October 1944

The Russian attack on the Theiss front on 5 October 1944 caused 2 Panzerarmee to withdraw slowly westwards, offering delaying tactics on account of 3 Hungarian Army being partly overrun. After the initial fighting at the Thiess, StuGs of 3 Battery formed the rearguard of the battle groups. The Russian units were hesitant to follow since they also had difficulties in supply. The brigade Tross and parts of 4 Battery were transferred on 11 October from Pancevo to Indija upon learning that a Russian spearhead was poised to enter Belgrade. The Brigade Staff and 1 Battery were transferred to the Semlin area (airfield) but when another spearhead of 3 Ukrainian Front moved up from the south-east to Belgrade, 1 Battery was sent to support the German units defending at Jakovo, Zeleznik and Sremcice south of the capital. Under growing enemy pressure, fighting in the mountains and woods upstream became increasingly difficult. The first losses in StuG crews and materials occurred while the head count of the accompanying infantry was reduced considerably. After the loss of several StuGs, 1 Battery was withdrawn and returned to Semlin near the Zemun airfield.

To clarify the situation, during the enemy attacks on the Theiss front, the Hungarian government was overthrown and in the confusion many Hungarian units on the Theiss front joined the new rulers. Some units remained with the Germans, including a Hungarian infantry battalion which operated for some months with Brigade 191. Because the Hungarian units had no unified leadership, some continued to side voluntarily with the Germans but gradually even these gave up their German allies and made the best of things that they could, although a few stayed with us to the capitulation and went with us into US captivity in Austria. There was later a Hungarian PoW camp at Annaberg near Salzburg from where the inmates were eventually allowed home or to migrate elsewhere. These examples show the difficulties which confronted the German leadership. The collapse of the southern front was accelerated by the loss of Hungary and finally became unstoppable.

As mentioned, after the Russian major offensive on 5 October 1944 along the entire southern front, the battle groups of 3 Ukrainian Front reached the southern area of Belgrade from where they attempted to occupy the Yugoslav capital with the help of partisans. The German occupying force including flak units and the Waffen-SS Division 'Prinz Eugen' inflicted very heavy casualties on the enemy here. The Russians had also reached the northern side of the city where the German defences buckled under the growing numerical superiority. 1 Battery joined forces with the Waffen-SS to free the German units which had been holding the Kalamegdan fortress and had been encircled.

1 Battery and infantry attacked from the main railway station towards the inner city. Passing through the first streets, they came under fire from anti-tank rifles and heavy infantry weapons located in the houses. The infantry remained behind and vanished. The battery's first casualties exemplified why the deployment of StuGs without infantry escort was not valid for street fighting. StuG commanders Sepp Weberndorfer and Wachtmeister Weisgerber were the first to be wounded by anti-tank rifle rounds. An StuG brought them back at once over the Organization Todt bridge to the battery Tross at Semlin.

The remaining six StuGs also suffered casualties while attempting to root out the nests of resistance in the houses. The fierceness of the fire to which they were subjected resulted in their being withdrawn from the street fighting. The Waffen-SS units also had very heavy casualties. To the present day there is no account regarding the fate of those trapped in the fortress. The Yugoslav capital was totally surrounded by the Soviets on 15 October 1944 and fell to them three days later. Only a few members of the German occupying force managed to slip through the encircling ring.

Croatia and Hungary, October–November 1944

After Belgrade was given up, Armee von Weichs withdrew fighting to Novi Sad towards Esseg in the German-occupied Batschka. The centre and right-wing of 2 Ukrainian Front, after setting out from the Salonta–Gyula–Arad line to attack across the Theiss to the north-west was forced to wheel north to avoid a dangerous flanking movement upon meeting German forces.

In the broad and flat Hungarian puszta, which was particularly suitable for panzers, major tank battles raged back and forth between 7 and 15 October, in the course of which Russian armoured and cavalry units were encircled south of Debreczen, suffered serious losses and were only saved from annihilation by battle units appearing from the rear. German losses were also heavy and included the loss of Grosswardein. The Russians were thus forced to abandon their original aim of breaking through across the Theiss and then heading north, however. This was all the more important for us when the German 8 Armee and 1 Hungarian Army were involved in a planned retreat east to west.

3 Battery attached to 2 Panzerarmee retreating from the Theiss front was continually engaged in battles with advancing Soviet forces. A critical point was the Vel canal, where there were no bridges for the StuGs. The help of the battle group was obtained to hold off the Russians to gain time for the StuGs to cross. A number were brought across by barge. The StuGs protecting the operation had some losses, Oberleutnant Werner being seriously wounded when an anti-tank round hit his StuG. New defensive positions were then set up around Sombor and Apatin.

When the enemy forces east of the Danube could no longer be contained, the German battle units and StuGs intended to cross the Danube at Batina and Gerechat in order to occupy better defensive positions on the western side. However, the Russians beat them to it and erected two bridgeheads there.

Under Soviet pressure 1 Battery had to be pulled back and by using delaying tactics reached Esseg (Osijek) via Neusatz (Novi Sad) and then occupied accommodation at Vukovar.

At this time the brigade was still receiving supplies from fourteen StuGs loading at Vinkovci railway station. Betrayed by partisans, the transport was bombed by aircraft before loading; eleven StuGs were destroyed.

1 Battery StuGs took over anti-partisan protection on the southern flank but here it remained quiet initially. In the first days of November, 1 Battery including the supplies staff was sent from Vukovar via Esseg north-west to the Hungarian frontier in order to join 3 Battery to defend at the Danube. On the way to the frontier they received orders from Armee to return to Vukovar and there join an Armeekorps. This practically separated them from Brigade.

This showed clearly that the German military commanders had lost the thread. The expression thereof was to be found not only in the inadequate contact between the various branches of the service, but also in the rising sense of panic, particularly among Staffs who had led a quiet life for several years and were not capable of directing defensive measures under difficult conditions. Their errors claimed many victims and affected StuG Brigade 191 substantially.

Thus in many cases the Brigade Staff was too far removed from activity, which made the task of command leadership difficult. For example, the brigade workshop lay far in the hinterland for reasons of safety, and therefore the repair of StuGs did not function satisfactorily.

Confusion in operations became the rule and demonstrated clearly the lack of understanding that many commanders possessed regarding the tactical value and limits of operational possibilities applicable to an StuG brigade. Personal objections by Brigade COs were barely heard out and in many cases simply ignored. It may be that anxiety about an imminent unpleasant end to the war even among persons at the higher command levels with bad nerves allowed confusion to develop such that erroneous decisions were frequently made and operational orders given regardless of the outcome that such orders would bring about.

On 12 November our CO, Hauptmann Kollböck, was on the way in his StuG to the 3 Battery defensive front. At a village north of Esseg, the StuG became involved in street fighting between our infantry and the Russians. When our CO dismounted in order to pass infantry ammunition from his StuG to a machine-gun group he was fatally wounded by mortar shrapnel. The brigade lost an irreproachable officer and CO, and holder of the German Cross in Gold. Since the formation of the Abteilung in 1940 until the hour of his death he had been with the unit constantly and was a much-liked and valued colleague and senior officer. He was buried at Esseg cemetery. Command of the brigade was taken over temporarily by Hauptmann Krech, commander of 4 Battery.

On 15 November a German battle group supported by 3 Battery attempted to narrow the enemy bridgehead at Batina. The assault was beaten off by determined Russian resistance. The German defences were accordingly pulled back a little on the morning of 16 November in order to set up a better position. An infantry party from the brigade was chosen and under the command of Leutnant Labusch transferred to the Apatin area. It occupied positions as outposts until 28 November and then returned intact to the Fünfkirchen area.

On 19 November, Russian battle units embarking upon an attack from the bridgehead were forced back by our infantry and 3 Battery StuGs. Over the next few days, however, the Russians succeeded in widening the bridgehead under cover of minor attacks.

Between 23 and 26 November the StuGs were frequently in action, often as a 'fire brigade' along the defensive fronts between Dubosenica-Udvar and Brangni. After these raids abated, our StuGs were pulled out of the line and sent to Szigetvar for R&R.

A general takes his leave of StuG Brigade 191 men, end of May 1944, Buzau, Romania.

Major Alfred Müller displaying his pleasure at a belated delivery of field post from home.

Another vehicle in the brigade car park was a Ford saloon of 1938/39.

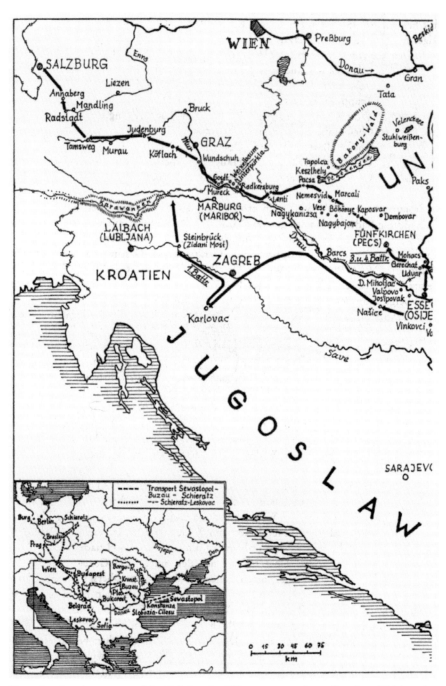

Map showing the course of StuG Brigade 191 operations from October 1944 to the war's end, May 1945.

Only a few vehicles and not much equipment could be got out, but the mass of men were shipped across the Black Sea from Sevastopol. On 30 May 1944 the brigade was loaded aboard rail transporters in Romania for reorganization in the Reich.

A quiet spot in the Staff car was of great value during the long railway journey!

A stop on the way somewhere in the Balkans.

The locomotives hauling the transport.

Most brigade men had to travel in cattle trucks.

A locomotive fireman of the Reichbahn.

In fine weather it was possible to enjoy the journey in the open air. At the time in this area the danger from low-flying fighter aircraft was not so great.

The transport passing through a Balkan gorge towards Vienna.

The rail journey to Schieratz near Breslau with many interruptions lasted until 30 June 1944, therefore four weeks!

At a stop on the railway journey on 15 June 1944, command of StuG Brigade 191 was transferred from Major Alfred Müller to his successor, Hauptmann Kollböck.

Soldiers of the brigade gave the departing commander the traditional 'Eyes right!' as they passed him. The march-past was watched by the new commander.

Near Vienna the brigade train met a transport carrying Tiger panzers. Most men of Brigade 191 had never seen one before.

At Schieratz north-east of Breslau, in July and August 1944 StuG Brigade 191 was reorganized into Heeres Sturmartillerie Brigade 191 and equipped with the new StuG III version G, with 7.5-cm cannon and optimized armour.

The brigade was transported out to southern Yugoslavia in September 1944 to cover the retreat of Army Group E.

A stop at one of the numerous railway stations and yards on the way to the Bulgarian frontier.

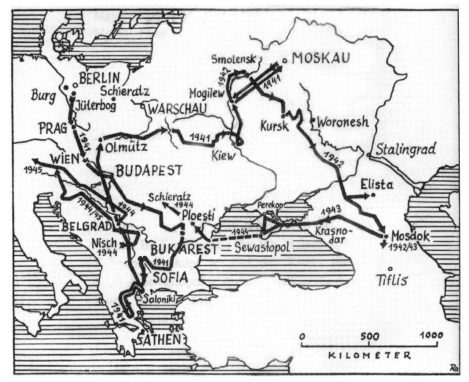

The operational route followed by StuG Buffalo Brigade from 1941 to 1945.

One of the few photos of Günther Möller, who fell at Kiev on 22 September 1941. He received the Knight's Cross posthumously.

The author of this book, Bruno Bork, served first as Hauptwachtmeister with the Staff Battery and later with 3 Battery, StuG Abteilung 191. After being wounded in action as an StuG commander in mid-1943 he was sent for officer training. He passed out as an Oberfähnrich (cadet, senior grade) and received his commission as Leutnant on 1 November 1944. On 30 March 1945 he was awarded the Iron Cross First Class and retired from active service on 21 April 1945 in the rank of Oberleutnant. He died on 27 March 1996.

'Gebirgs-Pionier-Bataillon 54 gives heartfelt congratulations to Sturmgeschütz Brigade 191 and its commanding officer for their 500th enemy tank destroyed.' Gömend, Hungary, 15 March 1945.

The StuG of Oberwachtmeister Riederl (far right in picture) crossing the Danube at Belgrade on 23 September 1944. From left to right: Unteroffiziers Grasenack, Raber and Plath, and Obergefreiter Bärenfänger.

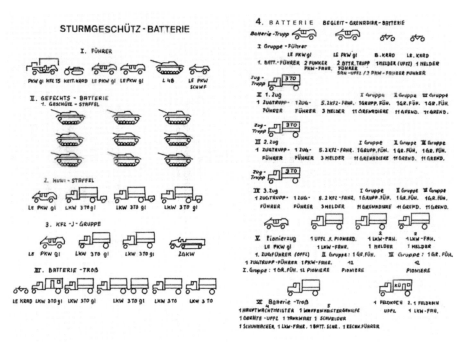

The organization of a StuG battery.

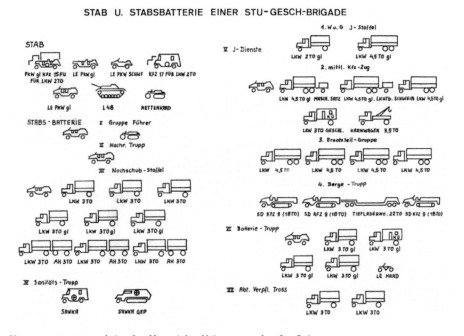

The organization of the Staff and Staff Battery of a StuG battery.

This was the main weapon of the 'assault artillery', the Sturmgeschütz III (on Panzer Mk III chassis). Versions A to E were deployed at the front into 1942, and from that year versions F and G were delivered.

StuG III version F was fitted with the 7.5-cm long barrel cannon which enabled Russian T-34 tanks to be engaged successfully at a range of 1,000 metres.

Side profile of an StuG version F. It differed from the later G version which had a modified upper structure and cast steel, rather rounded so-called 'pig's head', gun shielding.

Hauptmann Hoffmann-Schoenborn was CO of the heavy Artillery Abteilung 777 before transferring into the StuG Arm.

Major Hoffmann-Schoenborn, CO of StuG Abteilung 191 in Russia in 1941 during a visit to his old artillery unit, Abteilung 777.

Oberstleutnant Hoffmann-Schoenborn in black panzer-style uniform and wearing the Knight's Cross with Oak Leaves, 1942.

Oberst Hoffmann-Schoenborn as CO of the StuG School at Burg in 1943/44.

A photo signed by Hauptmann Alfred Müller received by Hermann Röhm as a souvenir of his CO.

Hauptmann Alfred Müller without cap.

Hauptmann Alfred Müller receiving the award of the Knight's Cross from Oberstleutnant Hoffmann-Schoenborn on 20 February 1943.